DEATH AND TAXES

DEATH AND TAXES

HOW SARS MADE HITMEN, DRUG DEALERS AND TAX DODGERS PAY THEIR DUES

JOHANN VAN LOGGERENBERG

Jonathan Ball Publishers
Johannesburg & Cape Town

Originally published in South Africa in 2018 by
JONATHAN BALL PUBLISHERS

A division of Media24 (Pty) Ltd
PO Box 33977
Jeppestown
2043

ISBN 9781868428090
ebook ISBN 9781868428106

Every effort has been made to trace the copyright holders and to obtain their permission for the use of copyright material. The publishers apologise for any errors or omissions and would be grateful to be notified of any corrections that should be incorporated in future editions of this book.

Twitter: www.twitter.com/JonathanBallPub
Facebook: www.facebook.com/JonathanBallPublishers
Blog: jonathanball.bookslive.co.za

Cover by publicide
Design and typesetting by Johan Koortzen
Editing by Tracey Hawthorne
Proofreading by Kelly Norwood-Young
Index by Sanet le Roux

Printed and bound by novus print solutions, a Novus Holdings Company
Set in 11 on 16.5pt Sabon MT Pro

I dedicate this book to my wife, Nicole. As always, thank you for the many hours of support and patience, advice and guidance, for listening, and, above all, for your unconditional love.

I also dedicate this book to all officials who continue to work at SARS: our country needs you now more than ever. You make us proud, and I wish for your continued success. Never give up and always stay true to the higher purpose.

Contents

PART 4: RAPID DESCENT

Author's note

I was a taxman for just over 16 years before I left the South African Revenue Service (SARS) in early 2015. In this book I share some of my experiences as a tax sleuth.

I always worked within the enforcement component of SARS in one or other capacity, and therefore my stories are limited to this sphere of SARS's business. Some of the cases we investigated received much public attention and my main focus will be on these. Some of these cases we won, others not.

SARS is a vital institution and pillar within our democracy because it's the primary mechanism by which the Government collects taxes to fund its programmes and services to the citizenry. The tax authority employs around 14 500 people at any given time. Of these, most work in the operational sections: they deal with the public in registering for tax, filing returns and being subjected to audits, for example; and with customs-and-excise staff at border posts, harbours and airports. Then there are the legal and policy division, human-resources management, the finance and information-technology components, and the administrative division that holds everything together. There was also the centralised Large Business Centre, dedicated solely to servicing large corporates and multinationals because they contribute such a large portion of tax to the fiscus.

So, within this broad framework, the enforcement component of SARS was really quite small (although, as you will come to learn, it punched well above its weight). This enforcement capacity came into play only when people failed in their legal obligations to SARS and where we believed we could assist the State in combating organised crime.

My stories take place against SARS's growth from a relatively unknown state department into one of the country's most efficient and trusted public institutions. However, sadly, where previous to 2015 we regularly read about successes achieved by SARS, since 2015 SARS has been in the news more often for false reports about a so-called 'rogue unit', and allegations of 'state capture' and corruption by some of its leaders. This book therefore also discusses developments in recent years and their impact on the institution, including the departure of over 55 executives within a matter of months, and the ultimate reported loss of over 500 staff in the 2016/17 fiscal year.

For several years I managed a small investigative unit that was falsely dubbed the 'rogue unit' by the *Sunday Times* newspaper. This unit consisted of 26 people at first, but by 2010 had dwindled to seven, and then finally to six people.

After the untrue accusations surfaced in the media in late 2014, reports continually seemed to imply that this was all I ever did at SARS – manage this small 'rogue unit'. I've said it before and I want to repeat it here: from when I took over the management of this fairly nondescript unit in early 2008, it accounted for less than 5% of my daily duties; it was a mere support unit to other larger units and external law-enforcement agencies.

When I left SARS, I intended to put my time there behind me and start a new life. I'm still trying to do that, even though some people continue to try and drag me and others into all kinds of dramas that I firmly believe are not in the interests of SARS and our country.

When Jonathan Ball Publishers asked me to consider writing a book about my experiences at SARS before my resignation, I reflected on certain key cases and decided to go ahead in the hope that, by sharing these stories and lessons learned, I could possibly assist my former colleagues and perhaps even aspirant SARS officials who're planning to dip their toes into big cases for the first time. I also hope that these stories may assist the public in general and the new management at SARS to reflect on how far SARS had come, and inspire them to pull things together and get the institution back to operating at the levels it used to.

A fear in writing this book is that I could be seen by some to be holding a grudge, but I can assure you that this is not the case. While saddened by the many negative stories about SARS that have dominated the media over recent years, I really bear no grudges. In fact, when I left SARS on 4 February 2015, the last man I shook hands with was the then newly appointed SARS commissioner, Tom Moyane and I meant it when I wished him well for his future endeavours.

In a strange twist of fate, while I was busy with the final edits of this book, President Cyril Ramaphosa suspended Moyane pending a disciplinary enquiry into various allegations against him. This followed within days after Ivan Pillay, myself and another individual received a summons from the South African Police Service (SAPS) to attend court on 9 April 2018 on a charge by the National Prosecuting Authority (NPA) of my supposedly having allowed a corrupt practice some time 'between August and September 2008'. Following our first court appearance, the matter was remanded to June 2018, and it's likely it will be referred to a higher court to a later date. It is, of course, a bogus charge, and one that I will defend vehemently – but these events demonstrate the continually shifting sands of our young and imperfect democracy in the wake of the state-capture revelations of recent years.

What started off as a relatively simple concept to tell multiple short stories, one after another, changed in time to a sequential string of critical events at SARS. In writing these stories, I've been somewhat limited by law in providing certain specifics about taxpayers and SARS operations that aren't in the public domain. I've had to dig around in old newspaper reports, court files and public records, and speak to a few old friends. Everything I share in this book is publicly available and verifiable, except where I state otherwise; it has also all been checked by lawyers. I make use of extensive endnotes for those bookworms who may wish to read more about the stories in this book and for legal reasons.

All the cases I worked on were dependent on team work, so while my name may have been made public in my association with these cases, please remember that the outcome was the result of a collective effort.

Johann van Loggerenberg

Foreword

Since 1999, the management of SARS has seen the role of the institution as part of the national effort to make South Africa succeed.

Given South Africa's location far from the main developed markets of the world, and with its colonial and apartheid history, it was always going to be difficult for us to be successful. Nothing short of a superhuman effort would be required to turn the promise of the negotiated solution of the early 1990s into reality.

Over time, we assembled at SARS a team from diverse backgrounds. We were Africans, Indians, coloureds and whites, with a sprinkling of non-South Africans. We made it explicit that there was a place and role for each one of us in SARS, provided there was commitment to the future of South Africa and to the future of SARS.

Although Johann (known as 'JvL' by friend and foe) was never in the national executive of SARS, he was a key participant in the new SARS team. A young former police official, aghast at the iniquities of apartheid, he committed himself to the new South Africa. Among all our staff, he made the most impact on the theory, policy and practice of enforcement. He gathered around him bright and energetic young people who were just as enthusiastic as he.

The SARS management team of which JvL was a part strove for the unity of all staff. We drew into action those who, because of their experience and interests, would not be negatively disposed to the new dispensation.

We quickly withdrew voluntary retirement packages – a poorly designed tool that in fact weakened the public service as it accelerated the departure of the most capable white members of staff. Those who weren't skilled and knowledgeable enough hesitated to test the market and stayed behind. Thereafter we retained much of the legacy staff, infusing it with new skills, perspectives and knowledge.

Over the next ten years, we succeeded in changing the demographics of SARS without forcing anybody out because of their skin colour, while thoroughly transforming the business of tax and customs.

We were advised early on not to make big technological changes; instead, we focused on changing our processes and bedding them down, streamlining our organisational structure, and improving our management capability. It was only from 2008 that we made significant technological changes to our systems.

SARS was reorganised into front offices, back offices and enforcement centres, enabling the standardisation and reengineering of our processes. Jobs were redesigned and levels of work reduced. We created an exciting and formidable institution. We had dyed-in-the-wool public servants for whom SARS was their first and only job. We had other 'firsts' – for those who came directly from the liberation struggle, SARS was their first formal employment. Still others were highly successful professionals and managers from the private sector, attracted by the vision of the senior team and its recent track record. Indeed, during that period, it was said that a stay at SARS considerably boosted one's CV.

At SARS we prided ourselves on our ability to implement and manage. We cared, and we were driven to succeed – we got things done:

As the main channel of revenue to the fiscus, in good faith we did what was ethical for a well-meaning government to be funded. In their book *Rogue: The Inside Story of SARS's Elite Crime-busting Unit*, JvL and Adrian Lackay refer to this as SARS's 'higher purpose'.

Our lodestar was the compliance philosophy: the basic tenet that, under conducive conditions, most people would do the right thing.

There are three levers that influence compliance behaviour: awareness, making it easy to do the right things and difficult to do the wrong things, and a credible enforcement capability.

Creating awareness was about informing and explaining to people the what, why and how of taxation; the second lever informed the design and management of systems to make compliance hassle-free; and the third lever was well organised and tightly managed so that we were fair to all, efficient and effective. We called this approach 'breadth, depth and leverage': we wanted to convey that SARS could reach each and every taxpayer.

When the criminal-justice system began to fail us, we complained, wrote memos and cajoled our counterparts. But we didn't stop there. We looked for other solutions and we found some of them right under our noses.

We began to place greater dependency on the remedies afforded by civil litigation. To this end, we amended legislation to increase the penalty provisions that we could levy. We sourced people in the required field and we learned. Some of our staff became specialists in insolvency and forfeiture of assets, among other things.

Our experience and our study of the illicit economy suggested that we try to understand it as a business with a value chain of suppliers, transporters, storage and warehousing, sellers, customers, market prices, payment systems, investments, substitutes and competition. Then we identified the crucial points and took actions to disrupt them. As JvL shows in *Rogue*, by the end of 2013, smugglers and producers of illicit tobacco products were on the ropes.

As I've noted, we saw our contribution as our national duty to South Africa. Over and above our normal duties at SARS, we tried to spread a 'good virus' from below. We assisted other state entities that pulled us in, including providing the software to Home Affairs for processing entries to and exits from South Africa for the 2010 World Cup, designing the new ID cards, supporting the Department of Health in the Eastern Cape, providing engineers and analysts to the Government Employee Pension Fund, initiating and coordinating the foundational work in researching procurement in state institutions, proposing and designing the Chief Procurement Office, and convening many workshops for public servants over the years that were centred on the SARS experience.

We worked incredibly hard and we were voracious learners. We made mistakes, but we corrected ourselves and steamed ahead. We mixed activism with good implementation skills. Our project-management expertise was tempered with systemic thinking. Above all, we had little tolerance for the dishonest and self-seeking politicking that seemed to permeate other state institutions.

SARS was named a 'preferred employer' in South Africa over many consecutive years, and in benchmarking exercises carried out by international institutions, SARS appeared among the top performers in the world in many of the key indicators.[i]

The facts show that SARS and some of its key officials came under attack from about 2001. From that time onwards, relentlessly, outlandish allegations against the SARS leadership were circulated. These so-called 'intelligence dossiers' were usually provided to the media, political parties and ministers of the Government, and very few politicians (of all parties) and senior public servants dealt with the information in a principled manner.

Nonetheless, our quick and thorough responses, including engagement with the criminal-justice system, kept the attackers at bay: as long as there was a stable, experienced political leadership of integrity, we at SARS could hold our own.

Over the years, we built up the most capable and feared enforcement capability in the State. Relatively few attempts at penetrating SARS and undermining its integrity succeeded. Indeed, we remained, until 2014, impervious to bribes, threats, political influence and the machinations of intelligence structures that had been infiltrated by criminals.

These disaffected elements, made up of former and existing SARS employees, tax evaders, criminals and political middlemen, naturally began to find each other. Since all attempts to weaken SARS failed, the only remaining solution was for the president to move against the

i This account would be incomplete without mentioning that, despite many attempts, we failed to have any impact on Crime Intelligence and the Gauteng Department of Health, who showed no enthusiasm at all for our help.

Finance Ministry and place a willing body at the head of the institution. In a matter of just a few months, the new heads managed to rid SARS of its most senior management, replacing them with predominantly non-tax executives of dubious integrity and capability.

The performance of SARS, despite all the propaganda from the new management from September 2014 to the time of writing (November 2017), has not inspired hope or confidence.

When the campaign to target and isolate JvL found some traction prior to the appointment of Tom Moyane, my response was simple: more than once, I said to the seemingly concerned members of staff, 'When you're as committed to the South Africa that's described in our Constitution, and you work as smart and hard as Johann, I'll take you seriously.'

This book covers some of the key cases in which JvL and his teams were involved, which tested our resolve and our ingenuity, and which in turn enabled us to improve our standards continually. I believe that there are important lessons to be taken from these cases that can inform the rebuilding of SARS and the criminal-justice system of South Africa.

Ivan Pillay
Former deputy SARS commissioner[1]

PART 1
EARLY DAYS

'Tax evasion, illicit financial flows and transfer pricing are contributors to the tax gap in any country, and the extent to which they're uncontrolled undermines the fiscal capacity of the various countries.'

– Pravin Gordhan, addressing the Conference on Illicit Financial Flows: Inter-Agency Cooperation and Good Tax Governance in Africa, University of Pretoria, July 2016

1

Tax activists

On 25 August 2016 – the so-called 'day of the warning statements' – I found myself sitting on a dodgy chair in a stuffy, gloomy room in Pretoria.

Old tables and chairs, and a dilapidated couch with stuffing sticking out of it, lined the walls of this social room-cum-kitchenette. Yellowing posters with anti-corruption slogans and internal notices were stuck to the walls, some curling up at the edges. An old fridge purred along, and a hot-water urn made a clicking sound as it switched on and off. The windows looked out onto the building next door.

From time to time, people would enter and make themselves a cup of tea or coffee, then walk out again. Some of them I knew well from my time at the South African Revenue Service (SARS) but my attempts at small talk failed repeatedly.

Far away I could hear people singing. One song I recognised clearly was the struggle song 'Senzeni na?' (What have we done?).

A few hours before, I, together with former SARS deputy commissioner Ivan Pillay and our lawyers, had entered the offices of the Hawks – the Directorate for Priority Crime Investigation, established in 2008 as an independent directorate within the South African Police Service (SAPS) – in Visagie Street. We had a date with what's known as the Crimes Against the State (CATS) unit of the Hawks, mandated to investigate terrorism, weapons of mass destruction, treason and subversion of our country's sovereignty.

Pillay was accused of pension fraud and of creating a 'rogue intelligence unit' at SARS, while I'd supposedly been unlawfully running the so-called rogue unit since 2010 and had involved myself with corrupt payments through a fundraiser for charitable causes. (As revealed in my

2016 book *Rogue: The Inside Story of SARS's Elite Crime-busting Unit*, which I co-wrote with Adrian Lackey, all were baseless allegations.)

As we approached the building a crowd awaited us, among whom I immediately recognised human-rights lawyer George Bizos and former constitutional judge and Freedom Under Law civil-rights activist Johann Kriegler. More familiar faces jumped out – those of human-rights activist Francis Antonie of the Helen Suzman Foundation, and Mark Heywood, the founder of Section27, a public-interest law centre promoting human rights. I also recognised Ben Theron and Wayne Duvenage from the Organisation Undoing Tax Abuse (OUTA), some members of Corruption Watch, including David Lewis, and people from other civil-rights groups.

Print, radio and television journalists were all over the place, with flashing cameras and camera crews.

My wife, Nicole, came towards me from the crowd. She took my hand and gave it a tight squeeze. We manoeuvred our way to the front doors, where we were met by an official who took us up to the designated floor where the CATS unit would question not only Pillay and me, but also Finance Minister Pravin Gordhan.

The three of us had been summoned to the Visagie Street headquarters in letters drafted on a Sunday and hand-delivered to our lawyers the following morning. We'd been instructed to appear before CATS on 25 August, for them to take down 'warning statements' with regard to their investigation into allegations of a 'rogue unit' at SARS, and in Gordhan's case into his approval of Pillay's early-retirement package and reappointment at SARS in 2010.

Gordhan, acting on legal advice, had declined to attend. Pillay and I, despite receiving the same legal advice, had decided to go – our situation was different to Gordhan's, as by then we had left Government.

We were welcomed by a smiling Brigadier Nyameka Xaba, the CATS head. He took us down a corridor to an office, and introduced us to two of his colleagues. They decided to interview Pillay first, and I was shown to the drab coffee room and told to stay put.

I sat there for two hours, waiting to be questioned by people I'd once regarded as fellow civil servants who I thought were also fighting the good fight. And as I sat, I reflected on my 16-year career at SARS and the events that had brought me to this moment in time.

I recalled my very first day at SARS, 17 years before. Back then, SARS had just started its journey from being a mainly administrative institution to a more modern and agile organisation that could serve our new democracy with fresh energy.

Many stories jumped to mind, some of which could provide excellent plotlines for crime thrillers. Most of them made me extremely proud for what we'd been able to achieve with fairly limited resources and an abundance of dedication – even right at the beginning, there were already quite a few big fishes to fry.

Many of the stories I thought of made me smile, although some made me angry and slightly melancholic, especially where our efforts had been thwarted by a lack of cooperation between different state departments or political meddling.

I thought of my former colleagues, some of whom had left SARS, others who'd remained; some had parted ways in less-than-ideal circumstances, and some had passed away.

Over the years I'd met some truly amazing people at SARS, all part of the vast number of success stories that reflected so well on our country, our Government and our revenue agency.

I resolved that day that no matter what happened, no matter what lay ahead for us, some of the stories would be told, one way or another ...

I first joined SARS in late 1998, and a few months later Ivan Pillay, who would go on to become deputy commissioner, was appointed general manager: Special Investigations. We had many planning sessions and meetings about different aspects of the institution that then Finance Minister Trevor Manuel, his deputy, Jabu Moleketi, and SARS commissioner Pravin Gordhan and his executive believed were achievable. (Pravin Gordhan joined SARS as deputy commissioner in

1998, and became commissioner in 1999.)

It was customary for Pillay to convene working sessions and meetings on weekends, when we were free from our daily work responsibilities. In some cases, these meetings were formal and related to our work; in others, they were simply broad discussions around strategy and planning. One of these meetings happened to take place at a nursery near Pillay's home on a Saturday morning. It was here that I first heard the term 'economic transformation', when Pillay explained how SARS was playing a pivotal part in the newly formed democratic government.

In his usual soft-spoken manner, pausing often to find the right words, he told us that while political freedom might have been achieved in South Africa in 1994, the struggle was nowhere near over. There was still much to be done, he said, and it would take many years, probably well beyond the lifetime of some of us at that meeting, to achieve genuine economic freedom.

Pillay said the political changes may have brought constitutional order, equality, human rights and political freedom, but that the lives of the black majority hadn't changed overnight. We should remember that those people who'd lived in South Africa during apartheid, both victims and beneficiaries of the regime, hadn't just disappeared on the night after the first democratic elections. South African society would feel the structural, psychological and economic effects of apartheid for many years to come.

SARS could help to ensure that South Africa became economically free from having to rely on outside donors and borrowing, Pillay told us, and at the same time become self-sufficient and able to fund the respective programmes Government wanted to implement to develop society. Tax was part of achieving this goal.

The idea that SARS employees were activists in striving for a better South Africa was being established. If SARS achieved its targets, the Government could fund its own initiatives, more grants could be paid to the destitute, more homes, schools, clinics, hospitals and police stations could be built, more state officials could be trained and deployed, municipal services could be expanded, electricity and water could be provided to people who'd never had access to these services, and, as a result, job opportunities and economic growth could be created.

While this is a slight oversimplification of the system and how economics works, it basically meant that if SARS could collect enough money per year, as required by Government, not only would citizens benefit from it, but our economy would grow and bring us closer to fiscal sovereignty. I think we all understood the importance of this.

While the governmental system had to be modernised and adapted to the times and the needs of all South Africans, neither Pillay nor Gordhan wanted to throw the proverbial baby out with the bathwater when it came to SARS employees. They recognised that many of the 'old order' employees had years of technical expertise and experience, and they didn't want to lose that capacity. In time, they began to identify those who'd embraced the political changes and wanted to contribute to our new democracy. There were instances where heads bumped, and a few dug in their heels and used every trick to frustrate and hamper change at SARS, but the vast majority moved forward to help make SARS a better institution.

In those early years we were inspired not only by the philosophy of individuals like Pillay but also by the leadership of Manuel, Moleketi and Gordhan.

Manuel had instituted what became informally known as 'Monday mornings', at which the SARS executive briefed him on matters of importance. The 'Monday mornings' practice would continue for many years, through the period when Gordhan was finance minister and Nhlanhla Nene deputy minister, and when the latter ultimately became minister. He was a hard taskmaster, but fair. He always wanted us to do better.

I started attending some of these meetings, usually just to sit in and be ready with details of particular matters if required. I distinctly recall my first such meeting. Manuel had expressed concern about the unscrupulous practice of using industrial alcohol to manufacture very cheap brands of consumer-alcohol products and selling these off to unsuspecting buyers – industrial alcohol is poisonous and can cause tremendous damage to the liver and other vital organs. Manuel knew everything there was to know about these 'poisoned alcohol' cases, from the brand names and selling prices to where they were being distributed. The practice was on the rise, and Manuel wanted us to do everything we could to track down those behind it and bring them to book.

I was tasked to brief him on our progress in these cases. We'd managed to identify and investigate the primary role-players in this racket – but Manuel wanted more, and he wanted it soon. That's how he was – in touch with what was happening in our country, aware that SARS could play a role in many areas that were troubling our land, and impatient when we took too long to catch the crooks.

The other thing that struck me that day was the man's focus. It was incredible. He'd had a long meeting the evening before; he was always in early and he'd probably had very little sleep. At times, as I continued with my briefing, he would close his eyes – I could see he was dead tired. Wondering if he'd fallen asleep, I hesitated for a second or two – and he instantly opened his eyes, looked straight at me and began firing off questions.

Gordhan was the same in many respects. Both men didn't suffer fools, didn't waste time and abhorred any form of corruption, no matter how small. Both had the rare capacity to deal with the big picture, the long-term aspects, issues that span lifetimes, strategies and tactics; and then, in an instant, be able to drill down to the minute details of the what, where, who, when and how. They effortlessly moved through these matters; it was second nature to them. They came up with questions and ideas that, no matter how hard we and our teams may have tried to prepare for our briefings with them, always managed to stretch our minds beyond what we were doing at any point in time. They always encouraged us to think outside the box, to move forward, to never give up.

Manuel and Gordhan had zero tolerance for people who came to meetings unprepared. They would catch the person out immediately, and the perpetrator wouldn't easily be let off the hook. Eventually we resorted to preparing two types of presentations for these men, one dealing with the big picture and strategy, and the other delving into the intricate details. And even then, they would both still, effortlessly, ask us questions and direct our thinking to aspects beyond those we'd brought to the table.

Both former anti-apartheid activists and underground operatives who'd suffered isolation through imprisonment, banning orders, torture and dirty tricks by the apartheid regime, Trevor Manuel and Pravin Gordhan are truly remarkable men. It's a shame that our country was robbed of such brilliant minds for so many years.

What they brought to us at SARS was the hope and belief that we could all be activists, and we could all contribute to making our country great.

2

Full circle

An urban legend doing the rounds in Durban in the 1980s and '90s told of a young man by the name of Barney who'd taken an arm of dagga[ii] 'on appro', then bought a one-way train ticket to Johannesburg, with a whole grilled chicken, a loaf of bread and a bottle of milk to sustain him on his journey. Once in the big city, Barney broke the arm up into sticks (small cigarillo-style rolled-up portions of dagga), which he spent the weekend selling, making a small profit on each sale. The demand for dagga in Johannesburg was at a high at the time, especially if it was Durban Poison[1] – users would pay extra for the special high the weed from the coastal city promised.

At the end of the weekend, so the story went, Barney used the profit to buy a ticket back to Durban and pay his supplier. He was left with just enough to buy a slightly bigger package of dagga for his next trip the following weekend.

The young man kept turning a profit in this way until he could recruit others to do similar trips to Johannesburg on his behalf. This is how, apparently, Barney turned his small business into a little empire.

According to this legend, Barney started diversifying his product offerings, investing in shipments of Mandrax[2], mainly from India. Soon enough, his small empire grew into a much larger one, and Barney became one of the largest importers, investors in imports and, later, manufacturers and dealers of Mandrax in Natal (today KwaZulu-Natal).

As time went by, Barney began to expand his reach beyond Durban, and beyond drug dealing. He ultimately invested in legitimate businesses

ii Dagga is the colloquial name for marijuana. An 'arm' of dagga is a quantity of the dried leaves rolled up in brown paper or newspaper, about the size of a man's forearm.

ranging from a nightclub and a jewellery store to a clothing business and even a butchery. He eventually got married and had a family for whom he built a mansion in the Durban suburb of Sydenham. He began to plough back into his community by donating generously to community projects and services.

That, at least, is how the urban legend goes.

It was 1994, the year of South Africa's first-ever democratic elections. I was in the prime of my life, barely 25 years old, with long, dark brown hair hanging down my back. Usually you'd find me unshaven and wearing sandals, jeans and a kurta (a long shirt of Indian origin). Working as a deep-cover agent for the police's Organised Crime Intelligence Unit, I'd been trying for a few years to get into the Mandrax market in Durban.

In retrospect, it strikes me as odd that I actually believed that as a white privileged Afrikaans-speaking boy – because that's what I was – I could actually go and live in Durban, hang around the taxi-ranks all day looking for dodgy deals, and somehow manage to deceive hardened and experienced drug dealers into believing that I wanted to join them. But, sure enough, there I was, trying to do just that on the side of a road in Sydenham, very close to the home of someone I'd only ever heard of.

Michael Tyrone Barnabas was an enigmatic entrepreneur who was well known and even revered (and also somewhat feared) in the area. He lived in a large facebrick home just off the highway in Sydenham, a township for Indians and coloured people.

It had taken me some months to gain the confidence of the man I was with, a taxi-driver called Calvin. I was trying to move closer to a group of people I knew were associated with Barnabas and people close to him. Just the week before, I'd participated in a controlled deal where I'd bought Mandrax from a dealer, with an interloper – an informant – by my side to assist me, so that this 'assistant' could spread the word that I was in the trade. Soon enough, the news that I was in the business of buying and selling Mandrax started doing the rounds.

That day Calvin and I were standing by the side of the road when Barnabas's gold Mercedes-Benz passed us. He was in the passenger seat, and his driver pulled up next to us. He rolled down his window and I finally came face to face with the man I'd heard so much about. Expensive golf shirt, chinos, expensive shoes and an expensive wristwatch, I noted.

Using one finger, Barnabas dropped his Ray-Ban Aviator sunglasses just a little. He had close-cropped hair and was clean shaven, with friendly eyes and a big smile – but you could also see that this wasn't someone you wanted to mess with. He just had that look about him.

He started the conversation – he'd heard about my Mandrax deal and wanted to know where I got my product from. Well, I wasn't going to behave as if I knew what he was talking about; that's not how the game of dealing in Mandrax works. People who trade in Mandrax and don't know each other don't just advertise the fact openly. You get to hear of each other and then 'test' each other out without actually admitting openly to what you're involved in. So I shook my head. [iii]

There were a few more ums and ahs, but it wasn't long before his driver, realising the conversation was headed for a dead end, started up the car and slowly started driving off.

As he rolled up his window, Barnabas winked at me.

For the next few years, I'd continue to try to infiltrate the groupings and circles associated with Barnabas, but with little success. However, I was able to collect enough information to lead the police to an illegal Mandrax-manufacturing plant, for which Barnabas and a number of others were charged.

In October 1999[3] an affidavit before the Durban High Court disclosed how two police undercover operations had been launched during previous years, one dating as far back as 1993, which had led to the identification of individuals involved in the Mandrax trade in the greater Durban area. It was in one of these two operations that I'd acted as an undercover

iii This is how infiltration works. You don't push hard to get in on deals. You signal surreptitiously, then hope that the person gets back to you. Sometimes they do, sometimes they don't.

police agent.[4] These court papers formed part of efforts by Government to seize over R50 million in assets that were allegedly the proceeds of selling illegal Mandrax tablets.

The subjects of these two undercover investigations, one of which was dubbed 'Operation Indiana', included Ronny Johnny Smith, described in the affidavit as 'the kingpin of a sophisticated and currently active drug syndicate'. The court papers further identified Asgar Hoosen 'Butch' Ebrahim, Andrew 'Maxi' Chetty and Vusi Radebe. Taped conversations were submitted that implicated others, such as one 'Barbara', Martin Luther, Nithia Chinnasamy (who was already on trial on a charge of murder), Bimbo Sagren Pillay (then facing charges for dealing in and conspiracy to deal in illicit drugs) – and none other than Michael Tyrone Barnabas.

Barnabas had previous convictions for a range of offences dating back as far as 1974, but up until then the police had been unable to get their man. Despite the best efforts of law-enforcement agencies, however, he was again acquitted. He was as elusive as ever.[5]

In the 1990s, while most of my peers were just starting their careers after doing their national service, or were busy with their studies, or were dating their future wives, I was pretending to be someone and something that I wasn't. My life wasn't balanced at all, and I was living under very unnatural conditions. I had nobody to trust and absolutely no support network.

Cut off from my family and with no real friends, my only link to any form of normality and sanity was my 'handler' – but even contact with him was limited to prearranged brief meetings, usually in a car park, during which I handed over information reports, answered questions and received new tasks.

In an interview with *City Press* newspaper many years later, in 2014, my handler said, 'Johann lost contact with his family. I was his father, his mother, his brother and his sister. Nobody knows what it was like to live a lie for 24 hours a day. He was on his own with no friends, no family, nothing. He was dealing with ruthless people and his exposure could mean death.'[6]

This may be the reason why, in November 1998, at the age of 29, I joined SARS. Although I'd also been offered a job at the then South African Secret Service which would likely have better suited my background as an undercover police agent, I think by then that living a life of secrecy had taken its toll, and I wanted to start a normal life.

At the time I joined the tax authority, it had only just become a single entity. As a hangover of the past, two separate investigative units existed under the former Customs & Excise and Inland Revenue departments. The so-called Inspectorate had offices in all the main cities in the country and conducted a type of audit of taxpayers known as a 'special tax review' (the forerunner of today's lifestyle audits); each inspector could select who to investigate and when to do so.

The Customs Special Investigations unit had offices in Pretoria, Durban, Port Elizabeth and Cape Town.

An operational agreement between SARS and the Commercial Crimes division of the police, and a High Court case concerning the constitutionality of private criminal investigations, were the primary legal mechanisms used by SARS to conduct criminal investigations into tax crimes.[7]

After amalgamation, these units were brought into a single division called Special Investigations. In 1999 Ivan Pillay was appointed as general manager for the Special Investigations division, later renamed National Special Investigations.

The intelligence unit I worked in fell under Special Investigations. Our mandate was to collect, collate and analyse data of previous and existing criminal investigations of tax and customs cases in order to determine trends; introduce what later became known as the Suspicious Activity Report System;[8] and direct tax and customs investigations more intelligently than having regional offices selecting and investigating cases as they deemed fit, which was the case at the time.

Our little intelligence unit was new in SARS, and it was viewed with some suspicion, mainly because investigators were no longer allowed to pick and choose who they wished to investigate.

A separate division under the Debt Collection Division called Prosecutions consisted of 'tracers' who primarily had to find errant taxpayers who'd failed to submit tax returns, and serve them with subpoenas issued by court. Prosecutors and two courts (Pretoria and Cape Town) were dedicated to SARS's outstanding-returns prosecutions.

Investigations weren't selected on any notion of priority or risk at the time, and usually resulted in admission-of-guilt fines. The result was that some people were subpoenaed for one outstanding return, while others who'd failed to submit returns for multiple years weren't addressed. As a result, the number of outstanding tax returns grew exponentially year by year.

By January 2000, as a newcomer, I had virtually no cases to my name and was still unsure of myself in the new job. We'd just started an experimental outfit called the Special Compliance Unit, the aim of which was to enable SARS to assist the State and its law-enforcement agencies to curb the rising levels of crime in our young democracy.[9] The unit, of which I was the manager, was a mixed bag of old hands, people with accounting and auditing skills, a few former policemen, two former prosecutors, and a handful of inexperienced newcomers who came to be referred to as 'people off the streets'. I insisted on the inclusion of these newcomers despite resistance from the old guard, who not only thought we didn't know what we were doing, but also viewed us through the tainted lens of a specific ideology. They didn't trust Gordhan, Pillay and other new employees, such as the manager of Customs and Excise, Vuso Shabalala, who hailed from a struggle background, and would constantly find reasons to sabotage any new concepts or ideas because they didn't want the 'new guys' to succeed. (While I shared their demographics, being Afrikaans-speaking and white, I sided with the 'commies', which was anathema to them.)

The complaint of the old guard was that tax and customs cases were too complicated to give to newcomers, and that it would be impossible for these 'people off the street' to investigate them successfully. But we soldiered on, assigning the newcomers to some of the more experienced employees who were prepared to work together in the new unit. We soon proved the naysayers wrong.

One of the first cases the Special Compliance Unit took on was that of Michael Barnabas. His case was part of a broader multi-agency national threat assessment and anti-organised crime drive. We contacted the police and managed to get copies of their old dockets on Barnabas, as well as the 1999 case before the Durban High Court. We worked day and night going through these files to see if we could pick up any useful information from a tax-collection perspective.

We were working out of a small office in Hatfield, Pretoria and had little in terms of equipment, laptops and printers. However, what we had between us, we shared. The energy and willingness among the group members to learn and work long hours was truly astounding. The police and prosecutors who'd been involved in the 1999 case were also extremely helpful and cooperative.

The experienced guys, the old hands on the team, told us that the only way in which we were going to understand Barnabas's finances would be to use the 'special tax review' methodology they'd perfected over the years. And so the case of *SARS v Michael Tyrone Barnabas and related entities* was born.

Our first step was to do a special tax review on Barnabas. This is where an investigator looks at someone's lifestyle and compares it to the assets, income and expenses declared by the person under investigation. A finding is then made as to whether that person is living within his means. The central method these inspectors relied on is known among accountants and auditors as a 'capital reconciliation'. In layman's terms, this means the auditor looks at the tangible and identifiable asset growth of an individual or company over a certain period, converts it into real value in monetary terms, and compares this to what the taxpayer has declared to the Receiver of Revenue for that same period.

Lifestyle audits are notoriously complicated. They require lots of time and effort. Not only are they heavily dependent on the inspector or investigator being able to acquire and utilise third-party information, but they're more often than not conducted on taxpayers who're recalcitrant or refuse to cooperate and try their best to hide their true income from the Receiver of Revenue.[10]

So these inspectors had to look at everything in respect of the submitted financials of a taxpayer, but they also had to look beyond that, seeking out undisclosed or hidden income.

The weakness of people who don't want to pay tax lies in their greed – ultimately, they usually want to live large and use the money they've amassed, and this is exactly what the special tax review relies on. The greedy spend their profits, and when they do, this can be identified and taken into account when a special tax review is done.

In the Barnabas case we did everything by the book. He was notified of the investigation and asked to produce his financial records for verification and audit. There was constant toing-and-froing of correspondence between our Hatfield office and his accountants and lawyers in Durban. Slowly but surely, we pieced together the case. In the end our findings suggested a very high figure.

However, we were told by the experienced guys that if we did an estimated assessment at that point, as we intended, if the matter went to tax court, it would be very difficult to prove. So we continued pressure-testing our evidence and were often sent back to the drawing board. Ultimately, we managed to refine the amount to just over R1,2 million in back taxes due to SARS.

We were confident of this amount and of the evidence supporting our findings. None of us had any intention of losing one of our first cases.

By May 2001 the case was ready. By then it had dawned on Barnabas that I was the very same person who'd hung out in his neighbourhood so many years before; he tried to make something of the fact that I'd worked as an undercover agent for the police in previous years, attempting to use this information to claim that the case against him was tainted. But he knew there was no point in fighting, and that the case against him was solid, and he asked for a meeting with me and a legal representative from SARS.

In June, a SARS lawyer and I flew to Durban. We met in law chambers in what was then Smith Street. It wasn't a very long meeting. Barnabas basically admitting that he accepted that he hadn't paid SARS the tax he should have, and that he wished to do so now, and that he was prepared to plead guilty to charges of tax evasion. As SARS officials we couldn't agree to his pleading guilty to tax-evasion charges, but we undertook to raise his admission of guilt with the police and the prosecuting authority.

After that meeting in Durban, Barnabas's legal representative made an interesting comment. He told me how his client, who'd been classified 'coloured', had struggled tremendously to start a legitimate business during the apartheid era. Bearing in mind that some of his unpaid taxes predated 1994, when democracy had arrived in our country, the advocate explained that people who'd suffered under the apartheid regime had deliberately evaded tax because they reasoned that they didn't want to fund an illegitimate government that would just use their money to further suppress the black majority.

Barnabas's counsel, a gentle and stately man who was himself an underground-liberation stalwart, told me in a soft voice of his own suffering at the hands of the apartheid regime, and shared how some of his clients had been detained and tortured by the security police in previous years, and of others who'd simply disappeared, never to be seen again. He made a huge impression on me and caused me to question a number of my own assumptions.[11]

That night I thought to myself: if Barnabas, who clearly had tremendous entrepreneurial and organisational skills, as well as drive and energy, had been born white, where would he have been in life now? Could he have become a hotel magnate or the owner of a string of nightclubs if he hadn't been limited by the colour of his skin? We'll never know but it certainly made me more aware of how people's backgrounds impact on their lives.

As we concluded our discussion that day in 2001, Barnabas didn't direct the slightest hint of ill-feeling or malice towards me, despite knowing by then that I wasn't who I'd pretended to be years before when we'd first met. In fact, it was clear to me that he, too, believed in our country's new prospects, and realised that this time around, taxes due were to be paid for the sake of our collective future. In his own way, he bought in to the higher purpose SARS was serving in collecting funds for the Government to develop our country.

The two of them remained seated when I stood up to leave, and as I walked through the door and turned back to wave goodbye, I could swear I saw Barnabas winking at me.

Barnabas pleaded guilty to charges of tax evasion in the Pretoria Commercial Crimes Court. He was sentenced to four years' imprisonment suspended for five years on condition that he continued cooperating with SARS to conclude his tax audit. 'When that, including interest and penalties, is calculated it is expected to be a substantial amount… We also have additional agreements with him regarding his business entities which will again involve a substantial recovery for us,' SARS's spokesperson reported.[12]

But the matter didn't end here.

On a typically humid April afternoon in 2003, in the tropical city of Durban, various cars descended from all directions on a house in Sydenham. Members of the local police, the newly established SARS Special Compliance Unit and the local SARS office jumped out of the cars and ran up to the house.

Barnabas's wife, Amelia, opened the door. She was told that SARS had obtained a court order to seize all assets in the house. She immediately tried to call her husband but failed to reach him. The officials allowed her to try again and again, but to no avail. Eventually she called the family lawyer.

Soon their daughter, Chantel, arrived with the family lawyer in tow. By then word had spread in the small suburb and a fairly large group of onlookers had gathered around the house and across the road. [13]

Because I didn't want anybody in the Special Compliance Unit to be accused of anything afterwards, I instructed that the entire process be video-recorded. This was the unit's first big case and we weren't going to take any chances.

The officials started the painstaking process of going through the house, writing up a complete inventory of everything. Large amounts of cash were found in several rooms.

But this wasn't the only address being visited by officials. Another was at a popular nightclub, Obsession, in the city centre, while yet another team was busy at a clothing store in a nearby shopping mall.

What had brought about these actions was a court order following the failure by Barnabas to settle all his debts with SARS. SARS had approached the Durban High Court and obtained the order because he'd failed to pay an agreed amount of over R4,3 million. The order had allowed the sheriff to seize all movable and immovable property that belonged to Barnabas, to sell it off on auction, and to use the returns to pay the back taxes to SARS.

The process took a long time and ran late into the night. By arrangement with the family lawyer, it was agreed to post two security guards outside the house so that the team could return the next day to seize all movable property, which included furniture, electronic goods, and hundreds of pairs of imported Sebago shoes estimated to be worth about R500 000. Other items seized included four motor vehicles, cameras, guns, jewellery, computer equipment and a large quantity of documents.

The media loved the story, with one newspaper warning other would-be tax evaders about the 'new' SARS, reporting that we would get them – no matter who or where they were.[14]

3
Dominoes

The man was nervous. He kept looking about, and constantly sought assurances from me that I'd come alone to meet him at the shopping mall in the east of Johannesburg. I could see he hadn't been sleeping well and was going through a difficult time.

I tried to reassure him, because he was the key to one of the largest projects we'd ever undertaken at SARS. He could explain to me how hundreds of millions of rands have been pilfered from the fiscus, and provide the evidence to prove who'd been involved and how they'd gone about their 'business' in the electronics industry: he held all the knowledge of the myriad schemes executed in the electronics industry during those years. But he would have to be brave to come clean about them – very brave.

So how did I end up at this meeting some time in 2001?

The year before, quite a few local representatives of brand holders (companies or people who hold a trademark or patent over a brand or name of any goods or services) and suppliers of some of the most famous brands of everyday items, such as computers, fridges, radios and televisions, had approached SARS to say that they were considering pulling their companies from the country. They explained that they could no longer compete against unscrupulous local importers and dealerships that were undervaluing imported goods, enabling them to sell their products to consumers at far below landed cost.[iv] What these famous

iv 'Landed cost' is the cumulative value of an item manufactured overseas and imported to South Africa, and includes the original price of the product, the cost of transporting it to South Africa, insurance fees, shipping and handling fees, and clearing agent's and storage fees. The seller would then add his markup for profit before selling it on to the consumer.

brand holders were saying to Government was that there were just too many people tricking SARS on the importation of their products, which gave them an unfair advantage in the market.

At that point the electronics sector consisted of nine major manufacturing firms directly employing almost 9 000 workers. The sector contributed about 2% to the GDP[1] and generated a turnover of around R7,7 billion in the retail sector alone.

If those brand holders were to leave our shores, it would result not only in the loss of taxes they would have paid to the fiscus, but significant job losses and a dent to our reputation as a country.

Something had to be done, and it had to be done quickly, because we needed to demonstrate to the sector, and those within it who were compliant, that the State did care, and was capable of dealing with unfair competitive behaviour. Time was not on our side.

Enter the enigmatic Shirish Soni, once an operative in the ANC as part of an underground cell of uMkhonto we Sizwe (MK), the military wing of the liberation movement. (Public records would later reveal that the cell he belonged to was commanded from Mozambique by ANC operative Ebrahim Ismail Ebrahim, who in turn reported to Jacob Zuma.) Soni had been arrested and detained several times by the notorious apartheid security police in the 1980s; on one occasion, they'd tortured him to within an inch of his life.

A tall, handsome vegetarian who's also a yoga expert, Soni has one of the sharpest business minds I've ever encountered. He was an entrepreneur and businessman in his own right before he joined SARS in 2000 as deputy head of Customs and Excise. With his abundance of grace and total lack of bitterness, he quickly became one of my mentors.

Soni was assigned the task to come up with a plan to deal with the undervaluations, misdeclarations and fraud that were rife in the electronics industry, in collaboration with Gene Ravele, a senior manager in the National Special Investigations division at the time.

Ravele also has a track record in the liberation struggle from his student days. He's from the northern part of the country and hails from royal lineage. Politically savvy and princely in manner, he was more observer and director in style than actual operative. Ravele was one of the first people I met at SARS when I started there; it was he who vetted my CV and ensured that I was suitable for the job.

One day Soni and Ravele called me to a meeting. SARS had just moved its head office from the drab building in what was then Visagie Street to its brand-new headquarters in Brooklyn, Pretoria, aptly named Lehae la SARS – 'the home of SARS' in Sotho.

It was in one of the nicely furnished new offices that I met with these two men. They told me about the case they were working on, and we all agreed that we had to act swiftly and across the entire spectrum of the electronics industry.

'Here's a pen, JvL,' said Soni, handing me a marker. 'Draw me the picture. How do we tackle this thing so that we make a major impact?'

On the whiteboard, I outlined a broad strategy for the electronics-industry project, to take on the myriad players who were dodging SARS and pushing legitimate companies out of the market. The plan had a few elements.

First, we had to put together a SARS team to dedicate time and effort to the case. The team would include a few old hands, two lawyers from the legal department and a couple of the new people, mostly from the Special Investigations division.

Second, we had to identify and collate all existing cases where Special Investigations, audit and customs people were already engaged in disputes with subjects in the electronics industry. This would enable us to possibly identify common denominators and understand the scope of the problem.

Third, we had to connect with the then SAPS Commercial Crimes Unit, the National Prosecuting Authority (NPA) and the erstwhile Scorpions.[2] Where possible, cases had to be fast-tracked through the criminal-justice system.

And finally, we needed a means to address role-players across the value chain. This meant that the smaller players, the middlemen, the financiers, the lawyers, the money-launderers, the bigger players and ultimately the very biggest ones, including listed companies, had to be identified.

The collation of cases immediately presented a difficulty for us as a management team. We were the 'new guys' at SARS and, as mentioned, some of the older hands viewed us with suspicion, continually reminding us how complicated cases were and that things couldn't happen the way we thought they could. This was a very difficult period at SARS, when the old guard, who were either jockeying for positions or were angry at having lost their privileged run of the range, were opposed to any kind of change.

Compounding this was the fact that there was no central case register, and the older Inspectorate and Customs Special Investigations case-management systems were all but nonexistent. I and a few others had to search for cases manually, relying on word of mouth and the grapevine to, first, identify the types of cases we were looking for, and then engage the investigators involved in those cases in order to understand what they'd done up to that point, who they were investigating, the modus operandi and the possible outcomes.

We had some success, but in some cases the investigators made it virtually impossible for us to understand their cases, simply refusing to engage or work with us. They seemed unable or unwilling to understand the concept of a broader, high-impact approach to a high-risk sector in our economy, preferring to engage at the transactional level of a single case only. We had a hell of a time dealing with them. I was subjected to most of the vitriol, since I was the 'sellout' who'd sided with the 'commies' – although ideologically opposed to the new Government, these guys were smart enough not to attack anyone else on the team who wasn't white.

Ultimately, however, we managed to get hold of most of the cases, which were at various stages of completion. None was at the stage where assessments could be issued, debts collected or criminal proceedings instituted. This was partly because the older Inspectorate and Special Investigations units didn't have a standard procedure that provided for measurable outcomes or a case-management system – investigators just plodded along with whatever case happened to fall in their lap, and they did their work pretty much however they chose to at any given time.

One advantage of this exercise was that it enabled SARS to begin to build and, in time, perfect a case-management system and investigations process, with measurable outcomes for investigators.

Another benefit of using the grapevine to look for cases was that I began to develop a broader understanding of the nature of the schemes in the electronics industry, and work out who was who, and the geographies and scale of the issues. It was, in fact, during this time that we stumbled across a case that at first glance seemed to have nothing to do with the electronics industry at all but turned out to be pivotal to our investigation.

It concerned a well-known Pretoria family, AA Tayob and his three sons, Rafik, Khaleed and Ryaaz, and their uncle, Abdul Rashid, who jointly owned several companies that allegedly owed R76 million to SARS in customs duties. They didn't have the funds to pay this amount and, as a result, the family businesses had collapsed; all except Rafik Tayob were declared bankrupt.[3]

The only remnant of this business empire was a biscuit factory, which itself was facing liquidation because Rafik was unable to pay back taxes due to SARS. The pre-sequestration process and ultimately the efforts to liquidate this factory proved to be very expensive; for instance, the liquidator, lawyers and SARS officials were sent to foreign countries at great cost to SARS in an effort to find assets there but returned empty-handed. The case had dragged on and on, and the bills for the lawyers and the liquidator grew to such a point that even if the sequestration order were made final in court, SARS would receive little or no money at all.[4]

While Rafik and his biscuit factory might not have led anywhere, we were really interested in his brother Ryaaz, who'd been involved in the electronics industry for many years and was firmly in our scope. However, the cases we'd worked on up until then, and the evidence we had in our possession, were simply too limited to use in a large-scale offensive focused on the entire value-chain of the industry. We needed a breakthrough – ideally, we had to get someone on the inside to speak to us.[5]

We had so little to work with that we would've followed up any possible lead for more information – so, we thought, why not try to get to Ryaaz via his brother? Soni, a SARS lawyer and I set up a meeting with Rafik to speak to him about his own case concerning the biscuit factory, in the hope that he'd be able to tell us more about the electronics industry – or, even better, to get his brother to talk to us about it.

Our first meeting was very informal. We asked Rafik whether he'd be prepared to bring his brother Ryaaz along at some point, with a view to helping us to better understand the electronics industry. We needed to know who the key players were, we said.

The rest of our discussion that day was about how the Tayob family had supported people in banned liberation movements, mainly the ANC, for many years, helping those seeking refuge from the security police or needing money. When activists were arrested and detained, the Tayob family helped to support their families and ensured that their legal fees were paid. It seemed that the Tayobs had also subscribed to a kind of ideological tax revolt – why pay money to a government that only used it to serve a privileged few, they argued; why fund the security apparatus that killed, detained and tortured people?

I understood this, but Soni – himself once an underground activist, detained and tortured while his family had no idea where he was or whether he was even alive – understood it better. And it was perhaps this connection that convinced Rafik to assist us. He said he'd ask his brother whether he was willing to meet with us.

It wasn't long before the call came – it was later revealed in court that investigators had been on Ryaaz's tail for about two years by then, and he was tired of being chased; he wanted closure. Yes, he wanted to come in, he said. Yes, he was guilty. Yes, he wanted to make things right.

I hastily put through a call to the NPA and the Scorpions, to ensure that we dealt with the matter openly and properly.

The following year Ryaaz Tayob pleaded guilty in the Commercial Crimes Court in Pretoria to 32 counts of contravening the Customs and Excise Act, relating to providing customs control with false documentation for imported electronic goods. He was sentenced to an effective 16 years' imprisonment, suspended for five years subject to his payment of R15 million to SARS.

As part of his sentence, Ryaaz was ordered to assist SARS in any investigations with whatever evidence he may have had regarding unlawful practices within the electronics industry, and that he did by providing us with substantial information and an affidavit implicating all those with whom he'd been involved.[6]

To my mind, that was the first domino to fall.

By December 2000, the SARS 'electronics industry' project was in full swing. Twelve containers of imported electronic goods valued at over R8 million had been detained by SARS; Mega Audio was the importer. Its owner, prominent businessman Kenneth McCleod, an associate of Tayob, was arrested by the Scorpions for various contraventions of customs laws. Within days, Mega Audio had been placed in liquidation.

It was later shown in court papers that at least R8 million-worth of televisions, hi-fis and other electronic goods had been procured overseas by McCleod and sold to retail chain Supreme Furnishers, a subsidiary of the large Profurn group which also owned well-known chain stores Hi-Fi Corporation and Morkels. But payments for these shipments had been made not to Mega Audio, as they should've been, but rather to McCleod or his associated companies, so SARS held on to the containers in Johannesburg until they were impounded by Mega Audio's liquidator.[7]

The second domino fell when McCleod was arrested and later convicted in the Pretoria Commercial Crimes Court on 31 counts of contravening tax and customs laws. He was given a suspended sentence on condition that he paid R15 million to SARS in lost customs duties and income taxes.

A major breakthrough came in the form of a whistleblower with insight into the workings of the electronics industry and who knew pretty much all of those involved. When Soni and I first approached him, he was genuinely scared for his life, but we knew that if we could convince him to talk to us, we'd crack the case wide open. We pleaded with him to do the right thing, and he said he'd think about it and get back to us.

And that's how I ended up at the meeting with the nervous, sleep-deprived man at the shopping mall in the east of Johannesburg in 2001. A few hours before, he'd called to say he wanted to meet with me privately – not as a SARS official, but as one human being to another. The thought did cross my mind that I might be being set up for a hijacking or something similar, but something in the man's voice made me drive to Johannesburg to see him.

We both smoked, so we sat outside. He started telling me about how he'd grown up: how poor he'd been and unable to afford to go to university when he finished school, but how someone had taken him under his wing and assisted him in paying for his studies. He shared his memories of apartheid South Africa, and of class and race struggles. 'When I got the opportunity to study at university, I worked like a slave so that I wouldn't disappoint the person who'd helped fund my studies. You know, I used to travel very long distances by train to get to class. Sometimes I'd miss the train and my classes,' he said.

At the end of the monologue, he looked me in the eye. 'Please, there's something you need to promise me,' he said. 'If I cooperate with the Scorpions, the NPA and SARS, you need to remember that I'm doing it for the right reason, and in honour of those people who faced similar difficulties as I did in my youth. I'm not doing it in a moment of weakness.'

It was important to him that I should know that he was deliberately choosing to go down a certain path because he wanted to help make South Africa a better place, and for no other reason.

I indicated that I understood his position, and we shook hands and parted ways.

The man was at the offices of the Scorpions first thing the next morning. In a process that lasted days, he set out facts and evidence that could assist us in our investigation. Among his revelations were aspects that pointed to the involvement of SARS officials who'd allegedly overlooked documents and facilitated the smuggling of goods. In this way, our informant added an entirely new dimension to the project, which now extended beyond the traders to include State officials in the scams.

That man did a brave thing: the stakes were high, and people in the industry would come to know that he'd assisted us. He also had his family to worry about.

Within a couple of days, the Scorpions and SARS had raided no fewer than 25 homes in Johannesburg and Pretoria, including those of 21 SARS customs officials and four former SARS employees. A female member of the old SARS anti-corruption unit in Johannesburg was arrested by the Scorpions, while 18 SARS officials were suspended pending further investigations.

The joint Scorpions, NPA and SARS teams that conducted these raids seized computers, other electronic equipment and documents from the homes of several officials who were alleged to have been involved in corruption and fraud in the electronics industry. Many were found to have assisted the various traders either directly or by looking the other way. An employee of auditing firm KPMG was also drawn into the net and investigated.[8]

Soon enough, many of the SARS officials who'd been implicated resigned from the tax authority.

Despite two unknown directors of the Profurn group suddenly fleeing the country, Profurn finally reached a settlement with SARS, agreeing to pay R26 million in outstanding tax and customs duties related to the purchase of imported electronic goods.[9]

As the criminal dockets would later show, the whistleblower helped the NPA, police and SARS beyond imagination. We were stretched to the limit and literally worked day and night, and most weekends.

By July 2001, the entire electronics industry in South Africa was wide awake to SARS's actions.[10]

The whistleblower identified an office block in Fordsburg, Johannesburg that was occupied by a businessman called Mohammed Bamath. In a specific office, we were told, many of the scams were conceived and executed with military precision. We were told which offices to look in specifically, and also what to look for.

Court records reveal how Bamath's scam worked. He submitted invoices to SARS reflecting fraudulent low values of imports, thereby paying less import duty than he should have. He then made photostats of genuine import documentation, using white-out to delete the lower values and overprinting them with higher values. These he presented to the bank as the real thing, enabling him to pay his foreign suppliers the real value of the purchases, with SARS being none the wiser.[v]

One Friday afternoon, a team of SARS officials arrived at Bamath's offices. We wanted to start the inspection immediately but Bamath wasn't present. By law, we had to at least afford him an opportunity to be present before we started searching the place.

I called him, and he said he was on his way. We agreed to wait. I went with a few others to a local restaurant and bought us all some cooldrinks and bunny-chows.[11]

As it got later, Bamath remained absent. At some point in the late afternoon, Soni arrived; he also called Bamath and got the same response: 'I'm on my way.'

v This scam wouldn't work today because SARS and the banks have a direct relationship, and third-party verification processes are in place.

Finally, we decided we couldn't wait any longer, and went ahead and conducted the search and seizure without Bamath there. The teams went through each office, painstakingly looking for relevant documents and other evidence.

Soni, another investigator and I were in Bamath's office when he finally arrived. We all sat down and spoke late into the night, with Soni playing the 'bad cop' and me the 'good cop'.

All the while the team was busy going through every document with a fine-tooth comb. Every time they found something incriminating, they'd come in to the office and confront Bamath with it.

Eventually, after midnight, Bamath gave in and accepted that he had to face his day in court.

Our next move was to call the NPA prosecutor assisting us on the case. 'No problem,' he said, half asleep, because by then it was after 01h00. 'He can come in on Monday and we'll settle the matter.'

A while later Bamath appeared in the Pretoria Commercial Crimes Court and was convicted on 81 counts of tax and customs fraud. He received a suspended sentence on condition that he paid the R13 million he owed to SARS.

Another role-player who was caught thanks to the whistleblower's information was Ahmed Bhorat, a Gauteng businessman who'd acted as a clearing agent. He was ordered by the Johannesburg Commercial Crimes Court to pay SARS R1,5 million in tax.

Kiran Naik, a Johannesburg lawyer, had to pay SARS over R4,3 million in outstanding taxes.

By October 2001, SARS and listed company Accord Technologies had also resolved a tax dispute, with Accord agreeing to pay to SARS R36,4 million.[12]

The hammer to hit the final nail in the coffin of the scam in the electronics industry came to us quite unexpectedly. One Saturday Soni and I, with a few others, were working through the mounds of paperwork in the electronics cases – there were hundreds of numbered and sealed boxes that had to be opened, inventoried and inspected, document by document, looking for possible links, evidence or any clue that would help us build our cases.

A SARS security official came into the boardroom and said there was a man at the gate who wanted to speak to me.

'Who is he?' I asked.

'No idea,' the security guy said. 'He didn't want to say who he was and asked to speak to only you.'

I wondered whether I should be worried – could this be someone wanting to identify me for some nefarious reason?

I followed the security guard to the main gate, where I found a man who said he was from a group of attorneys and that he represented someone who had reason to believe he was about to be raided and arrested by SARS and its partners at the NPA and the Scorpions. 'My client is sitting in my car just around the corner,' the attorney said. 'The car is idling and he'll drive away immediately if he's approached by anyone. He fears you may have a warrant of arrest for him and wishes to come clean with SARS and do the right thing.'

I was flabbergasted. I'd never heard of the man or of any company associated with him, yet here was his attorney, effectively trying to arrange to hand over his client, who seemed to believe that we were investigating him and were ready to make an arrest.

Keeping a straight face, I invited the attorney in. He accompanied me to the boardroom, where he made a call to his client to calm him down. Then he repeated to the others what he'd said to me.

Keeping my poker face – and noting that Soni instinctively did the same – I asked, 'What do you want, then? Or rather, if your client is guilty of customs fraud, what does he expect of us? Why is he here? And why are you here?'

'Well,' said the attorney, 'we were hoping that if he came clean, the State would keep it in mind when it came to criminal charges against him.'

We called the NPA, who arranged for a prosecutor and Scorpions official to meet with the client. Days later, Dean Su, a Chinese businessman and electronic goods importer, paid R3,4 million to SARS in outstanding customs duties. He was then convicted in the Pretoria Commercial Crimes Court for customs fraud and given a suspended prison sentence and a R500 000 fine payable to the NPA.[13]

The last domino had fallen.

This electronics-industry project was a significant example of collaboration between SARS, the police and the NPA in dealing with an industry that was so fraught with malfeasance that it threatened the fiscus, and would have led to many job losses if not halted in time.

'The fight against crime in South Africa took a significant step forward through SARS's two-pronged efforts, which focused on both internal as well as external elements,' read the *SARS Annual Report* for 2000/01. 'Externally, the most prominent was the clampdown on the retail trade – specifically in the electronics industry. SARS auditors, investigators and prosecutors set a new threshold in the Government's endeavour to marshal South Africans to new levels of tax and customs compliance. With the involvement of the South African Police Service and the NDPP [National Director of Public Prosecutions], eight people have already been criminally charged and nineteen SARS staff members are currently under investigation for corruption. Twenty-seven convictions were achieved with direct imprisonment totalling 121 years.'

4

Pay now, argue later

When I started working at SARS I spent many a night studying legislation and case law on tax, customs and excise matters in the hope of being able to understand more about what powers existed in law to conduct investigations and how best to do so. I discovered that legislation allowed SARS to put direct questions to a taxpayer, which the taxpayer was compelled to answer; failure to answer was in itself a criminal offence.[1]

I also discovered that SARS could use these powers when engaging third parties who may hold information on specific taxpayers. I found that the laws made provision for search-and-seizure warrants that could be used when a taxpayer didn't satisfactorily answer SARS.

What struck me at the time, however, and especially when I started reviewing existing and past audits and investigations as part of my orientation, was that it seemed that SARS didn't use its powers to their fullest extent. In fact, I could find no record of any significant searches conducted by SARS under tax-law warrants at the time.

I raised this during our regular planning and strategy sessions, which were chaired by Ivan Pillay as the general manager: Special Investigations, and it was resolved that as soon as the most appropriate case came up, we should begin to use these powers more effectively and start making examples of recalcitrant taxpayers.

Soon enough, such a case came along.

Metcash Trading Africa was what's known in the trade as a fast-moving consumer goods (FMCG) supplier and distributor. It had a vast network of supermarkets and convenience stores, fast-food and liquor outlets (many of which were 'cash and carry' shops, that is outlets that sell goods at high volumes for low prices), wholesale stores and retailers of basic consumer goods. It also sold and distributed goods to other, unconnected stores and outlets all over the country. The company was based in Johannesburg and had operations as far afield as Malawi, Namibia, Swaziland and Lesotho.

SARS had been in a tussle with Metcash for a while, with intermittent rumblings from the tax authority about Metcash's value-added tax (VAT) returns and payments, and in 1996 SARS gave Metcash formal notice that its VAT returns for July 1996 to June 1997 were considered problematic.

Matters finally came to a head in 1999, the year Pravin Gordhan became the SARS commissioner. In what was probably the biggest corporate case that SARS had tackled head-on, the Metcash offices were raided, and assessments were served alleging that fictitious transactions had been entered into by Metcash and/or its associated companies with four named close corporations.

Audits, correspondence, investigations and further meetings followed between SARS and Metcash. It was decided that Metcash should pay what was due immediately (R77 667 722,27) and argue later about the merits of the case – a situation allowed for by taxation law.[2]

Metcash was in trouble.[3]

Metro International, the holding company, immediately felt the brunt of shareholders selling off shares in the wake of the news.

Things started playing out rather nastily in the public domain. In a sponsored advertisement in the October 1999 edition of *Taxgram*, Metcash effectively accused SARS of having acted improperly in its investigations. 'Metro abhors the high-handed and bullying tactics used by SARS ... and feels that the commission arrangements existing between SARS and their investigators have given rise to the acts of SARS, and that SARS have failed to demonstrate the high standard of professional ethics or impartial, fair and equitable service, expected of a public administration,' the ad read.[4]

SARS responded with a press statement describing its open-door policy for the purposes of discussions with any taxpayer, and stressing that it was SARS policy to be accessible to taxpayers and that it invited frank discussions between it and taxpayers at any time.

Not surprisingly, Metcash objected to the SARS assessment; SARS considered the objection and disallowed it.

Metcash, which had the option to take its case to a special tax court to be independently considered and decided on, didn't go this route. Instead, the company brought an urgent application to block SARS from immediately collecting the tax debt, and a further order to declare that SARS had acted unconstitutionally by asking for payment of due taxes upfront.

Round one went to Metcash, with the High Court ruling in its favour that the 'pay now, argue later' sections in the tax legislation were unconstitutional.[5]

SARS took the High Court loss against Metcash on the chin, and went back to the drawing board. The issue was simple: if taxpayers could abuse the process of litigation through various means as a way to delay having to pay SARS any due taxes, the country would run out of money soon enough. By then, SARS was used to vexatious litigants who tried every trick in the book to delay having to pay their dues; in later years, we had cases that spanned decades. Imagine what would happen if we allowed all and sundry who happened to be in dispute with SARS to delay their tax payments?

Kosie Louw, then head of the Law Administration and Policy division of SARS,[6] had been part of the taxation system in South Africa for many years. A recognised expert on tax policy in South Africa and worldwide, he and his team of expert lawyers did tremendous legal research on tax policy and systems around the globe, and got multiple legal opinions from constitutional experts on the topic in relation to this case. As a result, SARS decided to take the matter to the Constitutional Court, under the lead of Louw and his able team of lawyers, flexing powers in law that had until that time rarely been used.

In its judgement, the court made one of the most beautiful statements in law when it comes to our Constitution (bearing in mind that our new democracy was only five years old at the time, and the Constitution even younger).

'The interim Constitution, which came into force in April 1994, was a legal watershed. It shifted constitutionalism, and with it all aspects of public law, from the realm of common law to the prescripts of a written constitution which is the supreme law. That is not to say that the principles of common law have ceased to be material to the development of public law. These well-established principles will continue to inform the content of administrative law and other aspects of public law, and will contribute to their future development. But there has been a fundamental change.

'Courts no longer have to claim space and push boundaries to find means of controlling public power. That control is vested in them under the Constitution, which defines the role of the courts, their powers in relation to other arms of government, and the constraints subject to which public power has to be exercised. Whereas previously constitutional law formed part of and was developed consistently with the common law, the roles have been reversed. The Constitution articulates and gives effect to the governing principles of constitutional law. Even if the common law constitutional principles continue to have application in matters not expressly dealt with by the Constitution (and that need not be decided in this case), the Constitution is the supreme law and the common law, insofar as it has any application, must be developed consistently with it and subject to constitutional control.'[7]

At the end of the trial the Court ruled, among other things, that the principle of 'pay now, argue later' for revenue authorities wasn't unique to South Africa and had, in fact, been adopted in many other open and democratic societies. The loss in the High Court was thus overturned by the Constitutional Court, and SARS won the battle. The Constitutional Court confirmed the legitimacy of the 'pay now, argue later' principle for SARS, and Metcash had to pay up.[8]

Following the judgement, Metcash and SARS began to talk, and the engagements were a lot more open and intended to seek a mutually acceptable resolution. On 6 November 2000 Metcash acceded to a settlement with SARS of R128 million.

Gordhan was quoted in the media as saying that the settlement didn't constitute any admission of wrongdoing by Metcash. He said the R128 million included around R80 million in tax that had been claimed by Metcash as a tax refund. 'Metcash claimed from SARS input tax in respect of transactions that were fictitious insofar as no goods were actually supplied, hence no input tax was claimable,' he said.[9]

As a direct result, Metcash shares rallied, gaining more than 3% as the market welcomed the settlement.

One thing became clear that year: SARS wasn't going to let big business off the hook merely because they were major players.

What's more, the notion of a social-compliance requirement in our newly democratic country suddenly came to the fore. If big corporate companies failed to comply with their social and legal contract to pay tax to enable the State to fund its programmes to uplift society, their shareholders weren't going to like it. A brand-new aspect of corporate governance, that of having the image of contributing to the fiscus to fund our young democracy, became a new trend.

But that wasn't the end of the Metcash case.

Let me pause here for a moment to describe the relationship between SARS and other state institutions during 2000 and 2001. When needed and to offer assistance where required, we had many interactions with the NPA, the police, the South African Secret Service and the National Intelligence Agency, Defence Intelligence and the police's Commercial Crimes detectives and Crime Intelligence division, as well as the priority focus areas of what was then known as the Office for Serious Economic Offences.

SARS staff were also trained by the intelligence services, with all staff in Criminal Investigations taking formal courses and completing programmes in criminal investigations developed by retired members of the Commercial Crimes division of the police.

The relationships between the NPA, the SAPS Commercial Crimes division and SARS were excellent, and this was evident in how we were able to work together on cases, and in the widely reported outcomes in those days. Those were the golden years when SARS's enforcement capability began to flex its muscles and become a force to be reckoned with.

During this time SARS established and I managed the Special Compliance Unit. It was the first focused unit that looked at significant cases and organised criminals from a SARS statutory perspective. It started with just two members, and later grew larger as we began focusing on organised-crime figures and complex cases.

In September 2002, the National Intelligence Agency and SARS concluded a memorandum of understanding in terms of which we agreed to cooperate to better fulfil our respective responsibilities. Among the various mutual agreements were that both parties would share information in pursuance of their respective legal mandates; that each party would from time to time engage in joint operations, and ensure that information provided in terms of the operational support would not jeopardise or undermine the interests of either of the parties; and, finally, that cooperation would be guided by mutually approved procedures and protocols.[10]

There were various exchanges of information on mutual cases we worked on, and several successful joint SARS/National Intelligence Agency actions in this period which resulted in, for example, a large cocaine bust at the then Johannesburg International Airport (now OR Tambo International Airport), for which one of my units provided cover for a National Intelligence Agency agent who pretended to be a SARS employee. SARS was also part of a committee chaired by the National Intelligence Agency and the NPA's Asset Forfeiture Unit, where a list of national priority crime figures was put together for all of us to work on together.

These activities should be viewed in the context of what was happening in the rest of the Government at the time. In his inaugural address in June 1999, then President Thabo Mbeki had announced that he was instructing a group of ministers to devise a government-wide strategy to combat crime within 14 days. A steering committee was established under the chairmanship of Pete Richer of the National Intelligence Agency, made up of the NPA, the SAPS, the South African National Defence Force (SANDF), the South African Secret Service, the Department of Correctional Services, the Department of Justice, the National Intelligence Agency and SARS. This later led to the establishment of the Directorate of Special Operations, or Scorpions, as well as a number of other operational agreements between various law-enforcement agencies and SARS.

What became clear from these proceedings was that SARS had quite a role to play in assisting other conventional law-enforcement agencies to combat crime.

It was the proverbial dark and stormy night when I received a phone-call from a representative of the NPA asking me to go immediately to a residential address on the East Rand. It concerned a case SARS had been working on for some years.

On my way, I stopped in Mamelodi to pick up a colleague in my rusty old Mazda 626. As we drove on through the storm, as if in some kind of horror movie, we both hoped this new lead would mean a breakthrough in our case.My colleague and I finally arrived at a facebrick house in a typical middle-class suburb. It was pouring with rain as we jumped out of the car and ran towards the gate, and by the time we were buzzed in, we were soaking wet.

The NPA official introduced us to the homeowner, who offered us coffee or tea, but we both declined because of the new SARS 'no gift' policy.[vi] And anyway, we wanted to get straight down to business.

vi This very strict policy, which stated that no SARS official could accept any form of gratification, included meals and refreshments.

We were there to discuss what was arguably one of the biggest tax cases in South Africa post-1994 but it all seemed surreal: we were dripping wet, and the owner's boisterous dogs kept jumping up on us; we didn't want to sit down for fear of ruining the furniture, so we stood at the dining-room table, on which laptops were open, and notebooks and papers strewn about.

It was explained to us that the homeowner – whom we now understood to be a witness – had insight into buying practices within Metcash. We were told how he'd approached the NPA, stating that he had insider information on how certain frauds were being perpetrated within Metcash. The authorities had started debriefing him, which is when they'd realised they needed us – we'd been asked to attend because the officials didn't understand the intricacies of exports and their tax implications, and the NPA officials hoped we'd be able to guide the interview.[11]

We were warned that the homeowner was being treated as a potential witness in a criminal case being considered by the prosecuting authority, and that we were under no circumstances to identify him.

The homeowner brought us towels, and we dried off and sat down.

If any VAT vendor exports goods out of South Africa, among other benefits due to the taxpayer is the VAT amount (14% at the time) on that transaction, which can be claimed back for the full value of the items sold and exported. So, theoretically, if someone claimed to have exported R1 million-worth of goods from South Africa, then technically that taxpayer could claim back R140 000 from SARS.

What this witness was telling us, and showing us by way of supporting documents, was that the buyers in the countries who were supposedly the recipients of the sold goods, didn't exist.[12]

And there was an added twist: in these types of businesses, selling agents, who were inside the business and trading on its behalf, received significant commissions on such deals. Some of these deals were substantial and therefore so were the commissions. So, apart from the tax implications of the fraud, individuals were also milking the internal system by earning massive commissions on transactions that had never occurred. It was fraud upon fraud, and the evidence to prove it was right there in front of us.

The very next day, 7 November 2000 – just after SARS and Metcash had agreed to a settlement – SARS announced that it was conducting a criminal probe into suspected tax fraud at the company. Investigations had found evidence that a series of tax-refund claims forwarded by third parties and some people within Metcash had been fictitious. 'We don't have evidence that the Metcash board was involved in this but we certainly have evidence that shows that certain members of Metcash staff were involved, and people outside of Metcash,' Gordhan said at a news conference.[13]

We worked that case very hard. The team at SARS, the investigators and auditors, the prosecuting authority and police officials all pulled together. It was a complex matter, and we had to sift through mountains of evidence and information. Slowly but surely, we built up a case that pointed to several individuals within and outside of Metcash who'd been using their buying and selling systems to generate fictitious transactions.

As SARS, our criminal investigations were limited, our policies and procedures premised on and informed by a 1995 High Court case that governed private investigations. In a nutshell, the court had ruled that any person (not only the police) could conduct a private investigation, and that this was a constitutional practice, provided that the functions of the police where criminal procedural legislation assigned specific powers to police officials weren't usurped. So as SARS employees we could gather evidence and information and affidavits, but we were unable to use certain parts of criminal procedure reserved for police officials, enabling them to obtain court-approved subpoenas and warning statements from suspects, for example.

So we collected whatever evidence we could, and sifted through boxes and boxes of documents provided to us. We built this case for the prosecuting authority, and the docket was finally ready and handed over to the NPA in early 2001.

Sadly, as the relationship between SARS and the NPA came under increasing pressure from the early 2000s, the Metcash case – and quite a few other big cases – died a silent death.

5

The Iron Duke

Never judge a book by its cover, the saying goes. Well, no other case in my life proved this more conclusively than *Irvin Khoza vs the Commissioner of the South African Revenue Service*.

How I first came to meet soccer administrator Irvin Khoza, aka 'the Iron Duke', played out rather publicly.[1] One day in August 2001, I was standing at international arrivals of the then Johannesburg International Airport, with a SARS team, waiting for a flight from Sweden. The team consisted of mainly auditors and one lawyer. We said very little to each other as we waited, our eyes glued to the announcement board.

I was anxious. In my hand I held two envelopes containing copies of a search-and-seizure warrant authorised by a judge in terms of the Income Tax Act.

The minutes felt like hours. Finally, the flight touched down and the arrivals board informed us that the passengers were disembarking. I looked at the team, shut my eyes for a few seconds and took a deep breath to compose myself, then gave the signal to go.

I immediately identified the man as he came through the arrivals gate. He was taller than I'd imagined, and very well dressed; in contrast to the other, dishevelled and clearly travel-weary passengers, he looked rested.

I walked up to him, put out my hand to greet him, and said, 'Mr Khoza, my name is Johann van Loggerenberg. I think by now you might know who I am but for the record let me identify myself. I'm from the South African Revenue Service. These people with me are all officials of the South African Revenue Service. I have with me a warrant, signed by a High Court judge, authorising the South African Revenue Service to search several premises associated with you.'

Khoza smiled and shook my hand. He was as cool as a cucumber. 'No problem,' he said. 'How does this work?'

I handed him a copy of the search warrant and asked him to sign it, which he promptly did. I advised him to make contact with his lawyers and said that we'd wait for him while he did so. I suggested that it would be best if his lawyers were with us when we executed the search warrant.

He made a call, then turned to me and said, 'I suggested that they meet us at my home. Is that good for you?'

I nodded. We all walked out of the airport, and I watched as he was driven off by a chauffeur. We hopped into our cars and travelled to Diepkloof in Soweto.[2]

Irvin Khoza was born in 1948 into humble circumstances in the township of Alexandra in Johannesburg. In the early 1970s he developed what soon became a successful shopping centre in Soweto. In about 1976, when he wasn't yet 30 years old, he became the general secretary of Orlando Pirates football club, also known as the Buccaneers – one of the top clubs in the country and a key player in the Premier Soccer League.

Khoza left the club around 1982 to pursue other business interests, and it soon became evident that he had the Midas touch – every new business venture went from strength to strength.

Although public records on the ensuing years are thin, it would seem that Khoza became involved in the struggle against the apartheid regime in the 1980s, with his most intense connection with the liberation movements between 1982 and 1992, when he was apparently primarily based in Zambia but frequently travelled on business to the so-called Frontline States.[3]

He returned to the Buccaneers in 1992, becoming their managing director and funder of the club. In no time, it was top of the football league.

When we first started investigating him, Khoza was something of an enigma. A number of rumours about his past had been aired in the media, and the reason I'd been so anxious that day at the airport was because of all the stories I'd heard or read. There were claims that he moved in unsavoury circles and mingled with drug dealers.[4]

He'd had a few scrapes with the law in his early life: he'd been convicted of insurance fraud in 1979 and received a sentence of R3 000 or 12 months' imprisonment, and had also been sentenced to R2 000 or nine months' imprisonment for insurance fraud in 1981 (it seems these records were later legally expunged). During the course of our background research on him, we also found that he had alleged links with an agent of the old apartheid regime's South African Defence Force.[5]

Although, when I was assigned the case and we started the investigation, I was apprehensive and even concerned for the safety of my team, our case against Khoza turned out to be much less dramatic than the rumours about him. Court records would later reveal that SARS was investigating him because he hadn't submitted tax returns from 1996 to 1999 and, as a consequence, the tax authority couldn't determine whether he'd paid accurate taxes.

In August 2001, when we got permission to execute the raid, the media caught wind of it and camped out in the street outside his home that day.

With the assistance of an assigned lawyer, we managed and coordinated searches at various premises throughout the day, and I oversaw the main team at Khoza's home in Soweto.[6]

Khoza was very gentlemanly throughout the process, even offering to arrange meals for us as the day dragged on (we had to decline). At one point he told me he was uncomfortable with the media outside, and we agreed that we'd go out together and to tell the gathered press that we had no comment and ask them to leave. Surprisingly, this worked, and most of them did leave.

Later that day Khoza asked me whether we possibly could speed up the process, as he didn't want his family to be exposed to the search. I agreed and pushed the teams hard but his wife Matina arrived before we'd finished, and she was equally gracious.[7]

Every so often, one of the investigators would come and ask me about a document. We'd look at it together to consider its relevance, then make the call whether we wanted to seize it. It was hard going but we finally finished and left the premises late that afternoon.

Following the search, Khoza immediately assembled a highly qualified team of advisers with a bulldog-like style, including advocate Andre Bezuidenhout, who could cite criminal-procedure law by heart; attorney Daniel Erasmus, probably the foremost private-practice attorney specialising in tax in the country; and Dr WAA Gouws, a chartered accountant with a keen eye for detail.

On our side, a small team worked on the case, with most of the slog shared between an auditor, an advocate, a lawyer and me. We started off working out of a storeroom behind the security entrance at head office, with few resources and access to very few auditors. All of us had other cases and responsibilities, and we were stretched pretty thin. Because the case was so high profile at the time, we were also expected to keep the SARS executive apprised of all developments. Let me tell you, it was tough and we slept very little, but we were determined to give it our best.

We dealt predominantly with what we called the 'civil side', referring to the actual financial audit and assessments; the Scorpions, the NPA and the police worked on the criminal case. At the time, Khoza hadn't been charged for tax evasion, but a case docket for contravening the Income Tax Act had been opened at the Johannesburg Central police station.[8]

We also made history by raiding the Sandton offices of Khoza's tax consultant, Andrew Pienaar – tax consultants and accountants weren't used to being raided by SARS.

Relations started souring when the matter was taken to the media. Erasmus, who usually did most of the talking, would typically accuse SARS of being a high-handed bully, which led to a ping-pong game in the press, with accusations flying both ways. Finally, however, we all managed to sit around a table and agree on a way forward.[9]

We had meeting after meeting with Khoza's team, with me leading most of the interactions. They really made us work hard. Gouws would prepare the numbers, Bezuidenhout would present complicated legal questions, and Erasmus would throw curve balls. After each meeting, we'd have to go back and rework our evidence, the numbers and our legal position. Round and round we went, week in and week out.

One positive spin-off of these tactics was that I learned a hell of a lot more about tax, and in fact began to study the relevant legislation and case law to prepare for our meetings. Each time I walked into a meeting with those three, I knew a little more than before.

In the second half of 2002, I received a call from Erasmus asking me whether I'd be prepared to meet with Khoza personally, informally and off the record. SARS had just opened its brand-new service centre in Randburg, and this venue suited Khoza. We met in a small boardroom; Khoza declined offers of coffee or tea.

We had a private and intimate talk. He spoke softly and looked me straight in the eye throughout. While I promised never to reveal the details, I can say this much: we didn't talk about his financial or tax affairs. It was a discussion between a young white South African who came from a privileged background thanks to a horrible apartheid regime, now working for the new democratic State, and an older black South African who'd been born in poverty, in a poor township created by that same apartheid regime to suppress black people, and who'd worked his way to the top despite all these challenges.

Remember I started this anecdote with the old saying 'never judge a book by its cover'? When I left that meeting that morning, I'd realised the truth in this adage. Khoza wasn't a 'bad' man, as some stories would have some believe. He was a true patriot, someone who loved his country, who'd sacrificed a lot for it, and who was busy investing in its future as a new democracy.

There were a few more interactions with Gouws, Bezuidenhout and Erasmus before we wrapped things up. Finally, in August 2002, SARS announced that Khoza had settled his personal-tax dispute, agreeing to pay an outstanding amount of about R7,2 million. He'd accepted personal tax liability totalling about R10,3 million, including interest and penalties, and had already paid about R3,1 million. 'We are comfortable that his personal liability has been established,' a SARS statement read.[10]

At the same time, SARS announced that the decision about Khoza's criminal prosecution for alleged tax evasion was up to the police and the NPA. A day or so later, the prosecuting authority issued a statement saying that prima-facie evidence existed to substantiate the original tax-evasion complaint. Evidence beyond the ambit of the original complaint had since come to light, media reports revealed, and was being investigated; there was a viable potential that further charges, among others relating to income-tax fraud, might be added to the existing charges.

In the same month, Khoza appeared in the Johannesburg Magistrates' Court. He was charged with four counts of contravening income-tax law relating to the years 1995 to 1999. The prosecutor asked for a postponement to complete the investigation.

Bezuidenhout, appearing for Khoza, objected to the postponement because by then the police had been investigating the case for a year, and he and the State had been negotiating since that June to bring the matter to a close. Bezuidenhout also mentioned that Khoza was on his way to Manchester in the United Kingdom to lead the South African delegation's bid to host the FIFA Soccer World Cup in 2010. He asked for the case to be struck from the court roll, as there was no indication of when the State's case would be completed. The matter was again postponed.

Then, in April 2003, it was reported that Khoza had appeared before the Johannesburg Regional Court on four charges under the Income Tax Act. He was cautioned and discharged after admitting that he'd negligently failed to ensure that his financial advisers had supplied correct information to SARS.[11]

In that same month, Khoza launched the official South African 2010 World Cup Soccer Bid in Cape Town.

The following year, then FIFA president Sepp Blatter announced in Zürich that South Africa would host the World Cup. The television cameras panned over to the South African delegation. Between our beloved Tata Nelson Mandela and Danny Jordaan, the head of the local organising committee, stood Irvin Khoza, the Iron Duke.

6

Wheels of Africa

It's a tale out of Africa, but it could have been made for Hollywood. An ambitious young mechanic buys a rundown fleet of trucks, then creates a thriving cargo-hauling business. Looking for a new challenge, he builds an auto plant and a string of dealerships. He angers rivals by offering deep discounts and superior service. Finally – after suffering lawsuits, corruption investigations and a costly price-cutting war – our protagonist goes bankrupt.

And let's not forget the rumours. Was he involved in the killing of a Daewoo executive? Did he really help finance an army in the Congo? Was he the victim of a Central Intelligence Agency plot?

It may sound like a movie script, but it's the true story of Billy Rautenbach.

— John Boley, 'The Rise and Fall of Billy Rautenbach: How a South African entrepreneur challenged the establishment – and lost'[1]

In December 1999, it became public knowledge that SARS and the Investigative Directorate of Serious Economic Offences were cooperating in an investigation into the affairs of Muller 'Billy' Conrad Rautenbach and his Wheels of Africa group, known for its assembly and sales of well-known car brands Hyundai and Volvo.

Wheels of Africa began as a humble family business. After he took it over, the Zimbabwe-born Rautenbach – the proverbial boy-genius entrepreneur – developed it into the largest truck-hauling company in Africa at the time. By the mid-1990s he'd built up a business empire spread across several African countries – to some he was known as the Napoleon of Africa – as well as having concerns in Australia and the United Kingdom.

No stranger to controversy, Rautenbach had become involved in mining in the Democratic Republic of the Congo (DRC) in 1998. Then DRC President Laurent Kabila sealed a deal with him to operate and run the state-owned Gecamines, and Rautenbach had, by all accounts, managed to substantially increase the profitability of the company.

But rumours started surfacing that Rautenbach was somehow involved in financing the war in the DRC,[2] even if he consistently denied these allegations. By then he had several properties in South Africa and a massive farm outside the Zimbabwean capital Harare, and he travelled all over the world on his Falcon jet.[3]

Rautenbach started the company Hyundai Motor Distributors and based its plant in the Botswana capital of Gaborone. Hyundai Motor Distributors, of which Rautenbach owned 50%, owned all 52 dealerships, 14 used-car outlets and a total of 34 mechanical shops throughout southern Africa.

Botswana and South Africa formed part of a common customs union, and there were certain rules and tariff treatments for the importation of what were known as 'semi-knocked-down' vehicles.

Goods imported to South Africa for local consumption typically attracted duties (a form of customs tax) which were determined according to the description of the goods and their tariffs. Customs rules stipulated what the tariffs were, whether the goods were allowed into the country and what other requirements had to accompany such imports. For instance, it was very difficult to import cars to South Africa, because, apart from the tariff regulations, permission had to first be obtained from the South African Bureau of Standards and the Department of Trade and Industry. This was primarily to protect the local motor-vehicle-manufacturer industry, but it also ensured that other manufacturers didn't dump substandard cars onto the South African market.

From time to time, local vehicle manufacturers needed to import vehicle parts or complete vehicles that they couldn't source locally, however, and they were then allowed to bring in partly assembled 'knock-downs' or 'semi-knock-downs', including engines, tyres and headlights. Lower duties were payable on these, and it was this loophole that formed the foundation of our SARS investigation.

SARS contended that Rautenbach had effectively imported through Mozambique completely built cars stripped of a few parts to comply with the 'knock-down' rules. After delivery in Botswana, the cars were reassembled and sold as 'manufactured in Botswana'. This way, Rautenbach paid 23% import duty to the Botswana revenue authority, and no additional tariff to the South African customs authorities once the vehicles were exported to South Africa.[4] Local manufacturers who played by the rules were required to pay a 115% tariff on fully imported cars.

The consequence of Rautenbach not paying the full and correct customs duties was that Hyundai Motor Distributors could sell its vehicles much cheaper in South Africa than its competitors. The pricing advantage also enabled Rautenbach's company to offer vehicles with air-conditioning, leather trim and fancy radios as 'standard', and the cars came with three-year warranties, which were unheard of at the time.

In no time, Hyundai Motor Distributors – whose outlets were, unlike its competitors, also open on Sundays – had taken the motor-vehicle market by storm and owned 10% of the market share.

In reaction, some local manufacturers approached the courts with an order seeking to prohibit Hyundai Motor Distributors from trading on Sundays, and failed.[5]

Their next step was to engage with the Department of Trade and Industry, the designers and regulators of import rules and regulations. Soon enough, the Department of Trade and Industry changed the rules for semi-knock-down imports, providing a clearer definition to avoid abuse. But Rautenbach was seemingly unaffected – he was in the process of expanding the Botswana plant at a cost of R250 million.

In May 1999 banks threatened to foreclose on Hyundai Motor Distributors. (It would later be revealed that the company may have overextended itself financially and that financiers gave Rautenbach hard cash to get out of that spot of bother.)[6]

By then, old hands John Bear and Albert Gouws from the Germiston SARS Special Investigations office had for some years been conducting a special tax review on Rautenbach and Wheels of Africa, which included Hyundai Motor Distributors and Swedish Truck Distributors.

Gouws, who was nearing retirement age, was always dressed in a suit and was a true gentleman. Bear, an understudy of Gouws who at first glance looked more like a rugby player than an auditor, was as sharp as a razor. These two men were key to the project from the word go.[7]

SARS's legal powers followed a sort of 'hierarchy' along a continuum, from least to most intrusive. So, first, SARS could invoke its powers to ask third parties such as banks for information about a taxpayer, and this information had to be provided; next was the right to ask questions directly of the taxpayer, who had to respond even if they incriminated themselves. And, finally, SARS could use more intrusive powers, such as search-and-seizure warrants and tax inquiries to subpoena and question witnesses – but these more intrusive mechanisms required the tax authority to apply to a High Court judge and demonstrate that all other methods had failed to provide answers.

In the Rautenbach/Wheels of Africa investigation, SARS was forced to opt for a search-and-seizure operation, which we planned meticulously in conjunction with the Investigative Directorate of Serious Economic Offences. At the time the warrant was issued, over 80 000 owners had bought cars from dealerships that relied on warranties and services issued by Rautenbach's company.[8]

On the morning of the raid, well before sunrise, we all gathered in the underground parking lot of SARS's head office and were divided into teams; each team was assigned a lawyer. The management team (of which I was part) would oversee the search at the headquarters of Hyundai Motor Distributors in Germiston on the East Rand, an imposing building comprising several floors, including Rautenbach's personal office.

The teams made their way to the respective premises, each armed with copies of the signed search warrants, the basis of which included allegations of customs and tax fraud, evidence of corrupt payments made to bank officials, and indications that Rautenbach had allegedly embezzled millions from Hyundai Motor Distributors and Swedish Truck Distributors from 1994 to 1999 – Gouws and Bear's hard work paying off.

In what would be one of the largest search-and-seizure operations executed by law-enforcement agencies in post-democratic South Africa, all teams would execute the search warrants at the same time, as soon as the offices opened.

The first stop of our team at the Germiston premises was Rautenbach's vast offices; Rautenbach himself wasn't there. The various teams began the painstaking task of searching desk by desk. It was a massive undertaking and included many desktop, laptop and server computers. Everything had to be done by the book.

In Rautenbach's personal office we found a large walk-in safe. We asked all his managers, but nobody knew the combination or had the keys. Then we asked Rautenbach, by telephone through his lawyers, for access to the safe but nothing was forthcoming. So, eventually, a locksmith was called.

It took him some time to come back to us, and the look on his face wasn't inspiring. 'I've never seen this kind of safe before in my life,' he said. 'I have no idea how to open it.'

Now, more than ever, I was convinced that the safe was our key. We called in a steel-cutting expert, who used a complicated gas mixture and blowtorch affair; we all had to stand far back and not look into the flame. The process was excruciatingly slow but, finally, after more than an hour, the safe was cracked.

Slowly the door swung open. We all moved closer.

In the dying light of the day, we saw that the safe was empty aside from a few documents and items of personal value. I pictured

Rautenbach somewhere far away, laughing his head off at us.

The search ended very late that night. Apart from the offices, we also raided homes and even an aircraft hangar. Inventories had to be made up, including each and every document and record taken by us; these inventories made up a book on their own. Three large trucks travelled from one location to the next, collecting the seized documents and records.

The fallout was immense. The Hyundai Motor Company in Korea issued a warning that it might not honour the warranties of cars built at the Botswana plant, and by December 1999, Hyundai Motor Distributors had gone into liquidation, leaving its showrooms in South Africa all but abandoned.

A month later, six South African companies that fell under Wheels of Africa were also placed into liquidation. Sweden's AB Volvo stepped in and began to negotiate to buy the assets of Wheels of Africa's truck and bus companies.

Within months, most of Rautenbach's South African and Botswana companies were in liquidation, leaving debts of more than R1 billion in South Africa and R900 million in Botswana.[9]

Rautenbach was nowhere to be found. 'He's down a mine in Zambia, waiting till it's safe to come out,' one businessman joked at the time.[10]

But it didn't take long for him to start fighting back. He brought an application in the High Court seeking to review and set aside the search warrant, and asking for all seized records to be returned to him; he cited as respondents virtually every law-enforcement agency in South Africa. The application also sought to interdict SARS from communicating any matters that came to its knowledge in the performance of its duties; it tried to interdict the director of Public Prosecutions from 'making any further defamatory statements' about Rautenbach; and it sought to have a section of the National Prosecuting Authority Act declared invalid because, according to Rautenbach, it was inconsistent with the Constitution.[11]

What this application also did, however, was bring the details of the case into the public domain. This afforded us the opportunity to put some facts straight, and in our responding affidavit, we were able to demonstrate the history of our investigations into Rautenbach and his companies. We asserted that where these companies were writing off for tax purposes operational costs in South Africa, these should rather have been borne by non-South African companies; we were able to demonstrate the large sums involved in the transport costs of vehicles being imported into South Africa; and we were able to show how travel and other expenses relating to non-South African activities were deducted, resulting in the South African taxpayer effectively subsidising the business and Rautenbach's private living expenses.

Irksomely, Rautenbach ultimately won the case on a technicality, because the search warrants had been obtained as part of a preparatory investigation that the High Court found to have been unconstitutional. But the judge then did something that was still rather rare at that point – he referred the matter to the Constitutional Court for confirmation.[12]

It was then that I met Rautenbach for the first time. He and his lawyers had arranged to see us, and on the day in question, I was standing outside the boardroom where the meeting was to take place, with people coming and going around me. A snappily dressed young man – I was 30 at the time, and he looked younger than me – with a quiet demeanour was also waiting, and we struck up a casual conversation.

When the rest of the attendees arrived, I made my way to the boardroom and the young guy followed; I assumed he was on Rautenbach's legal team. When we were all introduced, I was surprised to discover that the young man was Billy Rautenbach himself. (He also turned out to be ten years older than me!)

What struck me about him were his intensity and focus. We were dealing with complex issues, difficult legal concepts and technical interpretations of tariffs, and he was effectively facing off against a team of experts – but he was on top of everything and handled the meeting very well.

In August 2000 the Constitutional Court declared that the Investigative Directorate of Serious Economic Offences and SARS had been justified in raiding the various premises associated with Rautenbach, and that the relevant sections in law that had earlier been successfully challenged as unconstitutional were, in fact, not. Deputy Judge President Pius Langa said that the law properly balanced the right to privacy, as entrenched in the Bill of Rights, and the 'important interest' of the State in the effective investigation of criminal activity.

As part of the ongoing investigation, just one month later, the newly established Asset Forfeiture Unit obtained a provisional preservation order to lay claim to property belonging to Rautenbach, including a Falcon jet, a Bell helicopter, a house and six flats in Sandton, a Cape wine farm and a farm in KwaZulu-Natal.[13]

In April the following year, Rautenbach struck back, launching an application in the High Court to have the order set aside on the grounds that it had been obtained in his absence. He lost the case.

By then, the Independent Directorate of Serious Economic Offences team had begun preparing extradition papers to have Rautenbach brought back from Zimbabwe to be charged for fraud amounting to over R100 million, but Rautenbach fought on, and by October 2002 he'd won his case against the Asset Forfeiture Unit, with the Court ordering the return of all his assets.

Things went pear-shaped for us from this point, with the criminal case against Rautenbach floundering and the extradition never seen through.

I've often wondered why the wheels started coming off around that time. I think it may have had something to do with NPA officials and the newly established Scorpions becoming increasingly involved in matters of a political nature, and cherry-picking particular cases that would have some or other political consequence.

It was from then on that increased pressure was placed on me, my investigators and other people at SARS to participate in cases with the Scorpions, in ways that we weren't prepared to – the perception of not being independent and objective was something we at SARS wished to avoid.

The first cracks in what had up until then been a very good intergovernmental relationship started to appear.

Rautenbach went on to become a major shareholder in a DRC copper-mining company called Central African Mining and Exploration, and remained out of SARS's reach. His debts to us remained on our books but there was very little we could do unless the NPA succeeded in extraditing him to South Africa.

Then, in 2007, Rautenbach was arrested in the DRC and deported to Zimbabwe. The DRC government issued a statement saying that it was 'making strenuous efforts to clean up the mining sector in the country, and has taken seriously South African charges of fraud, corruption and other crimes against Rautenbach'. (The statement was drawn up and issued by British public-relations company Bell Pottinger – the same company later hired by the infamous Gupta family.)[14]

The NPA announced that it would adopt a wait-and-see approach before deciding whether or not to seek businessman Billy Rautenbach's extradition from Zimbabwe.

In the interim, Rautenbach continued living the high life in that country.

PART 2
THE RISE

'In addition to the many ongoing programmes that we have been implementing, Government will this year ... start the process of further modernising the systems of the South African Revenue Services, especially in respect of border control, and improve the work of the interdepartmental coordinating structures in this regard, intensify intelligence work with regard to organised crime, building on the successes that have been achieved in the last few months in dealing with cash-in-transit heists, drug trafficking and poaching of game and abalone ...'

– *Thabo Mbeki, in his State of the Nation Address to the Joint Sitting of Parliament, 9 February 2007*[1]

7

Many hands, light work

As we began to grapple with more and more cases that required not only the recoupment of lost taxes and duties but also criminal prosecutions, we started learning more about how SARS could fit into broader efforts by Government to combat crime.

To give this some context, SARS fulfilled the roles of law-enforcement agency, in addition to being an administrator and regulator. This dynamic raised considerations not found in conventional law-enforcement agencies, which engaged with people only when crimes were suspected or committed. In the case of SARS, its relationships with taxpayers, customs traders and licensees imposed continuous obligations on both sides: traders were required to register, file returns or submit certain documents regularly and make payments, and SARS in turn had to process these, verify them and in some cases pay refunds.

In the early years – around 1999 to 2001 – the public's and in particular other law-enforcement agencies' reliance on and expectations of SARS to address the illicit economy was very limited. This increased over time, from around 2000 onwards, however, and was given a further boost by developing statutory obligations, such as SARS's obligations in terms of legislation relating to organised crime (the Prevention of Organised Crime Act of 1998), asset forfeiture (around 1999), financial intelligence (which specifically referred to SARS as key stakeholder from 2001 onwards), corruption (the Prevention and Combating of Corrupt Practices Act in 2004), drugs (in terms of the Prevention of and Treatment for Substance Abuse Act of 2008, which required SARS to submit and act in accordance with an annual 'mini drug plan'), various policing law amendments, and Reserve Bank legislation.

From about 2002, as multiple changes occurred within the broader law-enforcement community and new units formed (such as the Asset Forfeiture Unit and the Directorate of Special Operations), a greater onus was placed on SARS to participate and assist in crime-fighting efforts.

At the same time, SARS had to satisfy its international obligations in respect of existing and ever-growing taxation agreements between South Africa and the rest of the world, and participate in and comply with the requirements of various international mutual trade and customs agreements, and work groups and cases in the World Customs Organisation.

If this weren't enough, SARS was also often called to various parliamentary committees to account for and explain what it was doing about illicit drugs, poaching of abalone, rhino and other wildlife, and other crimes that were troubling our country. The parliamentarians in various oversight committees were tough on us, and expected us to do and answer more each time we came to report back.[1]

A strategic decision was taken by the SARS management team to assist all our law-enforcement agencies in combating organised crime. We knew the State's resources were stretched thin, and that we would all have to do our bit to help curb crime in our new democracy. Besides, many organised-crime syndicates not only contravened legislation administered by SARS but made profits that were never declared for tax purposes.

SARS commissioner Pravin Gordhan had long realised that the illicit economy was untapped from a tax perspective – after all, taxes were due on income regardless of whether the source of the income was legitimate or not. Income was income, and therefore taxes must be paid on it. So even in those early days of SARS, we attempted to understand what was referred to as the 'tax gap' and the 'illicit economy'.

By the mid-2000s several agreements existed between SARS and law-enforcement agencies, including the Commercial Crimes division of the SAPS, the NPA, the Asset Forfeiture Unit, the National Intelligence Agency, the Border Police and Marine Coastal Management.

SARS had also agreed with the NPA to delegate a handful of SARS prosecutors to prosecute tax-related cases. This particular relationship grew to a point where SARS and the NPA entered into a more detailed agreement that resulted in SARS providing funding to the NPA for the creation of Special Tax Units, which included the funding of training of the NPA prosecutors in these units.

It was against this backdrop that, in 2004, then SARS commissioner Pravin Gordhan instructed us to begin to develop a proper strategy for SARS to deal with organised crime. This had to take into account the overall strategy of SARS, which was based on the premise that enforcement of the law was only one of three elements of SARS's compliance model, the others being education and service. When we applied this model, our approach was always to ensure that all taxpayers had an equal chance of being contacted by SARS ('breadth'), that SARS had the ability to investigate or audit complex cases in depth ('depth'), and that the results of all compliance actions could be replicated through all sectors of taxpayers and the economy ('leverage').

It's important to note that the behaviour of taxpayers had to dictate the response by SARS. For example, what may have started off as a seemingly acrimonious relationship could, over time, be resolved as the taxpayer came to realise his or her error. SARS legislation provided for all sorts of mechanisms for this, such as allowing taxpayers to pay fines, and customs traders to pay admissions of guilt and forfeitures. The Criminal Procedure Act allowed for guilty parties to plead guilty, and to plead for leniency from a criminal court or enter into a plea bargain, as long as the NPA consulted with SARS as complainant.

The process to develop a proper strategy for SARS to deal with the scourge of crime was based on the assumption that SARS played a key role in the economy.

The Illicit Economy Strategy was finalised after several drafts and inputs from different departments within SARS. We also consulted widely with other law-enforcement agencies, and relied heavily on a lot of the work done by them in terms of their own powers, capabilities, strategies and focus areas.

The context that SARS moved from within this strategy was threefold: one, that there were statutory obligations on SARS to address crimes in respect of tax, and customs and excise-related offences; two, that we accepted that South Africa faced a crime problem that was attributable primarily to the history of our nation; and three, that although SARS wasn't considered a primary law-enforcement role-player in South Africa, it, like all other government departments, would have to play a more significant role in fighting crime in order to assist the conventional criminal-justice system.

A person who would become another mentor to me at SARS was management and enterprise development specialist Goodnews Cadogan, a rare individual with a deep voice and an infectious laugh, who always had encouraging words for anybody who seemed down in the dumps. Cadogan, a humble man of superior intellect and aptitude, was an organisational design genius, able to simply explain the most intricate of concepts to any audience. He instinctively understood systems, the complex relationships between the law, process, policy and procedure, and the limitations within a state department. He made us think harder and ask more questions, and pushed us to consider the cause and effect of anything we did.

Under his guidance, a group of us developed a 'total compliance approach' that looked at the entire value chain of the relationships and legal obligations that existed between SARS and taxpayers and customs traders, taking into account the role of SARS within the broader governmental system and in relation to the citizenry. The SARS strategy dealing with organised crime was a critical part of Cadogan's total-compliance approach.[2] It was a no-brainer: tax criminality that had financial gain as motive, and the profit incentive for the crooks was automatically removed. At the same time, the likelihood of their being identified and held accountable was increased, and simultaneously the government was assisted in addressing the scourge of organised crime.

Cadogan and I would collaborate over several years not only to develop and strengthen the SARS strategy to deal with the illicit economy and organised crime, but also on a whole host of other strategic approaches that ultimately became embedded in the broader enforcement framework within which SARS operated.

We drew our basic case selection and prioritisation model from the laws administered by SARS, of which there were 34 in total at that time, from the better-known Customs and Excise Act and Income Tax Act to obscure legislation dating back to when Zimbabwe was still known as Rhodesia. These dictated that SARS was obliged to act on matters where tax and customs implications arose directly from crime. To assist us in narrowing our focus, we also took into account the economic impact of the crimes, their value and magnitude, prevalence, frequency and social impact on society. This led us to a further focus on theft and fraud from or aimed at government institutions, such as refund fraud or social-grants abuses, crimes affecting the health of people and crimes affecting the environment.

Following a fairly complex model, we made an artificial distinction between the formal and informal economies, and superimposed over these a third, 'illicit economy'. Effectively, it meant that the types of crimes we were to focus on spanned both the formal and informal parts of our economy, across the continuum of multinationals, large businesses, smaller businesses and the informal trade. Apart from these, there were also 'pure criminal enterprises' – syndicates set up to, for instance, smuggle and distribute illicit drugs. For each of these we had a particular tactic and plan.

In the formal economy, we narrowed our focus to organised tax and customs schemes within legitimate businesses – what we called 'corporate theft', which referred to individuals or groups who ripped off shareholders and investors, tax-avoidance schemes, organised schemes intended to defraud the public, and fraud aimed at government, such as tender fraud. And we narrowed our focus even further, to certain parts of the formal economy, in particular the banking and financial sector, the tobacco industry, clothing, textiles and footwear, and the construction sector.

In the informal economy, we focused on the taxi industry, illicit drugs, smuggling and counterfeit activities (particularly in the tobacco, and clothing and textile industries), the vehicle sector, copper theft, abalone and rhino poaching, and various refund scams and activities aimed at defrauding the State's welfare system.

This Illicit Economy Strategy set SARS on the path of doing its bit to help rid the country of the onslaught of organised crime.

8

Stashed cash

Following the 2016 publication of *Rogue: The Inside Story of SARS's Crime-Busting Unit*, co-authored by myself and Adrian Lackay, I was asked by Gareth Cliff in a radio interview which of the cases I'd worked on at SARS was the oddest or most startling. One I related very briefly, and one other – prime examples of how some tax evaders in our country operate – immediately came to mind.

For many tax evaders, one of their biggest problems is what to do with all the cash acquired by illegal means. Going to the bank is often not an option: if criminals banked all their cash, we at SARS would be able to calculate their ill-gotten gains without any trouble. So what to do?

It was late afternoon some time in the mid-2000s when I, along with a SARS team comprising officials from the then SARS Business Intelligence Unit, Customs and Excise division, Special Investigations and Special Compliance Unit, with some police officials to assist, converged on a certain property. We'd received a tip-off from a whistleblower that the home belonged to a customs clearing agent assisting the Triads – a transnational criminal organisation reportedly based in Hong Kong, Taiwan and Singapore – to smuggle goods into South Africa. Our basic checks had revealed that the clearing agent had run into trouble with SARS on many previous occasions, and our next step was to conduct an inspection of the site in terms of the Customs and Excise Act.

On our arrival, we found the gates to the premises locked and high levels of security, including alarm systems, guard dogs and an electric fence. We knew there were people on the premises because someone answered the buzzer; it was only when we announced ourselves as SARS officials that they suddenly fell quiet.

We had to move fast – we were concerned that they would try to destroy evidence while we sat outside the gate.

'Who's going to scale the fence?' I asked the team.

Former soldier Patrick Moeng, a guy who could really take care of himself when the situation demanded, and who would later become like a brother to me in the many investigations we did together, put up his hand. While we kept the guard dogs busy at the gate, Moeng jumped the fence at the back of the property, and made his way to the main entrance to open up for us. Within minutes he'd buzzed us in.

Once inside, we identified ourselves to the homeowner. We handed over the legal documents, then started the search of the premises. We began to walk through the house in the presence of the owner, going from one room to the next, peering into every nook and cranny of the palatial mansion. The opulent home had many bedrooms, and it was expensively furnished, including several big-screen televisions.

Some areas were clearly designated as office spaces, and we focused most of our efforts on those, finding and looking through thousands and thousands of documents to determine whether anything seemed strange or suspicious before we could lay seizure to them.

In movies this kind of exercise is often made out as a dramatic exploit by the hero of the story, but let me tell you, it's incredibly boring and repetitive, and it takes up much time. It requires constant concentration and an eye for detail. We had to scrutinise each document, trying to find exactly those clues that the evaders were trying to hide from us. In the odd event that we did find potential evidence, we then had to record in an inventory the exact location where we'd found the document, and its details. And once the documents and goods we'd seized had been boxed and sealed, these had to be transported to our offices and packed in an office or storage facility that had security and access control.

This process was extremely important, because it maintained the chain of evidence: as the State, we had to be able to demonstrate later to a court that we'd found a particular piece of evidence at a particular location, that it was indeed from that location, that it was found in the presence of someone who had control over it, that it was scrutinised in the presence of that same person, and that it was then sealed in a manner that would withstand any legal scrutiny at a later stage. If we failed to do this, the document could be challenged in court as never having been found at the premises, or, worse, having been tampered with or altered after its removal from the premises.

The search ran late into the night. At one point we discovered a safe under a carpet in one room but, alas, it contained documents and items of little use to our case.

Then Moeng noticed something about the staircase in the entrance hall. It had what appeared to be solid-wood panelling running all the way to the floor but closer inspection revealed seams that turned out to be hinges fitted between the panels. There were no obvious handles but we realised that the doors could be opened by pushing lightly on them and getting a grip on the panels. So, with Moeng on the one side and me on the other, we opened the 'doors' simultaneously – and cash in all sorts of denominations came crashing down on us. There was a proverbial mountain of money stashed away under the stairs.

Because we were there on a customs inspection, which only allowed us to detain goods defined in the Customs and Excise Act, we couldn't do anything about the cash. But we knew that somebody would have an interesting story to tell about all this money, so we immediately sealed off the area and got the South African Reserve Bank people in.

Many years later, Moeng reminded me of another event that occurred following these discoveries. During the process of our investigations, we were led to another clearing agent's premises and conducted another search-and-seizure exercise there. The clearing agent called Moeng and me to one side, and we expected him to spill the beans. Instead, he brazenly offered us a bribe of hundreds of thousands of rands; we could name our price, he said, if only we let the matter slide. Of course, we laughed him off but this made us even more determined to find all the evidence we needed.

In the end, we did find the evidence, and we were able to assess and schedule the culprits and collect the due revenue for the fiscus, including penalties and interest – although we never could establish the alleged links to the Triads.

In another case we were approached by the then fairly newly established Asset Forfeiture Unit, whose task was to lay claim to the proceeds of organised crime. Money or property that was suspected to be the proceeds or instrumentalities of organised crime could, once its owner was convicted, be forfeited to the State, going into the Criminal Assets Recovery Account, which in turn used the proceeds to compensate victims or fund other law-enforcement agencies and projects.

In the early years, there was a very good relationship between SARS and the Asset Forfeiture Unit. In one of the first cases they worked on, we were approached by the founder of the Unit, advocate Willie Hofmeyr, himself a struggle hero, accompanied by his then right-hand man, advocate Rudolf Mastenbroek. Hofmeyr explained to us that they'd been looking closely at a well-known businessman because of his involvement in illegal gambling dens and possible human-trafficking where people got caught up in prostitution rings. The businessman was very rich and had many law-enforcement officials in his pocket – the reason, apparently, why he hadn't yet been brought to book.

Mastenbroek was in charge of the matter and I instinctively liked him; we got along well in those years. The Asset Forfeiture Unit had collected sufficient evidence to justify executing a provisional preservation order, which would enable them to lay claim to many of the assets they had identified as possible proceeds of crime; and they wanted us to assist them from a customs point of view, because the man was also involved in the import and export of almost everything imaginable.

I met with the Asset Forfeiture Unit representatives and discussed the plan, which called on SARS to assist the unit on the day that they executed their provisional preservation order, to conduct inspections on site at a number of identified premises and see if we could find anything amiss: according to their information, the man had been involved in smuggling, in particular illegal gambling machines.

The day came, and by then we on the SARS team had done our homework and were ready with our own preliminary findings. The searches, which covered many premises at various locations throughout the city and outskirts, started very early in the morning and lasted the entire day, and involved a combination of Asset Forfeiture Unit staff, local police officials and our SARS teams. I oversaw several of the inspection groups.

We were required to inspect a large warehouse in one area, and a number of shops in the city area and on its fringes. When we entered the warehouse, I couldn't believe my eyes. The multistorey building was a little longer than the average sports field, and on floor after floor we encountered an enormous hotchpotch of goods stacked to the ceilings. You name it, it was there: old army boots, clothing, wind-up toys, canned food that was so out of date that the cans were rusted right through … It was physically impossible to do an inventory of the items, there was just so much there.

Deciding that there was nothing significant from our point of view in the warehouse, we moved to the identified shops in the city centre – general-dealer-type outlets of the kind that sell household cleaning materials, cheap clothing, appliances and bric-a-brac. And, again, when we entered the first store, I couldn't believe my eyes – although this time for a different reason. Lying in aisle after aisle were huge piles of rand notes in cash. In some cases, the money had been there for so long that a layer of dust and grime had settled on it.

And this was the case in store after store. They were all in equal states of disarray but virtually without fail each had heaps of rand notes piled up in the aisles. I asked a proprietor at one point how it was possible for them to keep that amount of cash just lying around in the shop. How would they know that it wouldn't get stolen? I asked.

The shopkeeper wasn't really in the mood to chat with me, but he looked me in the eye, and without any glimmer of facial expression, very seriously said, 'If anybody took any of our cash, they know what would happen to them ...'

From SARS's point of view, the case was a success to the extent that many illegal gambling machines were seized. Similarly, the Asset Forfeiture Unit managed to conclude one of their very first large asset-forfeiture preservations.

For some years to come, we at SARS enforcement worked very close with the Asset Forfeiture Unit on a number of matters. By 2006 it was reported that the unit had seized over R1 billion from alleged or proven criminals in the preceding seven years.[1]

9

King

Of all the tax cases that played themselves out in the public domain, *The Commissioner of SARS vs DC King* is probably the most fascinating. Lasting no fewer than 13 years from start to end, it began unceremoniously in a small office occupied by a loyal and dedicated 70-year-old SARS official with the unlikely name of Charles Chipps.

Born Carel Christoffel Ludewicus to a railway-station master and a farmer's daughter from Louis Trichardt, 'Mr Chipps' always hated his birth names. In a tribute to his father, Richard – one of four sons – told how his father changed his names to Charles Christopher Louis at the age of 21.

Mr Chipps became an auditing clerk at an accounting firm, studying at night to eventually qualify as a chartered accountant, then worked for several other companies before joining the then Receiver of Revenue (later SARS).

He was a generous man, and if he had any vices – he didn't smoke or drink – it was being a workaholic. In his 60s when he obtained his Higher Diploma in Tax, the 'painfully pedantic' Mr Chipps 'bragged' (according to Richard) 'that he had worked for 58 years', revelling in the power and authority being a special investigator gave him to 'bring down the bad guys'.[1]

Dave Cunningham King arrived in South Africa from Scotland in 1976 with almost no money, or so the story goes. Around 1994 he came up with the idea of starting a company to manage the treasury functions for government departments and parastatals. King pitched the idea of the company, Specialised Outsourcing, to well-known economist Magnus

Heystek during a round of golf, and invited him to join in the new venture. Heystek declined.

King went ahead with the concept and soon enough it became a favourite of small-cap fund managers.[vii] By 1995, Specialised Outsourcing had listed on the Johannesburg Stock Exchange at around R1,20 a share. During 1998/99, by which time the price had risen to R80 a share, King sold off most of his shares.

A magazine article at the time related how King had purchased a famous Irma Stern painting for more than R1 million. Mr Chipps, an avid reader, picked up on this titbit and decided to do a bit of sleuthing. In May 2000, Mr Chipps wrote a few letters to King, and received some answers. And soon enough he came to discover that all was not well with the buyer's tax affairs.[2]

One morning in early 2001, Mr Chipps came to see me – hobbling along on crutches after injuring his ankle had not stopped him from coming to work and doing what he loved best. In our broom closet of an office, he laid out the case. What started off in this way as a simple matter of a taxpayer not declaring all his income to SARS during the relevant tax years, would grow into a complex legal and technical web spanning more than a decade, many court cases, an international preservation order, and the seizure and sale of foreign assets as far afield as France.

Initiated by Mr Chipps, soon the so-called King team (mainly under my management) was expanded to include a number of auditors, internal and external lawyers, and accountants; Mr Chipps remained an integral part of it.

The first time I met Dave King, I was quite surprised: he was smaller than I'd imagined, softly spoken – he never raised his voice – and had piercing eyes. He was as sharp as a razor and extremely focused. He appeared somewhat irritated in the few interactions of which I was part,

vii 'Small cap' refers to companies with a small market capitalisation value; a company's market capitalisation is the market value of its outstanding shares.

because of what he called our 'unwillingness to bend'. I had to explain to him that his interactions with SARS weren't a business deal, and that we had to operate within the boundaries of our own statutes, and on behalf of the State, taxpayers and the country.

To give a sense of how we tackled these sorts of cases, first, we'd give the findings of one audit team to an entirely different audit team (sometimes specially comprised and including our best auditors and legal people), asking the new team to critique the findings. Once they'd conducted their review, they would interview the original audit team, conducting a sort of 'pressure test' to ensure that everything we did would not only withstand legal scrutiny but was solid in terms of accounting, the numbers, the manner in which our cases were constructed and the working papers that supported our work. The discussions would sometimes become rather heated, and often hard exchanges followed, but they were always conducted in good spirit, and we all accepted that we were doing this for the benefit of our country: there were never any hard feelings between people, even when we vehemently disagreed.

The essence of the SARS case against King was that he'd declared a taxable income of only R60 000 a year but at the same time was able to afford a lavish lifestyle, which included paying R1,76 million for a painting. In the course of the initial audit, it was found that King had made more than R1 billion in profit when he'd sold his shares in Specialised Outsourcing; the shares had tanked when these sales became public knowledge, causing other investors massive losses.[3]

The SARS case was based on the argument that King had restructured his holdings in such a manner as to avoid paying tax. It was later reported that he told a SARS tax inquiry[viii] that the assets were transferred from

viii A tax inquiry happens when SARS approaches a High Court judge and asks permission to conduct an inquiry based on evidence of non-compliance. It's a closed hearing and its contents may not be used by SARS in criminal proceedings – taxpayers who're subpoenaed to testify before such inquiries have an obligation to be truthful, even if it incriminates them.

his company, Ben Nevis, to an offshore company, Metlika, because of concerns he had about exchange control.

What would later become public was that in November 2000, when Mr Chipps had first started asking uncomfortable questions on behalf of SARS, one Steve Bougourd, a senior trust officer at the Bank of Bermuda, wrote to another bank official, Dave Hewitson, noting that Dave King wanted to 'dismantle' the structure of his finances, and transfer the assets of Ben Nevis into a new company, as the 'tax authorities are chasing him'. Less than a week later, a summary of a meeting at the bank with King included: 'DK [Dave King] ... is happy there is no problem from his point of view in closing the Ben Nevis company. His intention is just to present a blind alley to any revenue investigation.'[4]

And in March 2001, Bougourd sent another communiqué to another bank official, Adrian Fairbourn, noting: '[W]e are restructuring Ben Nevis to stop the South African taxman in his tracks. To kill two birds with one stone, we are also liquidating all investments, as he [Dave King] wishes to take stock, consolidate his position and think through his strategy going forward.' The Ben Nevis investments included a £10-million portfolio with Barclays Private Bank, and two Royal Skandia portfolios managed by Cape Town hedge-fund firm Alpha amounting to about £3 million.[5]

The effect of these actions was to try and make it difficult, if not impossible, for SARS to discover and lay claim to R500 million in cash and other assets concealed in Ben Nevis.

On 18 February 2002 SARS approached the court to urgently attach the assets of offshore entities Ben Nevis and Metlika, pending the outcome of an action to be instituted by SARS for the 'piercing of the corporate veil' between King and certain companies.[6] 'Piercing the corporate veil' is the legal jargon used to describe an action pursued against a company that ultimately leads to personal liability of the owners or shareholders, which opens up to risk the bank accounts, property and investments of those owners or shareholders – the corporate structure is the 'veil' that provides protection, and if that veil is pierced, there's no more protection.

The tax claims by SARS at the time were disclosed to be over R900 million in the hands of King and well over R1 billion against Ben Nevis.

SARS contended that King was involved in the transfer of assets out of his name, for instance, the property on which the family home was built was initially registered in the personal name of King, but later transferred to another entity named Talacar; similarly, a Ferrari and Mercedes S500 were both transferred from King to Talacar. Another example was how the R2,75 million King received for the sale of Premier Soccer League club Amazulu Soccer Club was, within minutes, simply transferred out of the country.[7]

SARS also argued that it was only after the tax authority had started asking questions that assets were transferred from Ben Nevis to Metlika.

King put up a legal fight of note. Among many other wranglings, in the initial civil proceedings brought by him against SARS, he argued that the profit on the sales of Specialised Outsourcing shares was of a capital-gain nature and therefore not taxable; and in any event, he said, the profit was derived offshore by a foreign entity. He attributed his living expenses to Ben Nevis as 'remuneration for work done' offshore.

In June 2002, in collaboration with the prosecuting authority and the Scorpions, King was arrested on 300 charges, including fraud, racketeering, money-laundering and tax evasion. He appeared in the Randburg Regional Court, where bail was set at R1 million. King had to surrender his British passport to the police and was prohibited from applying for a new one before the case was completed. He was also ordered to not leave South Africa.[8]

The case was postponed to September that year for further investigation, and was then continuously postponed for the next 13 years.[9]

A preservation order granted in September 2002 began, 'Scotsmen are known to be thrifty. The first respondent [King] is a Scot. He cannot be accused of squandering his money on the unnecessary payment of income tax.'[10]

Part of the preservation order was for a luxurious Falcon 900B executive jet worth about R200 million, which had been flown out of the country and parked at a maintenance facility at Le Bourget Airport near Paris, France. SARS wanted the Falcon sold and the proceeds kept in trust, pending the finalisation of the case against King.

The jet was registered in South Africa in the name of Hawker Air Services, the holding company of which was Metlika.[11] We had to rush to court again, and on 18 February 2003, the court ordered the return of the Falcon to South Africa. It was historical for SARS to have obtained such an order, which spanned the globe.[ix]

However, another of King's companies, Carmel Trading, opposed the application by SARS to have the jet sold off. In papers before court, it emerged that Rand Merchant Bank had been an undisclosed partner in the jet, holding a 99,8% interest, and that, despite the preservation order, in September 2002 Carmel claimed to have informally 'taken over' Rand Merchant Bank's interest in the jet. Carmel's contention was that it could do this because it wasn't bound by the preservation order.

Under normal circumstances, as the court stated, such a 'taking over' would have had the effect of putting an end to the existing partnership and creating a new one.[12] In the February 2003 extension by the court, to include the Falcon and order its return to the country, the court held that the sale of the interests in the Falcon to Carmel was 'a contrived transaction, *in fraudem legis*, to bypass the preservation order' and that Carmel was a mere tool of King under his direct control. (*In fraudem legis* means 'in fraud of law' and includes any act done with the fraudulent intention of evading law.)

The jet remained at Le Bourget and this led to SARS bringing a contempt-of-court application against, among others, King, Hawker and Carmel. King had by then resigned as director of Hawker, which was a way for him to avoid being held personally responsible for bringing back the jet.

ix With the help of the NPA, several court orders, both in South Africa and overseas, were obtained to freeze all of King's funds, including the assets in several trusts and business entities.

The court dismissed the contempt application, because the parties had 'displayed a willingness to cooperate in bringing about the return of the Falcon to South Africa' and therefore a committal would have been inappropriate. At the time, the court said that it had made an order that would 'hopefully have the effect of bringing the Falcon back'.[13]

It didn't.

And, in the meantime, King was reinstated as the sole director of Hawker.

Metlika, which was supposed to bear the cost of the return of the Falcon, withdrew its financial support; Carmel refused to make funds available for returning the jet, and refused to give consent to the sheriff to return it to South Africa. Carmel then sought to register the Falcon in Mauritius, and SARS had to obtain an interdict to prevent this. The matter went from one court to the next, ultimately ending up in the Supreme Court of Appeal.

In the end, SARS got to sell the Falcon in France, realising about R100 million.[14]

Thirteen years later, on 29 August 2013, the NPA and SARS issued the following media statement: 'Mr David Cunningham King, the accused in the case of *The State versus DC King* ... today entered a plea of guilty in the South Gauteng High Court ... on 41 counts of various contraventions of Section 75 of the Income Tax Act 58 of 1962 ...'

In terms of the agreement, King was sentenced to a fine of R80 000 or 24 months' imprisonment on each of the 41 counts – the maximum sentence provided for in the Income Tax Act. The effective sentence was a fine of R3,2 million or 984 months' (82 years') imprisonment.

King also agreed to pay R8,75 million to the Criminal Assets Recovery Account.

King had conceded his tax debt and agreed 'to a payment of R706,7 million ... in respect of his personal income tax and the tax liability of Ben Nevis, a King trust company managed out of Guernsey. The fraud charges against Mr King were not pursued by the State and Mr King accepted liability in respect of 41 lesser counts of contravening Section 75 of the Income Tax Act, including the failure to disclose information and the failure to provide correct information about incomes earned over a number of years.'[15]

The statement quoted King saying, 'When this tax dispute arose many years ago I took a conscious decision not to cooperate with the authorities. That was a mistake. I regret not engaging with the State sooner, as I have found them to be extremely firm but fair in their dealings with me once I fully engaged with them. I accept the fact that I have been non-compliant in the past and will rectify this …

'Part of the agreement is that my family and I will be filing all outstanding tax returns to ensure that we become fully compliant. My experience should serve as an example to taxpayers who find themselves in a similar position with SARS – rather seek early resolution and cooperate with SARS when asked by them to explain your tax affairs. I am delighted to finally put this behind me and to be able to actively resume my business career.'[16]

Of all the things this case demonstrated, it was that taxpayers may have believed that by hiding and moving assets offshore, they would be safe from SARS's ability to get to them. Wrong. The Supreme Court of Appeal case made it very clear that where a taxpayer was subject to the jurisdiction of the South African courts, our courts were able to make preservation orders even of assets located in foreign jurisdictions.

And that judgement went further, confirming that South African courts could order an asset for which a preservation order had been granted, even if located offshore, to be sold off and the proceeds held in trust pending the finalisation of litigation.

On 5 February 2012, 18 months before the King case finally wrapped up, Mr Chipps passed away at the age of 83. He never saw the fruits of his hard work. But part of Mr Chipps's legacy is that he will forever remain the quintessential SARS auditor.

'Heroes come in all shapes and sizes, and from the most unusual places,' began the introduction to a tribute to Carl Chipps in *BizNews* in September 2013. 'In an age when many public servants spend their workdays trying to extract the maximum from the system, the late Charles "Carl" Chipps was an outlier. He believed providence had provided him the skills and position to serve the common good. And he was determined to do this to the best of his ability.'[17]

10

The scams

As is the nature of crime, once a scam is exposed, those engaged in it quickly adapt the way in which they commit their crimes to avoid being detected. Still, most kinds of tax fraud operate on the same principle, and tax and customs authorities cooperate almost daily to try and find out what the workings of the latest scams are. Tax dodgers may get away with it once, and may even continue to get away with it for some years – but, inevitably, the taxman cometh.

During my time at SARS, I participated in researching and publishing manuals and textbooks on how to identify and deal with different kinds of fraud. We published many of our own case studies, and often used these in our inhouse training.

Some time in the early 2000s, I came across a book that told the story of drug smugglers in the 1960s who were known in the United States as 'the Eternal Brotherhood of Sunshine'. The book tells of a group of beach bums and surfers who started a shop from where they plied their trade, selling large amounts of LSD.[1] Two observations in the book by an investigator from the Internal Revenue Service have stuck with me through the years: when conducting tax investigations, the investigator always has the option of engaging directly with the subject almost from the word go; and, worldwide, tax and customs legislation places obligations on people to tell the truth when asked for information by tax authorities, regardless of the source of their income or how they hide it – failing to answer is in itself an offence. This is very different from the case of, for instance, a murder suspect, who can choose to remain silent so as not to incriminate himself.

These two aspects gave us as tax investigators a great advantage and were invaluable tools in our toolkit.

Probably the simplest form of tax fraud is where an individual simply fails to register for tax when required to do so. This is typically the case with people operating illegal profit-making enterprises or cash businesses, and those involved in criminal activities for financial gain.

A slight variation on this is the person who's registered for tax but who declares only some of his taxable income. Take, for instance, a consultant who gets paid regular commissions, which he declares in his tax returns; but who also owns a holiday home that he rents out and which income he doesn't declare, and as a consequence he pays less income tax than he should. This often happens with individuals who have multiple income streams and not a single salary.

A third variation is a taxpayer who doesn't submit tax returns as and when required, leaving SARS to guess how much he earned and paid tax on.

Failing to register for tax when required to do so, failing to submit returns when you have to, and failing to declare your income accurately are all statutory offences in law. It can get worse, as all of these misdemeanours could technically also amount to common-law fraud, which means that not only may the perpetrator end up having to pay up to 200% in penalties and compound interest to SARS (depending on the value owed and the time elapsed since payment was due), but he could end up in jail and with a criminal record.

It's not that easy for salaried employees with a single income to commit tax fraud – by law, employers have to deduct tax from their employees' salaries and pay it to SARS – but some still manage to dodge their taxes. How? Well, certain things may be deducted for taxable purposes on a tax return, such as medical-aid contributions, retirement-fund and pension contributions, and travel expenses when the car is used for work purposes. Those employees intent on evading tax may get creative with these numbers, overstating or falsifying records of such payments – although it has become increasingly difficult to do this, as SARS requests proof and has access to retirement funds, pension administrators and medical-aid service providers.

The last and most significant type of tax evasion (excluding, for the moment, those who operate businesses as sole proprietors) is where a person fails to declare a type of income that is taxable by describing it as something else or not at all – this includes 'donations', which are taxable for any amounts received over R100 000 in a tax year.

Professional gamblers, investors or money-lenders may not declare the money they make, thinking of it as 'one off' or the result of pure luck – and ignoring the fact that the activity that generated the income is actually a trade or a business, so to speak, and solely intended to make money.

In South Africa, as in most parts of the world, any form of income is taxable, regardless of the nature of the trade. You may be a diamond smuggler or a police informant, run a 419 scam, operate or participate in a pyramid scheme or investment fraud scam, sell illegal drugs or smuggle tobacco – whatever business you're in, the profits made on those trades are taxable.

Corporate income-tax evasion or fraud is more complicated but is essentially premised on the same formula. The slight difference is that for businesses – and here I now include individuals who run businesses as sole proprietors, in their own name – money spent in the production of their income is tax deductible. This includes travel, advertising, phonecalls, buying raw materials, importing goods or buying things to sell onwards, among others.

In the case of companies, the tax rate is set. If the business is a sole proprietor, the taxpayer is taxed in accordance with a sliding scale that goes up to 45% (at the time of writing) of tax on profit if the income exceeds R1,5 million. These individual tax scales are set annually during the Budget Speech by the Ministry of Finance.

Corporates scam the tax man in a similar fashion to individuals. In its most basic form, there's the practice of conducting sales in cash, which are not recorded and therefore never declared; or only a portion of the income is declared for tax purposes.

Some corporates claim expenses on the basis that that they were spent in the production of income, whereas in fact they were not. This is where you see individuals basically using their businesses to pay for their lifestyle and living expenses, and setting these off against the expenses of the business. This not only reduces the amount of income tax the business ends up paying to SARS, but the individual also benefits from the money without declaring it in his own name as a benefit.

It's at this point that these types of offences become more complicated to investigate. You literally have to follow the money, and often, what may have started as a corporate income-tax case, soon enough evolves into a personal income-tax case as well.

Businesses employ people, and this is where the third most common type of income-tax evasion occurs. Often tax is deducted by the employer, supposedly for tax purposes on behalf of the employee, but never paid to SARS. I've even seen employers and employees collude on this, with both sharing the tax that's actually due to SARS.

Lastly, having an overdue debt to SARS is also a form of tax evasion.

Tax experts refer to income tax as a 'direct tax' because you're taxed directly on what you earn. 'Indirect taxes' include value-added tax (VAT).

Simply explained, VAT works like this. The first buyer of a product, let's say the owner of a small book store, pays 15% of the sales value of whatever is bought, let's say books in bulk. The seller collects that 15% on behalf of SARS.[2] The book seller then adds a little profit to his books, and sells them to another buyer for his marked-up price plus 15% VAT, which he too collects for SARS. In this way, in theory, the 15% VAT paid by the original buyer is passed down the line, ultimately ending up in the hands of SARS.

Normally done every second month (or monthly if the business's turnover is massive), VAT-registered vendors[3] complete a VAT 201 form and submit this to SARS, together with any VAT payments due. Each vendor in the line will set off what VAT he collected in that period against the VAT paid for the same period, which will typically give either a positive balance, meaning that VAT should be paid to SARS, or a negative balance, in which case the vendor will be refunded by SARS.

The simplest form of VAT fraud is when a vendor charges VAT on a sale and pockets the money. The 15% indirect tax is never passed on to any other vendor and/or recorded in any accounting journal. In fact, many such evaders aren't even VAT-registered – they just act as if they are, charging VAT and keeping the money.

A slightly more complicated form of VAT fraud is when a VAT-registered vendor accepts payment in cash, doesn't record those transactions for tax purposes, and pockets those takings. The rest they collect properly and pay on, but the cash deals are the ones to watch.

In order for SARS to verify VAT returns – the VAT 201s – the tax authority requires invoices and proof of payments from the vendor from time to time. This allows SARS to add and subtract to see if the vendor's calculations were accurate, and also to compare the vendor's submissions with those of the other VAT vendors in that set of transactions – and here's where the big fraudsters play. They set up companies to invoice each other without any real transactions taking place, and submit fraudulent invoices that show that VAT was paid when in reality it wasn't. In fact, some of the more sophisticated scamsters set up dud companies solely to defraud SARS of VAT by way of refunds. In this way, hundreds of millions have been stolen by many crooks over many years.

I'll deal with import and export scams a bit later, but it's worth mentioning here that big crooks who deal across borders also scheme their way out of having to pay VAT. In a nutshell, when goods are imported from somewhere outside of the common customs area,[4] VAT is charged by SARS on the value of those goods. If you're a crook, this means you'll want to declare a lower value for the goods than you really paid for them, thereby reducing the amount of VAT payable to SARS. This way, once your goods are in South Africa, you'll also benefit by having goods available to the free market at a lower cost than those of your honest competitors. In my own experience, the electronics industry, clothing and footwear, textiles and the tobacco sector have been most affected by this sort of practice over the years. The scale on which these scams run is unimaginable.

Because SARS places trust in vendors to collect VAT on the State's behalf (in other words, that money never belongs to the vendor), not only do these scams amount to common-law fraud and VAT evasion, but people who steal VAT in this way may also face theft charges.

So the next time you see a bargain that seems too good to be true, please think twice before you buy it. If a shop owner tells you, 'I can give you a better deal if you pay cash,' don't fall for it. And do ask for a receipt and check that VAT is reflected on it, together with the business's name and unique VAT registration number. By doing this, you may very well save that little bit of tax that otherwise we'll all have to subsidise when others don't pay their dues.

Excise duty is another form of indirect tax. These taxes are what are commonly known as 'sin taxes', because governments across the world levy excise duties on goods of a non-essential or luxury nature, such as alcohol and cigarettes, cosmetics and perfume.

Excise duty works similarly to VAT but doesn't pass through the various levels of payees. The manufacturer of the luxury goods is required to be registered with SARS and obtain a licence, and then strictly control and report how much it manufactures. The duty is levied on the amount of goods produced, which can be measured in various ways, for example, sticks of tobacco or litres of alcohol. In much the same way as VAT, the manufacturer must submit standard forms to SARS within specified periods and pay the excise duty at the same time.

In order for the crooks to jimmy the system, they do two things. First, they find ways to under-record the raw materials acquired for the manufacturing process; and, second, they under-report the volumes they manufacture. The consequence is that they don't pay as much excise duty to SARS as they're supposed to. The tobacco industry is rife with this practice.

This brings me to imports. South Africa has a protectionist economy, meaning we levy import duties on imported goods that can be made locally. The duty payable is calculated on three aspects: one, an accurate description of the goods and the applicable tariff payable; two, the value of the goods; and, three, the volume.

There are four main ways that criminals finagle the system. The first way is straightforward smuggling,[x] with goods being brought into the country and simply not declared to SARS at all. An example of this would be smuggled tobacco, usually hidden in baggage, false areas in vehicles and containers, or among genuine goods; and these may not always come through official ports of entry, such as border crossings, airports and harbours.

But people smuggle not only illegal and controlled goods such as arms and drugs, but also perfectly legitimate goods, solely in order to avoid having to pay import duties and VAT. Our clothing, textile and tobacco industries, in particular, have been tremendously affected by this.

The second way is what's commonly referred to as 'undervaluation'. Suppliers of goods, especially in countries in the Far East, are often quite happy to provide a local buyer with two invoices for the same set of goods bought: one reflects the actual value paid for the goods, and the other shows a far lower value, usually in US dollars. In some cases, importers manufacture their own fraudulent invoices. The effect of this is obvious: when the customs duty is calculated, it's done on the lower value depicted on the fake invoice, which is supplied to SARS if required, and this results in lower duties and VAT paid on the imports.

The third scam involves what's commonly known as 'misdeclaration', which means that either the scamster chooses a different tariff category that attracts a lower duty, and describes the imported goods accordingly;

x Interestingly, there's no such offence as 'smuggling' in South African law. If the goods being smuggled are illegal, the smuggler will be charged with the offence of non-declaration or misdeclaration to customs.

or that he declares less of the goods being imported in terms of volume than what is really the case. Both result in lower duties and VAT being paid to SARS.

The fourth scam deals with the way in which imports are classified. In some cases, goods entering South Africa attract no duties or VAT because they're 'in transit', meaning that South Africa isn't their final destination – they're en route elsewhere, such as Lesotho, Swaziland or another Africa country, for example. Theoretically, importers should pay duty and VAT on imports, and once they export the goods (even if it's on the same day), they can claim this back from SARS – but given the huge quantities of goods transiting through South Africa on a daily basis, this would cause an unmanageable mountain of paperwork.

So what do the crooks do? They declare the goods as 'in transit', and get corrupt officials to enter the goods as if exported (and sometimes even go so far as to export empty containers, called 'ghost exports') but in truth the goods are delivered somewhere in South Africa for local consumption. The effect? Zero duties and VAT paid.

A variation of the 'in transit' scam is the 'in bond' scam. Once goods have landed in South Africa, the importer/trader may choose to delay the payment of duties, and in this case, traders can register and license bonded warehouses with SARS. The goods are then placed in the bonded warehouse for a specified period (at present no more than two years). The concept is sound, because it enables businesses to import goods that they may need to manufacture things from, or perhaps add value to, usually intended for export to another country. It also gives manufacturers that supply the local market a breather from a cash-flow perspective, as they only have to pay duties and VAT on the goods once they're removed from the bonded warehouse. In much the same way as the 'in transit' scam works, the 'in bond' goods never really leave South Africa.

The scale of the problem, especially considering how small the resource base of SARS is, is made clear by a smuggler who once said to me, 'You see, JvL, for me it's like betting on the horses. I bet on a few in each race. I can't lose. I bring in a container through East London, I bring another through Beit Bridge, I bring in another by air and another through Durban. You stop one and fine me? No problem. I pay your fine with the money I've made on any one of the other containers that got through …'

On the export side of things, the scams are less complicated, since fewer opportunities exist for criminals to evade tax: no duties or taxes are levied on any exports other than diamonds. The primary crime in export is where illegal goods – usually illicit substances such as dagga – are exported from South Africa to other countries.

Of course, the 'in transit' and 'in bond' scams both depend on the ability of the criminals to somehow fake exports too.

There are two more scams related to imports and exports. One, called 'round-tripping', capitalises on the fact that when you export goods from South Africa, be they excisable or if you had to pay VAT on them, you can claim this back. It works the same way as the 'in transit' and 'in bond' scams, except that in this case, the traders would export the goods to another country, claim the benefits, and then sneakily bring the goods back into South Africa. In this way, they also wouldn't have to pay taxes on the sale of the goods, and in fact in many cases could even claim a (fraudulent) refund.

The other scam is 'ghost exports': by claiming to have exported goods, but instead diverting them into the local market, customs traders score big by not having to pay duties and VAT.

Some scams rely on corrupt officials. One big scam of the late 2000s, for example, was where legitimate taxpayers who expected real refunds never got them, and later discovered that their bank details had been changed at SARS – something that could only have happened with inside knowledge and access to the system. The net effect was that genuine refunds were 'hijacked' by criminals, and it was very difficult to trace the culprits.

In other cases, corrupt officials created refunds that weren't due and authorised their payout, and sometimes even had contacts within the banks who would open up false bank accounts for just this purpose.

Another prolific scam was straightforward extortion. Sometimes crooks impersonated SARS officials and then 'assessed' taxpayers, usually offering a 'discount' or to make tax problems go away for a fee. Sometimes these impersonators did, in fact, have people within SARS who worked closely with them, but in other cases it was pure nonsense.

Other rather common scams were those aimed at abusing or fraudulently benefiting from various trade schemes that the Department of Trade and Industry would introduce to give impetus to economic growth. The most abused of these, in my experience, were the motor-vehicle incentive programme and duty credit certificates (DCCs) in the clothing and textile sector. Both these programmes relied on proof of exporting locally manufactured goods to qualify for discounts on duty due on imports, so crooks would either overstate their exports, or simply claim to have exported goods when in fact they hadn't.

These basic tricks that tax evaders use to circumvent their obligations to the taxman aren't unique to South Africa, and the world over they remain challenges in even the most modern of economies. And when you superimpose the scams on each other, regularly and for many years on end, the multidimensionality of the crookery is staggering. For instance, the tobacco manufacturer who undervalues imported tobacco not only gets away with lower import duty and VAT, but also lower excise duties. As a result of the sale of the undeclared product, income is generated that's not declared by the business.

Many of the cases described in this book fall into this multi-dimensional category; few were ever as simple as unbundling only one scam. It was always a case of trying to see the whole picture and hold liable all beneficiaries of the proceeds of tax evasion.

This is what makes tax and customs investigations so complex. All these transactions are conducted in order to deceive, hide and obfuscate evidence. SARS auditors and investigators have to obtain information from other jurisdictions and try to do the numbers using access to third-party data, all the while building as solid a case as possible that will withstand scrutiny in the courts. Often SARS officials have to deal with accounting records – or the lack thereof – dating back many years and consisting of literally thousands and thousands of transactions; and in no case would the perpetrator have left evidence openly for them to just pick up.

This is what I believe the small band of women and men at SARS managed to develop over the years – the means to understand the scams, and the knowledge and expertise to know where and how best to collect the evidence to build the cases. We were constantly looking out for and trying to understand the latest frauds and methodologies.

And if the cases were dragged through one court or the other, with our opponents using every legal trick and obfuscation to fight back, we stayed the course.

In contrast, I can think of quite a few criminal cases that were started by the police, the NPA and the Scorpions, and which caved in after some years because witnesses became forgetful or died, investigators and prosecutors came and went, and new people took over longstanding and complex case dockets. Not us. We stuck to our cases, whatever it took. And where we had to do the heavy lifting for the police or prosecutors, we did so without complaining. Whatever was required of us to see cases through, we committed to that.

I'd like to believe that criminals knew that once we were on to them, we weren't going to go away easily. In that sense, I believe we received respect of a different kind from criminals when we tackled them.

At the same time, we weren't draconian in our approach. SARS legislation that dealt with enforcement issues was much wider than the legislation dealing with the relationship between a policeman and a suspect, or a prosecutor and the accused. SARS's laws – in line with the rules and regulations that guide tax authorities of many modern economies worldwide – allowed for wider enforcement, including settlements and compromises.

Where those we investigated respected the rule of law, and where such cases were meritorious, and taxpayers genuinely showed remorse, and managed to pass the stringent settlement committees (and provided the prosecuting authority agreed in criminal matters), they were resolved in a manner best suited for the fiscus and continued economic growth of the country. Unless the enterprise we were investigating was a criminal syndicate or fraudulent entity designed to pilfer from the State, we had to take cognisance of the impact that closing down a business would have in terms of jobs lost, loss of future taxes, and our efforts to grow the tax base. Closing down a legitimate business was always a last resort.

One thing I'm not prepared to give away here are the ways in which we bust these scams, regardless of their complexity or how deeply the evidence may have been hidden. Every scam has weaknesses – you can take my word for that.

I'll also not divulge how best those engaged in these activities can be caught. All of these scams leave traces and evidence, which you can find if you know how and where to look for it. It all starts with an interest in understanding your opponent and a willingness to put in the effort. And you must never give up, because it's what the smart crooks hope you'll do.

One thing my 16 years at SARS, and the thousands of cases in which I was involved, taught me, was if the right investigator or auditor latches on to you, you can run, you can hide, you may think you've got away with it, you can even think you're very smart and believe deeply that you've left no traces of your misdeeds – but boy, would you be wrong.

PART 3
FISSURES

It has become commonplace 'for certain individuals with an interest in perverting the course of justice to compile dossiers, files and information which purport to uncover corruption, but [which] are in fact a concoction of some fact and much fiction. Such dossiers are then distributed to the media, certain law-enforcement agencies and political players in the hope of disrupting or thwarting a SARS action.'

– *SARS spokesperson Adrian Lackay, discussing a backlash in which SARS investigators became the target of false allegations to discredit them, July 2014*[1]

11

Dirty tricks

The idea of a small unit to develop a dedicated capacity within the National Intelligence Agency to support SARS in economic crimes – what would later inaccurately be called the 'rogue unit' – came about after various proposals discussed between the two entities.

The primary participants in these discussions were Ivan Pillay and Pete Richer, employed at the time by the National Intelligence Agency but later to join SARS as general manager: Risk in what was then known as the Business Intelligence Unit. The thinking at the time was that the unit, located within the National Intelligence Agency, would be dedicated to supporting SARS in combating illicit trade.

SARS official Andries 'Skollie' Janse van Rensburg was tasked to work with Richer on this, and towards the end of 2006, SARS agreed to fund, recruit and train in tax and customs law a number of people for the unit who would ultimately be transferred to the National Intelligence Agency. In earlier years, SARS had done exactly the same for the prosecuting authority by recruiting inhouse prosecutors, and funding and setting up what later became known as Special Tax Units.

As far as I can recall, a detailed legal opinion by the National Intelligence Agency's legal department and another from SARS lawyers gave the concept the go-ahead. A memorandum of understanding was drawn up by the National Intelligence Agency and approved up to the deputy-director general level; approval was also obtained verbally from the then Minister of Intelligence Ronnie Kasrils. Just one signature was awaited, that of director-general of the National Intelligence Agency Manala Manzini; for reasons unknown to me, he never signed off on it.

In anticipation of giving effect to the concept, a proposal was simultaneously presented to the then Minister of Finance Trevor Manuel, who approved it in February 2007. The proposal explicitly stated that SARS did not have the capacity to intercept and monitor communications. It also noted that SARS would recruit and train staff, and fund them, and that the National Intelligence Agency would at a later stage take them over and 'ring-fence' the unit, meaning that it would be dedicated to supporting SARS and not be openly advertised on account of the high-risk work in which they were to engage.

The plan envisaged that SARS would provide for the personnel cost of the unit. The amounts provided for over a three-year period were R12 million in the first year, rising to R18 million by the third year. No provision was made at that time for any equipment or other capital expenditure.

For reasons unknown to me, no aspect of this plan was implemented by the National Intelligence Agency, who suddenly went cold on us, and we at SARS had to make the best of what we'd put in place on our side. With the benefit of hindsight, I suspect that there were all sorts of power struggles and machinations going on at the National Intelligence Agency, which led to their taking their eye off this particular ball.

The hope remained for some years to come that, ultimately, the National Intelligence Agency would realise the benefits of the concept and cooperate with SARS, and for this reason the unit was managed in a manner so as to ensure that when this happened, the transfer would be easy. At one stage there were even attempts to convince the police Crime Intelligence division to take them over. Everybody made the right noises, and everybody agreed, but when it came to doing anything, it was always left to SARS alone. Draft memoranda of understanding were compiled with both the National Intelligence Agency and police Crime Intelligence Service, but were relegated to the dustbin when neither agency followed through on their agreements with SARS.

The small unit, consisting of about 12 internal SARS transfers and a similar number of externally appointed people, mostly law-enforcement officials, was turned into a fully fledged SARS unit and named the Special

Projects Unit. Janse van Rensburg, as its manager, reported to Pillay at the time.

By this time, in 2007, I was the manager of a division known as Special Projects, and we interacted somewhat with the Special Projects Unit on some cases. I also assisted them with the formulation of their mandate, procedures and processes, job descriptions, key performance measures, training, and so forth.

The unit worked very closely with other law-enforcement agencies from the start, so I could never understand why, many years later, some would say it was 'ultra secret' and 'covert', and its existence was supposedly 'denied'. The unit was instrumental in what remains one of the largest busts in modern history – that of an illegal abalone plant in KwaZulu-Natal in 2007 – and was called on in other cases to testify in open criminal trials. Witnesses identified by the unit gave sworn statements in certain cases, and were subsequently subpoenaed by the NPA to testify in open criminal trials, and in other cases by SARS to testify in tax inquiries, tax court cases and liquidation inquiries.[1]

By early 2008, Janse van Rensburg had left SARS after a series of tragic personal events, and the Special Projects Unit came under my division. By then I'd been promoted and managed several other investigative units. Because of the similarity of the unit names, the Special Projects Unit was renamed the National Research Group. It took up very little of my time; there was certainly no clue then of the hullabaloo that would engulf us some years later because of this nondescript little unit.

This unit, mentioned by its respective names over the years, also featured prominently in bestselling books and in the media, always openly associated with SARS, from as far back as 2010.[4] It was most certainly not covert, secret or denied. We did, however, manage its investigations as discreetly as possible, and we protected its members, cases and work – for good reason.

At a 2012 national management forum attended by more than 300 SARS managers from all over the country, the then chief officer: Tax and

Customs Enforcement Investigations, Gene Ravele, dedicated an entire hour to discussing the unit, which had by then been named the High-risk Investigations Unit, explaining exactly what it did. He informed the attendees that the unit investigated cases that posed grave risk to our people, and it did not 'intercept taxpayers' communications'.

By 2008 SARS had formally adopted and refined its strategy to deal with the illicit economy. This strategy took into account operational agreements between the SAPS, the Asset Forfeiture Unit, the Marine Coastal Management division, the Border Police, the National Intelligence Agency and SARS, which were entered into in an attempt to combat and prevent offences as contemplated in laws administered by SARS. It also took into account a memorandum of understanding between SARS and the NPA, which set out the strengthening of the relationship between these two institutions in the field of information sharing, joint enforcement action and combating transnational crimes and financial crimes. This strategy identified specific focus areas where SARS believed it could play a supportive role in the financial and criminal-justice system.

I'd also by then concluded a number of short courses on business management, tax, customs and excise, and various computer programs, and concluded a part-time postgraduate certificate programme in business management at the University of the Witwatersrand Business School.

In 2009, when Jacob Zuma took office, he announced that our commissioner at the time, Pravin Gordhan, was to be the Minister of Finance. Our then head of corporate services, George 'Oupa' Magashula, was appointed as the new SARS commissioner, while Pillay and Edward Kieswetter, then chief operations officer, became deputy commissioners.

It was at this time that a whole new phase of modernisation began within SARS. What had started back in 2004 as a very rudimentary system of e-filing of tax returns, by 2007 had become closer to what we now experience online, and had been extended to include a revamp of customs systems, risk engines, access to third-party data, and case section and management systems. Suddenly, customs clients were able to effortlessly apply for licences and registrations, and declare transactions online, while tax returns for individuals were being prepopulated (to name but a few of the technological advances).

SARS was entering a new phase of smarter systems and leaner processes and procedures. The measurement of production and workloads also became easier, and the human-resources management and financial systems were revamped and updated to the extent that all managers (including myself) had to approve payroll and leave applications online every month.

What was one of SARS's strengths then started turning into one of its weaknesses.

The tax authority's successes had some pernicious side-effects. Suddenly, there were increasing demands from other parts of government for SARS to intervene in areas beyond its mandate. Sometimes the public would come to SARS, expecting us to deal with crimes, rather than going to the police or the NPA because, according to them, they'd lost faith in the criminal-justice system. Many would openly state that SARS was the only government department that still functioned.

Sometimes, when SARS acted jointly with other law-enforcement agencies, unhealthy rivalries sprang up. The fallout of this included the issuing of press statements claiming successes solely for a particular institution, in order to actively hamper or thwart investigations in which SARS was the primary complainant or investigative body.

Suddenly, SARS, and especially its frontline enforcement staff, began attracting the attention of hardened criminals. They were frequently subjected to smear attacks and, later, threats of and real physical injury.

These first fissures started showing around the mid-2000s.

To safeguard and promote the rights of citizens, South African law demarcated institutions and separated the powers and functions for investigation, prosecution and judgement. The trouble was that this noble objective translated in practice into a fragmented and weakened criminal-justice system. This lack of alignment and management of the justice system had, among other consequences, disjointed proper handling of cases entering the system, from complaints through to investigations to prosecutions.

Many institutions within the justice system had been weakened over the years by ineffective operating models, unstable leadership and internecine conflicts. Institutions of the state must avoid all forms of bias, including political; and SARS had indeed scrupulously avoided bias, especially party-political bias, in its practices.

But, over time, as SARS began to impact on organised crime and significant tax evaders and customs smugglers, and because of the 'no gift' policy introduced in 1999, bribery and corruption were replaced by threats to the safety of SARS investigators and customs officials. There were even instances where SARS officials received death threats, their homes were broken into under very suspicious circumstances, and laptops with key evidence were stolen. Indeed, a number of SARS enforcement officials from different units had been physically assaulted over the years, including being shot at.

In one case, an investigator looking into the tobacco industry was seriously wounded in his driveway. The shooters were never apprehended. 'This was the second time he had been attacked,' then SARS spokesperson Adrian Lackay told the media, adding that there'd been other incidents too. 'We believe that our officials are under threat,' he said, noting that after several high-profile busts, syndicates were believed to target top customs officials, and that security around some of the SARS units and cases was being improved. 'Often they will first attempt to bribe officials. If that fails, then criminals may resort to violence. Security always has to be a consideration when conducting major investigations.'[2]

On top of this, the expectations of other law-enforcement agencies of SARS were often unrealistically high, with the proverbial silver bullet being sought. Very often, SARS's limitations in the exchange of information in legislation were interpreted by other law-enforcement agencies as a reluctance to cooperate. And, importantly, the workforce of SARS wasn't growing at the same rate as the demands on the tax authority.

The inability of other law-enforcement agencies to completely understand these dynamics, combined with the complexities that come with tax and customs investigations, caused the relationships between SARS and other agencies to begin to break down.

Another trend emerged, with those under investigation using tactics such as leveraging influential people and politicians, and discrediting staff by spreading false rumours that were distributed to the media, law-enforcement agencies and political parties.

In some cases, false criminal complaints were found to have been registered against SARS officials involved in investigations. In one instance, I urgently had to arrange for lawyers to intervene when the SAPS arrived at the home of a SARS investigator intending to arrest him. In at least three other matters I can recall and in which I was personally involved, SARS had to, with great difficulty, convince the SAPS that the complaints registered against SARS investigators were false, and intended solely to discredit and hamper SARS investigations.[3]

In 2012, while we were investigating international fugitive and convicted murderer and drug dealer Radovan Krejcir, the High-risk Investigations Unit received a tip-off that SARS offices were going to be bombed.[xi] None of our law-enforcement agencies stepped in to protect us, and we were left to fend for ourselves.

SARS was also increasingly being placed in the spotlight through the actions of people believed to be disgruntled former SARS employees, who released 'intelligence dossiers' and 'reports' containing various allegations against SARS. These documents were usually sent to political parties, media houses, parliamentary bodies, subjects under

xi In 2012, a homemade bomb went off in one of Krecjir's pawn shops. Officially, police stated that an unknown man had walked into the shop and left a bag containing the bomb on the floor. According to journalist Mandy Wiener, one theory (which she described in her 2018 book *Ministry of Crime: An Underworld Explored* (Pan Macmillan)) was that the explosives, apparently meant for my SARS office, had detonated accidentally. This seems to tally with the information we had back then.

investigation by SARS, and politicians. The most common accusations were alleged discrimination against African employees and in particular senior managers; that SARS had a 'covert unit' spying on people illegally; and that SARS had illegally intercepted communications. These improprieties were usually attributed to Pillay or me, and sometimes to Gordhan, Ravele and certain investigators involved in mainly tobacco-related investigations.

SARS always responded to allegations of this nature, including addressing correspondence to the Presidency, the national police commissioner, the State Security Agency and the Public Protector, from 2009 right up to 2014. Not a single one of these letters ever received a reply.

Despite all of this, the allegations resurfaced continually, often with slight adaptions if the originals were found wanting.

The mid-2000s were also somewhat tumultuous because of a massive turf war between the police and the Scorpions – all of which had a serious knock-on effect on the rest of the criminal-justice system, from which I believe we have yet to recover.

Needless to say, these events impacted on SARS and our own cases, and ultimately, in my view, the interests of justice suffered tremendously.

12

Death and taxes

Nothing in life is certain except death and taxes, or so the saying goes.[1]

Over the years, criminals have come to realise this truth – just ask American mobster Al Capone, whose murderous seven-year reign as a crime boss in Prohibition-era Chicago was brought to an end when he was arrested, prosecuted and jailed for tax evasion.

Indeed, as I've been at pains to point out, as far as tax authorities are concerned, *all* forms of income – legitimate or otherwise – are subject to tax. And on this premise of tax law, tax authorities worldwide assist law-enforcement agencies to curb crime.

When mining magnate Brett Kebble was shot and killed in September 2005 in what was later described as an 'assisted suicide', the killers were unknown. That changed after Michael 'Mickey' Schultz, Faizal 'Kappie' Smith and Nigel McGurk were arrested in 2006 by the then Scorpions.

That case was intertwined with a few others, most notably our investigations into drug lord Glenn Agliotti, and businessmen Dave King and Billy Rautenbach.

Around 2005, the Scorpions started an investigation into allegations of financial mismanagement and fraud related to Kebble and listed companies JCI and Randgold & Exploration. The investigation had been sparked by a report to the Scorpions by audit firm KPMG, in which it was alleged that Kebble and others had conspired to steal R3 billion in assets, mainly in the form of shares that were secretly transferred out of the two companies.

At the same time, there was a whole host of interactions between the Scorpions and the police, which turned up the heat in what seemed to be a turf battle between the two. Coupled with this were the suggestions that the Scorpions were serving particular political and commercial agendas.

The Scorpions arrested Agliotti, ostensibly for his involvement in Kebble's murder, but it seemed that they were actually more interested in Agliotti's relationship with then police commissioner Jackie Selebi; and, in exchange for his testimony against Selebi, Agliotti and the three gunmen were given indemnity from prosecution for their role in the murder.

Which brings me to Dave King. At the height of the acrimony between King and SARS, in late 2008, a strange sequence of events played itself out. King made the startling claim that he'd settled with SARS, and that, as a result, the assets held offshore had to be lifted and the monies released. But King wouldn't disclose who at SARS he'd dealt with, nor provide any details of the agreement. It was very odd indeed.

There was pandemonium at SARS as we tried to find out if anybody at the tax authority had indeed met with King and entered into any such agreement, and also what the 'settlement' had been and its legal basis. But nothing and nobody came to the fore. It was just a mystery.

By this time, SARS had formed the Anti-corruption and Security Unit under another struggle activist Clifford Collings, whose members began combing the streets, looking for leads that would point to this 'settlement', but to no avail.

The truth, which emerged later, was stranger than fiction.[2]

Back in 2008, the then head of SARS human resources and corporate services, Oupa Magashula, walked into the office one Monday morning and told a strange story. He and his family had gone for Sunday lunch to a restaurant in Muldersdrift outside Johannesburg. They were frequent guests there, so, on his arrival, and as usual, Magashula had exchanged greetings and chit-chat with the restaurant manager. In the course of the conversation, the manager had mentioned lightheartedly how SARS officials must love his eatery, as another senior SARS official, Leonard Radebe, had been there just the other day, having lunch with Dave King.

Radebe was a rising star in SARS at the time, having swiftly moved through the ranks from customs manager in KwaZulu-Natal to general manager of SARS's entire Customs and Excise department by 2008.

What was curious about the reported meeting with King is that Radebe had no reason to have discussions with the businessman, as there were no customs- or excise-related aspects whatsoever to the SARS case against King.

And, even more curiously, when asked about his relationship with King, Radebe denied ever having met him.

To try to get to the bottom of the mystery, Magashula and I went to the Muldersdrift restaurant that week, armed with a SARS prospectus featuring photographs of all SARS executive members, but with the names blacked out. The restaurant manager unhesitatingly identified Radebe by his photograph.

Collings and I then interviewed Radebe, who remained adamant that he'd never met King and didn't know anything about him. I asked Radebe if he'd be prepared to state this under oath, and he agreed.

So, for an entire day, I sat crafting the questions and his answers in the form of an affidavit. Once I'd finished, and Radebe had signed it, Collings and I advised him to carefully consider the implications of having stated under oath that he didn't know King and had never met him, because an eyewitness had placed him on a certain date and time at a certain restaurant in the presence of the businessman.

That weekend, on the Sunday, Radebe contacted me via cellphone, asking to meet. I met with him alone, at a car wash near his home; Collings was nearby, on standby.

Radebe told me that he'd given the matter some thought and confessed that he did indeed know King and had met with him on a number of occasions. How this had come about was through a man called Jacques 'JJ' Nel, a former riot-squad policeman in private security, who he'd met some years before in Durban. Radebe had remained friends with Nel, even after moving to Pretoria to head up SARS's Customs and Excise division, and they played golf regularly.

On a certain day, after a golf game, Radebe, a passenger in Nel's car, had gone with Nel to the home of none other than Glenn Agliotti. Agliotti had served them pasta and they'd had conversations about various things, including the King case. Radebe told me that Agliotti had tried to create the impression that he knew King well and was acting for him in his dispute with SARS.

This all happened during the period that Agliotti, soon to be the star State witness against Selebi, was being kept under constant watch by the Scorpions. We'd heard that the Scorpions had installed CCTV cameras at Agliotti's home, so naturally we tried to get from them any footage of the day that Radebe told us he was at Agliotti's home. The Scorpions weren't cooperative, however, and we didn't get it.

During the meeting at the car wash, Radebe asked me to shred the affidavit he'd signed the previous Friday, because it showed that he'd lied to SARS. I told him that I could unfortunately not do so.

That week, Leonard Radebe resigned from SARS. He would later tell the *Mail & Guardian*, 'I resigned because I wanted to protect the reputation of SARS and because it was the honourable thing to do.'[3]

That same week, King called a media briefing, naming Radebe as the person he claimed had brokered the 'settlement' with SARS. King claimed not to have known that Radebe was a customs official or a member of SARS's executive committee until he'd googled his name. According to King, Radebe had attended a board meeting during which Gordhan had expressed his desire to settle the King matter.[4] According to King, Radebe had taken it on himself to broker an agreement with King.[5]

When Radebe was approached by the media, he denied King's version of events. He said that he'd met with King, but never formally on behalf of Gordhan; he said that his interaction with King had been informal at all times, and never for the purpose of discussing his case. Radebe claimed that he'd been introduced to King by some of his associates, who in hindsight had misled him regarding the true nature of King's motives.[6]

Radebe added that whenever he met with King, it was always in the presence of Nel and a man called Noel Clegg, who told Radebe that he did VAT work for King relating to a Stellenbosch wine farm. 'At no stage have I ever negotiated with King,' Radebe said. (*Moneyweb* reported that Radebe resigned when he became aware of how King had misled him and his associates.[7])

The matter led us to uncover a host of other frauds and misrepresentations, some of which had affected SARS, and which also implicated Agliotti and Nel. They all formed part of a criminal complaint registered with the head of the police's Commercial Crimes Unit at the time, General Hans Meiring, and his team. But all our efforts to try and get law-enforcement agencies to investigate them fell on deaf ears.

The criminal case died a quiet death, with virtually no appetite within the police or the NPA to pursue the matter. I believe this may be partially attributable to the fact that the case implicated Glenn Agliotti – the star State witness in the intended cases against Jackie Selebi.

It was among my most frustrating periods at SARS. When we raised the issues implicating Agliotti at one meeting with the NPA, a very senior law-enforcement official told me that he couldn't take the evidence from me because then he'd be obliged to make it available to the defence team of Selebi, and that, he said, would affect the credibility of the State's witness, namely Agliotti.

From the perspective of King's case, at least, we were able to show that there was no agreement between him and SARS, and the matter continued without further interference.

But the twists and turns of the case were not yet over.

Billy Rautenbach and Glenn Agliotti had met 'serendipitously' in Zimbabwe, and this – according to court records – was how Rautenbach had 'learned about the relationship between Agliotti and Selebi'.[8]

Rautenbach had told Agliotti that he had a 'legal issue with SARS' and didn't want to return to South Africa since he was afraid of being arrested. It seems Agliotti then assured him that, thanks to his connection with Selebi, he could get Rautenbach's 'problems to go away'. In return he asked for a fee of US$100 000. Accordingly, Agliotti supposedly arranged for Selebi to meet with one of Rautenbach's attorneys in April 2005 in a hotel in Sandton to discuss Rautenbach's 'dilemma'.

Selebi consistently denied having received any bribes in exchange for this interaction.[9]

One of the witnesses the NPA sought to use in Jackie Selebi's corruption trial, which started in October 2009, was none other than Billy Rautenbach. Their predicament was that we at SARS hadn't forgotten about Rautenbach, and were still ready to pounce on him the minute he entered South Africa. As it turned out, the NPA had – without telling us – been in discussions with Rautenbach and his lawyers about securing his testimony in the Selebi trial and ensuring that he came to South Africa to do so.

A few months before the Selebi trial began, I learned through media enquiries that Rautenbach had entered into a plea-bargain with the NPA, pleading guilty to 326 charges of fraud as a representative of one of his companies, SA Botswana Hauliers, in the specialised Commercial Crimes Court in Pretoria. He'd agreed to pay a fine of R40 million, plus an additional amount of R15 million in several instalments to the Asset Forfeiture Unit's Criminal Assets Recovery Account.

I immediately put in a call to advocate Willie Hofmeyr at the NPA. Surely, I asked him, we as SARS should have been consulted in the process?

The result was that I had to sit down with some of my investigators and very hastily work out what amounts were still due to SARS by Billy Rautenbach, following the myriad liquidations of his older companies; and the result of that was that Rautenbach agreed to pay R15 million to SARS.

During the Selebi trial, it became clear to me why Rautenbach was so desperately needed. Glenn Agliotti testified that he'd paid Selebi US$90 000 in three instalments of US$30 000 each. But Agliotti's testimony wasn't accepted by the court.

Evidence led did show that Agliotti had flown to Lubumbashi in the

DRC, where Rautenbach had handed him $100 000; this would suggest that Agliotti had kept a portion, or perhaps all, of the money. Rautenbach was accepted by the court as a reliable witness and his testimony wasn't challenged. What happened to the US$100 000 paid by Rautenbach to Agliotti is anybody's guess.

In 2010, Selebi was convicted for corruption, but not for the US$100 000 transaction. He was convicted for accepting bribes worth less than R170 000 from Agliotti, in exchange for showing him top-secret police reports, and received a 15-year jail sentence.

The Asset Forfeiture Unit successfully applied for the confiscation of Selebi's assets worth a measly R230 000, and made up mainly of the money the court found he'd received from Agliotti, with interest.

Agliotti was found not to have been a reliable witness during the trial and lost the opportunity to be given indemnity from prosecution. Despite this, he was never tried for his part in the corruption.

By the time Selebi started serving his sentence, he'd been diagnosed as terminally ill. He was granted medical parole and died in January 2015.

At the time of writing, Glenn Agliotti and the three shooters – plus a host of others implicated in the R3-billion loss to JCI – were still walking the streets as free men.

In 2010, one of the shooters in the Kebble murder, Michael Schultz, took the stand to explain what had happened. Something in his testimony caught my attention: he claimed that the three accomplices were promised payment of R2 million for their 'services', although he'd received less than that.

Naturally, this required SARS to take a closer look at where that money had come from and where it had gone.

Taxpayers are required to submit either an annual tax return to SARS (if they're employees), or two provisional tax returns per year, wherein they state their income and allowable expenses. The amount earned that's taxable is measured against a sliding scale (the more you earn, the more tax you pay); this is called a 'tax bracket'.

When SARS conducts an audit, the tax authority essentially verifies what the taxpayer has declared. If there's a shortfall, the taxpayer must pay up. And if it turns out that the taxpayer wilfully and fraudulently lied on their return, they not only have to pay the tax owing, but SARS levies additional taxes of up to 200% of the amount, together with punitive compound interest calculated from the period when the money was due.

Because the shooters in the Kebble murder case – Schultz, Faizal Smith and Nigel McGurk – had failed to pay their taxes, even after they'd been audited, their tax woes became public knowledge in 2012 when the Central Projects Unit – a small unit under my management – obtained civil judgements against all three of them. Court records reflect that Schultz owed R243 000 in back taxes for the years 2005 to 2009, Smith owed R647 000, and McGurk owed around R1 800 000.

In Schultz's case, it would be revealed that SARS had assessed his earnings at R785 000 for that period. Asked to explain the source of R400 000 for 'services rendered', he'd allegedly replied, 'I received this money for Mr Brett Kebble's assisted suicide.'[10]

Another underworld character with a link to Glenn Agliotti who didn't pay his taxes was Calla Botha, a former member of the murky apartheid intelligence structures who was implicated in the 1989 murder of anti-apartheid activist David Webster. Botha had been the driver for Ferdi Barnard, the former Civil Cooperation Bureau hit-squad operative who'd shot Webster.

Botha applied for amnesty at the Truth and Reconciliation Commission,[11] describing in his testimony how Barnard had approached him to assist in Webster's murder. Barnard had been paid R15 000, Botha said, of which R5 000 had been paid to him for his 'assistance'. Botha didn't get amnesty, but to date has never been charged for his role in the coldblooded assassination, which he described as 'the perfect murder'.[12]

Botha might have escaped criminal prosecution, but he had a date with us at SARS. Since 2006, when Agliotti had disclosed (in an unrelated matter) aspects of Botha's undeclared income which immediately raised red flags for us, the Central Projects Unit had been digging into his financial affairs as part of a longer-term project I'd started informally named Unfinished Business. (I had by then listed a number of former apartheid security-forces operatives who'd allegedly creamed money from state coffers in the dying days of the regime, and who we'd found to not have been tax compliant.) We'd been trying for some time and with great difficulty to get Botha to disclose his financial affairs to us.

By 2011, Botha was running a business called Black Hawk Security and living the good life in a luxurious home in Krugersdorp, with a villa on the banks of the Vaal, driving around in an expensive BMW with personalised number plates and flying around in a private helicopter. We were after him for an amount of between R10 and R15 million, and intended bringing criminal charges against him for tax evasion.[13]

In May that year, Botha approached the Pretoria High Court, asking it to set aside the warrant of arrest that we'd obtained. In doing so, he placed his tax affairs and the fact that we'd been investigating him in the public domain.

The court agreed to set aside the warrant of arrest on condition that Botha appeared before a SARS tax inquiry.

Tax inquiries are very effective if used correctly, but they require months of planning, behind-the-scenes preparation and deep insight into the taxpayer, potential witnesses and their financial affairs. But by this time, the Central Projects Unit was operating like a well-oiled machine and required very little direction. Once a case was allocated to them, they had the formula down pat: if taxpayers failed to cooperate, they were able to execute tax inquiries and asset preservations without any hassle.[14] During the tax inquiry Botha confessed that he'd submitted only three tax returns in the preceding 21 years, the last in 2001. He also pled poverty, claiming that he lived just above the breadline.[15]

The case was still midstream when, in 2014, all hell broke loose at SARS.

13

419s

In April 2017, the Hawks arrested one Elvis Ramosebudi on charges of conspiracy to commit murder.

What made this case so sensational was the fact that Ramosebudi had allegedly written letters to two seemingly opposed groups of people, offering both his allegiance, support and the willingness to assassinate those who appeared to be their 'enemies'. On the one side was the infamous Gupta family,[1] supposed proponents of 'radical economic transformation'[2] but with links to allegations of fraud, corruption and state capture; and on the other was the Oppenheimer family, supposed opponents of radical economic transformation and accused of being anti-transformationist 'white monopoly capital'.[3]

For the Gupta family, Ramosebudi supposedly offered to assassinate, among others, the former Public Protector Thuli Madonsela, who'd made damning allegations against the Gupta family in 'State of Capture', her last report before her term ended; and former deputy Finance Minister Mcebisi Jonas, who'd revealed how the Guptas had allegedly offered him a bribe of R600 million to take up the position of finance minister. For this, Ramosebudi asked for R75 million to be deposited directly into his bank account.

In the case of the Oppenheimer family, the assassination targets were the 'beneficiaries of state capture', including the Gupta family, and the fee was a R60-million 'sponsorship'.

When these letters were made public, I considered them to be nothing more than advance-fee fraud, or 419 scams. These con tricks, which get their name from the relevant section of the Nigerian criminal code, work quite simply. The scamsters send out letters making some or other proposal, usually of a nature that would lead to some benefit to the party (a job, money, access to the winnings of a lottery). The trick is that for the addressee to gain the benefit, they have to pay a small 'administrative fee' or something of that sort – and then another, and soon enough, another. Many people have been fleeced in this way, and often these crimes remain unreported, because those who have been scammed are unwilling to admit publicly that they were illegally going to share in the spoils of stolen gold or lotto winnings or whatever the scam set forth.

What struck me about the case against Ramosebudi was the fact that the Hawks, and later the NPA, seemed to want to cling to the 'conspiracy to commit murder' charge only, almost as if they themselves truly believed the content of the letters – which, when read in conjunction with each other, just screamed 'scam'. During Ramosebudi's bail hearing, it emerged that the Hawks had been observing him for almost seven months, and that he'd acted alone and had no accomplices, and that there was no evidence of his possessing any arms.

Then the NPA decided to change the charges to the more serious 'incitement to commit murder', giving even more credibility to the letters. ('Conspiracy' implies an agreement to commit a crime; 'incitement' implies encouragement to commit a crime.)

When he received bail, the magistrate remarked that there was nothing suggesting that Ramosebudi was capable of carrying out the alleged assassinations. Describing the plot as 'immature', the magistrate actually questioned whether it wasn't perhaps a so-called 419 scam, because Ramosebudi didn't have guns, nor had he recruited anyone.[4]

Ramosebudi's case got me thinking about similar such cases I'd come across at SARS over the years – one of them being the case of a hysterical man, screaming for Pravin Gordhan in the SARS head-office reception some time late in 2007.

'Where's Pravin?' the man shouted in a heavy Indian accent. 'I want my money! Where is he?'

SARS security officials were trying to calm him down but he would have none of it.

What on earth is this about? I wondered, as I rushed into the reception area.

I eventually managed to sit him down and gave him a cup of warm sweet tea. He was extremely emotional, tears streaming down his face. When he finally calmed down enough to talk, he told me that he was a landowner from northern India who rented out land to subsistence farmers. He'd been a rich man, he said, but now was poor because of what had happened to him.

Slowly the story emerged. He'd received an unsolicited email one day, telling of a significant amount of money held in trust in South Africa. The email invited him to share in the spoils, provided that he kept quiet about it, and that he permitted one of his business bank accounts to be used as a recipient for the money. The money would be released in South Africa in due course, provided certain 'administrative formalities' were concluded, the email noted, including 'SARS authorisation'. Would this gentleman be so kind as to help 'free up' the money, for which he would get a significant 'reward'?

He replied in the affirmative, and the game was on.

Soon enough, he received further emails, with attachments, including letters that appeared to come from SARS, on SARS letterheads and signed by 'P Gordhan'. The letters, although poorly written, were full of legalese, and packed with codes and references – they seemed legit to him.

There was one catch, said one email. SARS required 'stamp duties' in US dollars to be paid into a South African-held bank account – would the gentleman please help? It wasn't much, and it would speed up the process.

And so the fleecing began.

Each email that arrived subsequently told of more and more 'red tape' and 'administrative burdens', always requiring some or other payment. The man continued to cough up, looking forward to eventually counting his spoils. He paid and paid and paid.

With, finally, all the 'administrative hurdles' cleared, the scheme got even more sophisticated. The money was as good is in the man's bank account, the scamsters assured him. Just a few more days, except ... this P Gordhan of SARS was now making life difficult. He was the boss at SARS, and if he said no, the money wouldn't be released. You know those South Africans, right? All corrupt. Even this P Gordhan was crooked – all that was required was to grease his palm, give him his cut of the spoils upfront. They'd make it up to the man, the emails assured him, as soon as P Gordhan had released the money.

The man checked out 'P Gordhan' on the internet, and sure enough, Pravin Gordhan was the boss at SARS. So he paid up.

Then the emails stopped.

The man sent email after email, with no response.

The scamsters had taken what they could from him and moved on to their next victim.

So this gentleman from India had decided to take matters into his own hands, and booked a flight to South Africa. He was going to confront Pravin Gordhan and get what was owing to him.

It was terribly sad for me to have to slowly take the man through the documents he'd brought with him. I showed him real SARS letters, comparing them with those sent to him, and pointed out the obvious and most visible differences; we compared the fake signature with the real one. I described in detail to him how these types of scams worked. And I watched his shoulders slump in submission as it dawned on him how he'd been fooled.

Eventually, he walked away, a very disappointed man. After a few steps he half-turned, looking at the file in his hand and clearly wanting to say something. But then just waved at me and kept walking.

I saw many of these scams in my years at SARS, particularly the ones that used fake SARS letterheads and names of people to advance their frauds, and I was always amazed at how easily people could be fooled.

SARS eventually published a link on its website called 'Scams and Phishing Attacks', detailing some of the scams and calling on the public to be aware of them and report them immediately to the tax authority. Many were reported to the law-enforcement agencies; few were ever investigated and prosecuted by them.

One day a man called Frans Richards came to see me.[5] Claiming to be an agent for the State Security Agency – the government department with overall responsibility for civilian intelligence operations – he was at pains to demonstrate how connected he was to President Zuma, to the extent that he opened a folder he had with him, showing me a photo of him standing next to the president. I wasn't impressed at all: long before the days of 'selfies', it was a known trick for someone to sidle up to a politician or other famous person and get someone else to snap a photo of them together; and, anyway, the photo could easily have been photoshopped.

I didn't care but I did consider it a bit unprofessional of a State Security Agency agent to try and impress me in this manner. There was no need: we were colleagues and working towards the same goal.

But as if that weren't enough, Richards then hauled out his cellphone and showed me in his contact list the names and phone numbers of very influential people, including some very senior people at the State Security Agency. He invited me to call them as character references, but I declined.

Richards then removed a few pieces of paper from the folder and handed them to me. Looking me straight in the eye, he told me that the documents were undeniable, factual, irrefutable evidence of billions in cash, which had come from the late Libyan leader Muammar Gaddaffi, been processed by SARS Customs and were now stored in a state warehouse.

If a man who was supposedly an adviser to the Presidency, and who had the phone numbers of some pretty serious and powerful people on his phone, believed that a waybill was irrefutable proof of an import of millions from Libya associated with Gadaffi, who was I to contest it? If he said the 'waybill' was a genuine, and therefore absolute proof of the import, and that it had been handled by SARS and kept in a Customs warehouse, then who was I to challenge him?

When I asked him why, if he knew exactly where the money was, the State Security Agency didn't simply go and fetch it, he told me there was a possible reward or commission in it for him – but that certain 'administrative formalities' would have to be completed …

But who am I to judge? After all, I was also taken for a ride, by another State Security Agency agent, from November 2013 onwards, despite my ability to smell a 419 scam a mile away.

14

Charlie and the rhinos

In July 2011, it was widely reported in the media that Thai national Chumlong Lemtongthai had been arrested by the Hawks for illegal trading in rhino horns, in what was described as the culmination of a year-long investigation led by SARS. Members of the Hawks had swooped on a house in Edenvale on the East Rand early one Saturday morning and arrested Lemtongthai just hours before he was due to fly out of the country. It was their second raid on that house.

About a month before, SARS investigator Charles 'Charlie' van Niekerk and his team had arrived at OR Tambo airport, ready for the next important step in their investigation into Lemtongthai. Van Niekerk had been tracking him for some time, and had picked up that he was entering the country that day.

As soon as Lemtongthai joined the queue for the customs channel, Van Niekerk gave a signal to the customs officials and they pulled him aside.

Van Niekerk, an old hand with police and intelligence experience, knew exactly what he was looking for. They asked the man for his laptop and cellphone, which he handed over, together with forms concerning the trade in 50 rhino horns and other documents. After undergoing some questioning, he was allowed to leave, and the laptop and cellphone were returned to him a few days later.

Lemtongthai was a director of Thai company Xaysavang Trading Export-Import, based in Laos, a small nation bordering China, Thailand, Myanmar, Vietnam and Cambodia. Xaysavang had by then gained notoriety in wildlife circles for its involvement in trading in protected animals and animal products, including rhino horns, and lion bones, teeth and claws.

Investigating rhino poachers is dangerous and difficult. The poachers carry firearms and don't hesitate to shoot. The transactions and nature of the operations are secretive, and a lot of money is at stake for the criminals involved. To give you a sense of this, in November 2012, the Hawks, in conjunction with a police task force, received information about alleged poachers near Sabi Sand private game reserve in Skukuza. 'When our team confronted the four men, they opened fire on the police, who returned fire. One of the poachers was killed, another is in hospital, while the other two were arrested,' a spokesman told the media.[1] The Hawks confiscated a hunting rifle, an axe, a saw and vehicle used by the alleged poachers.

In South Africa, rhino hunting is legal in certain circumstances: if someone wants to hunt a rhino, they must not only pay vast sums to the game farms that keep rhinos, but also register with the local authorities, who keep a detailed record of the hunt (and the export of the trophy if the animal was hunted by a foreign visitor).

This created a loophole, called 'pseudo hunting'. Poachers would bring poor foreign women to South Africa under the pretext of offering jobs, fooling the women into thinking that they could earn money for their families. Once the women arrived in the country, their passports were taken from them, and they'd be forced into prostitution with the threat of not being given back their passports and that harm would come to their families if they didn't do as they were told. Their names and passports were then used to apply to hunt rhino and export the trophies.

On the day the rhino was shot, the woman in question would be brought to the game farm and made to pose next to the dead rhino, complete with a big hunting-rifle in hand. This was supposed to serve as proof that she had shot the rhino.

When Lemtongthai was arrested by the Hawks, five such Thai 'hunters' were also found at the house. They had apparently just returned from North West province, where they were believed to have 'shot' at least five rhinos.

The group of women had arrived in the country in June 2011,

together with Lemtongthai – the day that Van Niekerk, his team and customs officials had briefly detained the Thai national at OR Tambo, and confiscated his laptop and cellphone.

Chumlong Lemtongthai was ultimately found to have been involved in the killing of at least 26 rhinos, every one of which had been shot after hunting permits had been issued to him and others who fronted for him – women hired to mislead the authorities into believing that professional hunters had shot the rhinos. After the hunting permits had been cleared by Customs and Nature Conservation, Lemtongthai had changed the address of the consignees on the CITES (Convention on International Trade in Endangered Species of Wild Fauna and Flora) permits[2] so that the rhino horns ended up in Laos.

In 2012 Lemtongthai was charged in the Kempton Park Regional Court on 26 counts of contravening the Customs and Excise Act by unlawfully and intentionally making improper use of documents to export rhino horn. He was also charged on 26 counts of contravening the National Environmental Management Biodiversity Act by unlawfully and intentionally trading in rhino horn.

On 5 November he tendered a plea of guilty and was convicted, receiving an effective 40-year prison sentence.[3] This was unprecedented, and a first for both SARS and the State's law-enforcement agencies.

SARS spokesman Adrian Lackay welcomed the sentence, saying, 'It sets a very strong legal precedent for possible future prosecutions of this nature and also indicates the seriousness with which the courts interpret and implement legislation … to protect our natural resources, in particular rhinos.'[4]

But why, you might wonder, did Lemtongthai plead guilty on all the charges in the face of such a lengthy prison sentence?

A year or so before all this happened, Charlie van Niekerk had come into my office one day and expressed frustration: he felt he could do more, he said, and deal with more sophisticated matters.

I'd known him for many years, and he was an extremely dedicated and skilled investigator, a clever man with lots of energy. A former police official and intelligence officer, and a prolific reader, Van Niekerk was one of those unique personalities who become almost obsessed with understanding what they're investigating on a tactical, operational and strategic level. Once on a case, the man hardly slept, and he was as dogged as they come. He was also a really nice guy, full of practical jokes and laughter when the mood struck him.

Around the time he came to see me, SARS was under tremendous pressure, and continually had to answer to Parliament about what we were doing as part of larger governmental efforts to curb the illegal poaching of rhino. By then, South African National Parks (Sanparks) had announced that the country had lost 528 rhinos in less than one calendar year, and there was a lot of public pressure on Government to deal with the problem.

We at SARS formed part of a multi-agency task team to deal with rhino poaching, and I assigned the portfolio to Charlie van Niekerk. He got stuck in immediately, engaging with the Hawks, the police, Sanparks, the NPA and private conservationist groupings. He met with hunters, traders, police officials, informants and anybody he thought might be able to give him more insight into the trade in illegal rhino horns. He engaged the various licensing and permit-issuing departments. He worked day and night for many months, often travelling across the country to attend conferences and joint governmental-agency sittings on the topic. Some of us began to refer to him not just as 'Charlie' but as 'Charlie and the rhinos'.

Van Niekerk began to put the pieces of the picture together, and soon enough he'd solved the riddle of 'pseudo hunting' and identified the main subjects involved in the pipeline between the Thai-based company and South Africa.

He came to see me and briefed a few of us on his bigger view of the illicit trade in rhino horn, including the fact that Chumlong Lemtongthai played a key role. If we could get to him, Van Niekerk believed, we would make a significant leap in combating rhino-poaching.

One Friday afternoon, Charlie and I, together with a lawyer from SARS and Lindsay Mudaley, a very experienced SARS criminal investigator, worked through the case and what Charlie had put together. It dawned on us that the customs-and-excise legislation was perfect for SARS to use to collect as much evidence as possible against Lemtongthai, specifically because he travelled regularly to and from South Africa, and probably had evidence on him when doing so – he had to smuggle the rhino horn out somehow, after all, to circumvent SARS's Customs department. And that's what had resulted in the detention and inspection of Lemtongthai's laptop and cellphone as he passed through customs back in June 2011 (the Customs and Excise Act allowed for such detentions if reasonable suspicions of criminality existed).

What had been found was a veritable treasure trove of evidence, setting out in detail exactly how Lemtongthai's operation worked in South Africa, including the dates and times couriers entered and left the country, where they stayed, financial transactions, how they used carriers for the cash used to pay for these operations in South Africa, dates and specifics about the 26 'hunts', and even photos of the smuggled rhino horns.

This indisputable evidence was precisely what the NPA and the Hawks needed to prosecute Lemtongthai, and was in fact so devastating for the Thai national that he opted to plead guilty and hope that the courts would be lenient on him.

In November 2011, Charlie, SARS investigators and members of the Hawks swooped on another Edenvale house and arrested two Thai businessmen, Punpitak Chunchom and Phichet Thongpai, for the illegal possession of lion bones. Chunchom and Thongpai pleaded guilty in the Germiston Regional Court to not having the requisite permit to possess the lion teeth and claws found in one of their bags. They were each fined R10 000, with an additional fine of R100 000 or five years' imprisonment suspended for five years, and they were sent back home.[xii]

Shortly afterwards, a media statement reported the arrest of two Thai nationals. The men, who'd been detained at OR Tambo after their flight from Thailand had landed, were formally arrested and handed over to police while investigations continue.

'The one suspect has a criminal record in South Africa for smuggling animal products like lion bones. He was previously convicted in a South African court, was fined R10 000, which he paid and then left the country. We believe that the aim of his return was to get involved in further illicit activities,' SARS spokesman Adrian Lackay said.

The second suspect was arrested for allegedly not declaring a large amount of foreign currency which was found in his luggage by customs officials.

Lackay indicated that both suspects were believed to be closely associated with alleged rhino-poaching kingpin Chumlong Lemtongthai, and that they were central figures in an international poaching syndicate.

'Today is another successful chapter of investigations into rhino-horn poaching and smuggling. Crime Line congratulates SARS and the Hawks for today's arrest and for tirelessly working to make an impact on the scourge of rhino poaching,' Crime Line[5] coordinator Marisa Oosthuizen said.[6]

It was an important arrest, noted Yolan Friedmann, the chief executive officer at the time of the Endangered Wildlife Trust, because it meant that 'we are starting to get into the syndicates' at the top, rather than operating just at the level of the poachers on the ground.[7]

The investigations had required the Hawks, SARS, the Department of Environmental Affairs, Sanparks and the NPA to work together closely. It was indeed an incredible success for all the state agencies involved, and an example of how all could work together as one system to address crime challenges.

xii It wasn't Punpitak Chunchom's first brush with the law – in September 2008, he and four others were arrested in Mpumalanga after they offered an undercover police agent US$60 000 for three rhino horns. Unfortunately, the case against Chunchom and two others was later withdrawn.

To date, Chumlong Lemtongthai is the most senior figure in the rhino-horn trade convicted and sentenced in South Africa. His syndicate spanned South Africa, Thailand, Laos and Vietnam.[8]

Charlie van Niekerk became a foremost expert on rhino poaching in South Africa, with a deep sense of understanding how the networks were set up and operate, fund their activities and move their contraband across the globe. The effort involved in developing this insight took several years of absolute dedication, and he continued to represent SARS at multi-agency committees and conferences, civil-society-organised meetings and on international platforms.[9]

One day, he walked into my office with a beautiful hand-drawn picture of a rhino on a little stand. He gave it to me in appreciation for what he considered the privilege of having been given the opportunity to work on the cases. It wasn't necessary, because we were just doing our work, but I really appreciated the gesture, and that drawing stood proudly in a prominent place on my bookcase for the remaining years that I was at SARS.

In 2013 Van Niekerk received the annual SARS Amakwhezi award as part of the then SARS Illicit Economy Team, as well as SARS's Amakwhezi Commissioner's Award, an accolade afforded only a few people who've made a national contribution to taking the SARS image and mandate forward in the most positive and visible way.

Sadly, for both the State and SARS, 'Charlie and the rhinos' left the tax authority in 2015 to join a private conservationist group.

15

How the 'rogues' helped to save the Springbok

Towards the end of the first decade of the new millennium, South Africa was on the brink of losing something very dear to many people – our ability to manufacture uniforms for our national sport teams.

Late one night, in a small restaurant in Cape Town, a very worried Shirish Soni, then head of SARS Customs operations, and I discussed this disconcerting matter over cups of coffee and tea. We'd been trying to do something about this grave state of affairs for a long time, and that day we'd come across a document that could be the key to solving the dilemma – if only we could determine who'd written it and why.

'JvL, get those high-risk guys down here,' Soni said. 'We can start early tomorrow morning, and call everyone in the business, and just ask. There's no harm in trying. Let's just ask each and every one of the people there.'

I made the call. Even though it was late, Johnny de Waal, a member of SARS's High-risk Investigative Unit (the former National Research Group, and the outfit later defamed in the media as a 'rogue unit'), answered. 'I'll send Gertjie Jute and Keith Hector down tomorrow,' he said.

Soni and I returned to our hotel to get some rest. A long day lay ahead of us.

South Africa's national flower, the king protea, and our national animal, the springbok, are used as emblems for most of our national sport teams. These emblems must be patented, licensed and trademarked to ensure that they're not used by anyone wanting to make clothing or for other purposes, which would dilute the brand.

By the mid-2000s, the national rugby squad was wearing a jersey bearing the king protea and a leaping springbok, together with clothing brand Canterbury's trademark three Cs. Canterbury International SA was owned by Fifth Element Marketing, which was a subsidiary of Brimstone Investment Corporation, one of the largest empowerment firms in South Africa. Canterbury owned the licensing rights to manufacture Canterbury sportswear, including the Springbok rugby jersey and jerseys for a variety of Super 14 and provincial rugby teams.

In early 2009, in a small public announcement that attracted hardly any attention, Brimstone announced that it had applied to put Fifth Element into liquidation.[1] The reason given was that between 1998 and 2008 the clothing, footwear and textile manufacturing sector in South Africa had shed about a million jobs, and the industry was being crippled by a variety of scams and smuggling.

What had once been a thriving manufacturing sector had been under significant pressure for a long time. The situation had become even more severe in the run-up to the 2010 FIFA Soccer World Cup, with counterfeit football jerseys and paraphernalia streaming into the country and being openly sold on every street corner and at every fleamarket.

If Fifth Element were liquidated, South Africa could lose the means to manufacture and distribute not only the clothing worn by our national sports heroes, but also similar clothing that fans bought (replicas). This would be disastrous.

When I came to meet the leaders of the South African Clothing and Textile Workers' Union (SACTWU) around this time, I learned a few things that contributed to my determination to try and do whatever I could to help. I listened as some told me how this sector employed predominantly women: women who were mothers, women who kept their families going financially, women who fed their children and did the best they could. I was told that the majority of those million-plus people who'd lost their jobs over the years were women, and that this affected not only the employees themselves but also their families.

SACTWU and its leadership impressed me with their dedication in trying to work with SARS in dealing with what they believed to be part of the problem: smuggling, under-invoicing of imported clothing, footwear and textiles, and counterfeit goods. Not only that, but this labour union was prepared, together with its worker-members, to use its own pension funds to invest in its own businesses.

In its quest to fight the illicit trade that was ruining the livelihoods of its members, SACTWU had been to the police, the Department of Trade and Industry and just about everywhere else, and it was now looking to SARS to help. The bleeding of jobs had to stop.

The import duty imposed on clothing, textiles and footwear was already among the highest, as part of Government's efforts to curb dumping[xiii] and under-invoicing. But that alone wasn't going to help. We had to do more.

I must admit, I felt overwhelmed by the challenge. Hundreds of thousands of large containers arrived at South African ports of entry every day, and – in a situation similar to everywhere else in the world – SARS simply did not have the capacity to check each and every one. It was a physical impossibility.

To help visualise what SARS faced daily in terms of imports, consider the statement, issued in 2011 when SARS announced to the media its customs modernisation programme, that a staggering R1,5-trillion worth of goods moves through South Africa's borders each year. Each year, more than 160 000 trucks move through Beit Bridge border post alone – equating to an average of twenty trucks per hour, 24 hours a day, or a new truck every three minutes – and a further 60 000 move through Lebombo. That is an average of over 600 trucks a day at these two border posts alone.[2]

The only way that we could ensure that those carrying legitimate goods moved swiftly and unimpeded through the borders, and that those carrying illicit goods did not, was by adopting a targeted-risk-assessment approach. And even then, checking the containers that brought in clothing, textiles and footwear wasn't simple or straightforward. Different items

xiii 'Dumping' refers to the practice of a country or company exporting products at a price that's lower in the foreign importing market than in the exporter's domestic market.

and types of textiles attracted different tariffs, and materials came with different descriptions. So one 12-metre-long container could be packed with T-shirts of different grains of cotton, for instance, and you'd have to be an expert in cotton to spot the differences.

The total enforcement capacity of SARS was never more than about 1 500 people, scattered across the country, who had to deal with a tax base of more than 11 million taxpayers. We were a thin line of defence pitted against a high-volume problem – but we were determined to make a difference.

I took my inspiration from three sources. One was the SACTWU representatives themselves – they asked the most obvious questions, and helped us to understand the nature and magnitude of the problem. They were also able to pinpoint particular geographic areas in South Africa where they believed storage facilities, manufacturers and warehouses involved in illegal practices were concentrated.

My second source of inspiration was Cuban revolutionary Che Guevara's booklet *Guerrilla Warfare*, a manual that drew on his experiences as a participant in the 1953-59 Cuban Revolution. The parts I'd read dealt with the 'foco theory' of revolution by way of guerrilla warfare: a vanguard of cadres of small, fast-moving paramilitary groups providing a focus (in Spanish, *foco*) for popular discontent against a sitting regime.

My third source of ideas was Shirish Soni, who'd been involved in the clothing industry and knew it inside out – during the apartheid era, Soni had used his textile factory as a means to employ underground operatives, pay their legal fees and provide cover for them. (As a result, Soni's factory had become the target of security forces and he'd had a very difficult time, including torture and solitary incarceration.)

Using these sources and insight, I formulated our basic plan. It required us to use the few resources at our disposal and engage with other state agencies to develop small, fast-moving groups to impact on the 'enemy'.

By the end of 2008, some of the fruits of our actions had become public knowledge by way of SARS reports issued, public announcements and media articles. In November that year, the media reported how 300 officials from the SARS National Enforcement Unit (which was under my management) and 30 police officers had raided five shops and 13 storerooms in a shopping mall in the Joburg city centre, which was known as a hotspot for counterfeit and illegal imports. They'd seized sports shoes, tracksuits, socks and sweaters worth hundreds of thousands of rands, suspected of being either illegally imported or counterfeit.

Peter Posthumus, then the manager of the National Enforcement Unit, was quoted as saying that the police and SARS had confiscated goods when store owners had been unable to produce tax or import-duty documents, and that inspectors and attorneys from brand holders would inspect the goods to ascertain if they were counterfeit. 'If shop owners don't come forward with their tax and import-duties documentation by tomorrow, their goods will be detained in storage for a period of 30 days, and if they don't come within that period, the goods will be seized by the State,' he said.[3]

The following month, the media reported that barely three months after the opening of China Town, a factory-shop complex in the Cape Town suburb of Ottery, 37 of its 47 outlets had been closed in SARS raids because the owners couldn't provide the tax officers with proof that their merchandise had been brought into the country legally.

'Initially, all 47 shops had been closed, but hours later the owners of 10 had provided documents showing where their merchandise was from,' the report noted. 'By the afternoon, 37 of the shops remained closed. They would remain so until the owners could provide the necessary documents, [SARS spokesperson Adrian] Lackay said.'

'We're working together with organised labour to identify how goods come into our country and how they find their way into retail outlets in the country,' Lackay told the media. 'We're finding goods are coming here through places like Botswana, Namibia and Mozambique.' He continued, 'This is very worrying for SARS and organised labour. It has a detrimental effect and makes it difficult to sustain jobs because some businesses can't compete with the illicit goods being brought in.'[4]

By early 2009, similar raids in Limpopo had netted fake clothes worth R3,5 million.

Soon enough, we'd got the help of not only the police, but also the Department of Labour and Department of Home Affairs' immigration division to join our 'foco' approach; and Soni had also by then allocated dedicated SARS customs officials to assist in these raids.

In September 2009, SARS concluded raids in various areas in KwaZulu-Natal, together with the Durban Metropolitan Police, the police, the Department of Health and the Department of Home Affairs. SARS seized 400 tons of clothing, textiles and goods valued at R60 million.

One of these raid areas was quite isolated, and involved many Chinese-speaking factory owners and warehouse managers; the town we focused on consisted mainly of clothing and textile manufacturers and storage facilities. Because of the anticipated language barrier, I arranged for an approved Chinese interpreter to accompany us – she would prove invaluable in not only bridging the language gap but also educating us in Chinese customs and how best to deal with nationals of Chinese origin without shaming them. One of the upshots was that we actually made a few friends in that town.

A small group of people from various SARS and customs units stayed at a hotel almost an hour away from the town. We would leave before daybreak every morning to travel to the town, arriving there as the businesses were opening. We would then break up into different groups to conduct our inspections and raids.

The police had an operational centre in the town, where I'd drop in there every day to pick up new leads and keep track of progress as we went along.

In the evenings, we'd all travel back to the hotel to have dinner, and before we went to bed, I'd get everyone together and we'd reflect on the day; team leaders would give me feedback, and we'd alter and adapt our plans for the next day if necessary. Then it was showers and rest, so that we could be up the next day before dawn to start all over again.

We camped there for an entire week, and systematically went through virtually all the businesses and warehouses. It was a long week but proved well worth it.

During raids in Durban, 85 stores were inspected, of which 47 were closed for failing to provide proof of import declarations for the goods on sale.

SACTWU issued a press release acknowledging our efforts, noting that it welcomed SARS raids of illegal clothing and extending 'deep appreciation' for this 'very important intervention'.[5]

In October 2009, SARS officials again visited China Town in Ottery, as well as Inyanga Junction in Manenberg, Durban Street in Bellville and warehouses in Lansdowne. Almost 300 tons of clothing valued at R45 million were seized. This included four tons of counterfeit branded sportswear valued at R600 000. At the same time, Immigration arrested four foreign nationals for contraventions of the Immigration Act.

And that wasn't all. Behind the scenes, we'd started engaging all the major clothing retailers, and had designed a basic vetting system for them to ensure that those importers and agents through whom they purchased imported clothing were tax compliant – we'd found some unscrupulous importers selling merchandise to major retailers at very attractive prices, obviously because they were cheating during the import process, and the retailers knew nothing of this. Every single major retailer welcomed and adopted the system across the board.

We also developed 'self-auditing' programmes for major importers and retailers, and, by agreement, got most of them to secure the services of external audit firms to conduct these audits and provide SARS with the results. A few very big audits were handled by the SARS Large Business Centre, all of them successful.

And so, day after day, week after week, we continued our planned inspections and raids all over the country. Some of the people would finish their inspections in one province, then fly or drive immediately to the next to continue there. By operating these 'foco guerrilla teams', we created the perception of massive SARS teams omnipresent throughout the country, and it worked very well.

What added great impetus to our efforts was the increase in tariffs introduced by the Department of Trade and Industry on these clothing and textile products, making them more expensive to import and so giving local manufacturers a competitive price advantage.

At the same time, a new price-reference system was negotiated by representatives of Government, labour and business which made it much easier for SARS officials to identify fraudulent amounts on invoices for clothing imports. The system was also used to identify suspicious transactions by comparing declared import values with historical transaction prices. Soon, SARS customs operations were announcing regular successful seizures of contraband coming in at our ports of entry.

In December 2010, we took the strategy a level further. Usually a quiet period because many SARS officials take annual leave over the festive season, December also happened to be the most attractive time for sales of counterfeit, smuggled and undervalued goods – and we weren't going to let the sellers off the hook just because of the holidays. SARS staff agreed to stagger their leave over the month, and at the same time we worked out a calendar to cover the different geolocations countrywide – so, for instance, week one was the Western Cape and North West, the following week covered Gauteng and KwaZulu-Natal, and so on. We allocated small teams of people and developed their travel plans to the regions according to the calendar, while checking which officials weren't on leave in the various regions, and adding them to our smaller teams.

By early 2011, the new SARS customs risk-management system had focused attention on textiles and other imported products, and more specifically on undervaluations. Benchmark prices, determined in conjunction with the industry and labour, assisted in setting rules against which potential undervaluation of similar commodities could be identified. These consignments were then stopped and detained by SARS, and put through a multi-level approval process that included reference to a valuation database containing the relevant reference pricing.

SARS reported the seizure of 7 348 937 clothing pieces estimated at R1,1 billion for the 2010/11 financial year alone. By comparison, in the 2015/16 financial year, only 495 436 items with a value of R8,7 million were impounded. Typically, SARS would auction goods of value to recoup losses to the state or donate goods for charitable purposes, but when it came to clothing, textiles and footwear, SARS took the principled position of having these destroyed or shredded into small rags to be used to manufacture blankets, cloths and mops.

It was at the start of this campaign that Soni and I had come to be in Cape Town that evening in early 2009. We'd been at a clothing manufacturer all day, working closely with the Brimstone managers and auditors, delving into the case. By then there was already some panic in the market, with several retailers expressing concern about time running out to place orders in order to obtain enough stock to meet the expected fan frenzy for Springbok jerseys when the British and Irish Lions arrived for their tour at the end of May that year.

When Brimstone instructed its lawyers to instigate a full forensic investigation and to cooperate with SARS, we started interviewing one person after another at Fifth Element, until one came forward and told us how his manager had instructed him to destroy a box of documents containing incriminating evidence. The employee, who hadn't destroyed the documents and had instead taken them home, agreed to go and fetch the box for us.

Working through the documents, I came across an affidavit that basically described how Fifth Element was being used by insiders to commit customs fraud. An employee of the company had been running a racket of his own, using it to place orders for goods in the Far East, then arranging for these to be undervalued on import and thereby paying less customs duty, then selling the merchandise on to unsuspecting buyers. Fifth Element and its directors had no clue what one of their employees was up to.

Although quite detailed, the affidavit was insufficient on its own to make a case – and it was here that the high-risk unit's Gertjie Jute and Keith Hector could assist.

They arrived by plane the next morning and within hours were able to identify the author of the document by analysing the embedded electronic markings of the attachment of an email, interviewing certain staff, and narrowing it down to a specific computer at the company. From there, it was a matter of going to the owner of the computer and asking him about it.

It took some convincing, because naturally people are scared in these sorts of situations, but both he and the person who'd given us the box of documents were brave enough to tell us about the scam and work with us, including providing us with witness statements. Within a day or so, the case was cracked.

The results led to our identifying local and foreign bank accounts, including one in Hong Kong, which I personally and immediately referred to the NPA's Asset Forfeiture Unit. We also registered a criminal case with the police of customs fraud and tax evasion, and I tried my best to push that case through the system.[6]

In February 2009, Brimstone issued a notice stating that three of their companies had been placed in voluntary liquidation after SARS had briefed Brimstone that possible serious financial and criminal irregularities had been uncovered.

Had Brimstone's auditors and the whistleblowers not cooperated so well with us, and had we not worked so closely with the company in order to solve the issue, there would have been far-reaching implications for retailers who relied on sales of replica sports apparel, our local sponsored athletes wouldn't have had kit to wear at their national events, and jobs would've been lost. Brimstone was able to enter into agreements with sponsored teams to supply everything from bags, tracksuits, practice wear and several sets of playing kit, right on time.

SARS and the 'rogues' had helped save the day.

In the following year, 2014, there were significant disruptions in SARS following a malicious campaign about the so-called 'rogue unit'. It picked up speed from October 2014 and ultimately led to an exodus of almost the entire leadership of SARS, and many more specialists and investigators from early 2015, many never publicly reported on over this time.

In March 2017, I read a news report about how SACTWU had staged a march *against* SARS at the SARS headquarters in Pretoria 'in an attempt at highlighting the negative impact of a lack of enforcement and inspection of imported goods at South Africa's customs points'. In what SACTWU researchers described as 'a near collapse in goods confiscated', only R8,7-million-worth was impounded. 'For 2015/16, only 495 436 items were confiscated, which is less than 7% of goods confiscated in 2011/12,' the report stated.

Dr Nick Steen, the chief executive officer of Sheraton Textiles who'd helped SARS set up the price-reference system, said that 'there was a feeling that there is "a lot of disarray" in SARS'. 'While there are still some dedicated officials at entry level in SARS, at a senior level, it is dysfunctional. The system is no longer set up to police illegal imports. There is high leakage and things are not working in SARS the way they used to. Unfortunately, SARS and the country lose out. Every illegal import is a lost revenue collection opportunity,' he said.

While there had been ongoing requests to meet with and discuss the crisis with SARS, this was simply 'glossed over', Eksteen noted, and the report concluded that the union's behaviour was a manifestation of its frustration.[7]

The High-risk Investigations Unit, a little unit which by 2010 comprised of only seven people, formed part of a rather small component within SARS that was trying to do its bit towards eradicating organised crime from both a tax and a customs perspective. Many people, including those who were critical of this unit, didn't appreciate the fact that all the different investigative units I managed operated as a whole. Each complemented the other and was dependent on the outputs of the others.

It's a sad fact that the disbandment of this capability left South Africa and the State much the poorer. Most if not all tax and customs authorities around the world have enforcement capacities that deal with organised crime. I can't understand why SARS suddenly no longer saw fit to contribute to fighting crime when it was so well placed to do so.

16

Oh Tannenbaum, oh Tannenbaum

Late on a winter's Friday afternoon in 2009, a few of us were travelling from Pretoria to Johannesburg to an address we had for a company we were investigating. The traffic was moving at a snail's pace, and we were using the car heaters to stay warm – none of us had expected to be going on this trip, so none of us was appropriately dressed.

But there was no time to waste: we needed to get there, and fast.

When we turned in to the office block, we were met by security officials at the gate. 'Everybody has gone home already,' we were told. 'Come back on Monday.'

I produced the documentation indicating the purpose of our visit, and the security officials understood and let us in. They showed us to the right building and accompanied us to the floor of the business.

When we arrived there, the offices were in disarray, a paper-shredder full to the brim, boxes lying about. *Certainly not a multibillion-rand business, by the looks of it*, I thought.

A pyramid scheme offers an 'investor' the means to generate income personally through the recruitment of new 'investors'; Ponzi schemes masquerade as investment opportunities, asking for money and promising unrealistically high returns. Neither lasts.

Both have a limited lifespan to the extent that they're able to attract sufficient 'investors' to keep using some of the new inflow to pay the older 'investors', but because they have to grow in size to stay alive, and have no legitimate business activities or profit of financial trading by which to do so, they reach a critical point where the payments to 'investors' can no longer be sustained. Then they collapse, taking with them the money of their 'investors', which is often people's life savings.

We've had a few of these in South Africa, some sophisticated and others so ridiculous it's hard to believe that people were actually fooled by them.

One of the more famous South African pyramid schemes was the 'Kubus' scam. In the 1980s there was a wave of excitement about an investment scheme that required 'investors' to buy, for R500 a pop, dried, ground-up cheese that produced a thick milk, called 'kubus' culture. The 'investors' were required to send small amounts of this kubus to a man named Adriaan Niewoudt, ostensibly as an ingredient for facial creams, for which he paid R10 a time. He in turn would simply grind up the kubus again, repackage it and send it off to new unsuspecting 'investors'.

Sounds stupid, right? Yet thousands of people bought into it and the scheme had turned around R140 million before it went belly-up.

A more recent scam was the Krion Ponzi scheme. Marietjie Prinsloo and her family started it in 1998 and it operated until 2002, turning over R1,5 billion from almost 14 000 investors in those four years, but leaving many in poverty when it collapsed; many investors were pensioners who'd put their retirement packages into the scheme.

'Although meticulous records were kept of moneys received from and returns owing to investors, none of the entities, incorporated or otherwise, kept books of account or published financial statements, and only Krion Financial Services Ltd opened a bank account (and then only for a period of about three months in 2002). The liquidators' task was especially complicated by the practice of Ms Prinsloo, as the driving force behind the operation of the scheme, of moving from one corporate identity to another successively and as it suited her and, particularly, during a period when there were official enquiries being made into her affairs. On such occasions the assets and liabilities of the discarded entity were simply taken over holus bolus by the one that followed.'[1]

The hard work on this case, which started in 2002 and came to a close in 2010, was a multidisciplinary effort by investigators, auditors and prosecutors from the NPA, the police, the South African Reserve Bank and SARS. Much credit should go to the criminal investigators and auditors of the SARS Special Investigations/Criminal Investigations Unit, who played a critical role in securing Prinsloo a jail sentence of over 25 years in June 2010. She was convicted on 122 000 counts, including racketeering, money-laundering and fraud.

Five other members of her family were convicted on the same day for theft, fraud, tax fraud and contraventions of several acts, including the Banks Act, the Insolvency Act and the Companies Act, receiving sentences of between five and 12 years.

None of the convicted took responsibility for their actions, with Marietjie Prinsloo blaming her attorneys and her co-accused in turn blaming her.

The most significant aspect of the court findings and sentence, which made history in the sense that it was a first for SARS, was that Prinsloo got a prison sentence for failing to submit tax returns.

The Grand Scam by journalist and newspaper editor Rob Rose is probably the most in-depth telling of the largest Ponzi scheme in the history of South Africa.[2] It doesn't have a happy ending, I'm afraid.

Barry Tannenbaum's grandfather was one of the founders of global healthcare company Adcock Ingram. He looked and played the part: he came from a wealthy family and clearly had the inside track on business.

Tannenbaum used his companies, Frankel International and Frankel Chemicals, as vehicles to offer 'investments' to people, for which they would receive interest of over 216% per year. On paper this appeared to be a lucrative and promising legitimate business of buying active pharmaceutical ingredients from foreign countries, to be sold on to generic drug makers to make antiretroviral drugs. 'Investors' were required to make deposits into Tannenbaum's Rand Merchant Bank private account, the inflows to which were found to amount to R3 156 487 235, and the outflows (the 'repayments with interest') to R3 053 156 652. The figures are so huge you may not notice a little discrepancy of about R103 million. I'll come back to it later.

Tannenbaum would explain to investors how, in order to avoid 'red tape involved with borrowing from banks', he would rather borrow money from investors and repay them tenfold in a few months.[3]

The scheme grew and grew, reaching out tentacles to Germany, Brazil, the United Kingdom, Australia, Switzerland, the United Arab Emirates, the United States and India.

Tannenbaum would show prospects purchase orders from major pharmaceutical companies such as Adcock Ingram, Aspen and Novartis valued at millions at a time; one such order amounted to over R700 million, and one investor put R100 million into the scheme.

Soon enough, Tannenbaum was joined by Johannesburg attorneys Dean Rees and Darryl Leigh, with Rees acting as an 'agent' for Tannenbaum.

The scheme continued growing, with more and more people wanting in. It reached a point where more than R12 billion had passed through various bank accounts, and 'feeder' Ponzi schemes were growing alongside it – smaller iterations of the main scheme, aimed at pooling smaller 'investments' to make up single bigger 'investments'.

More than 880 people fell for the scam. Wealthy British businessmen Philip Green and Richard Kirk and his brother Andy were investors; the Kirk family lost £17 million in the scheme. Other victims included former Pick n Pay chief executive officer Sean Summers, who was 'fortunate in that, while he is believed to have put more than R20 million into the scheme … hasn't lost everything'; Allan Rock, a professional tennis coach; accountant Howard Lowenthal; broker Wayne Gadden; and Uraj Tewary, a call-centre administrator who invested his wife's pension and some other family money. And, of course, if brokers and CEOs were investing, and their names were casually dropped, this seemed to provide further proof of legitimacy and value.

The Tannenbaums, Reeses and Leighs lived it up for the years 2007 to 2009, while the scam ran its course. They travelled the world, staying in five-star hotels. In what one witness described as a 'breathtaking' spending spree, Rees blew almost R5 million on watches for himself and bling for his wife, Dominique, sent limousines to pick up friends and investors for dinner parties through a luxury concierge service, and even flew his personal jeweller to St Tropez on the French Riviera to deliver a five-carat diamond ring worth R1,7 million to Dominique. Rees allegedly bragged about a villa in Lausanne, Switzerland that he'd bought for R65 million, and a Ferrari 599 sports car that he garaged in South Africa. On a trip to St Tropez in September 2008, Rees hired a 53-metre luxury yacht, equipped with a Jacuzzi and a helicopter landing pad, for a birthday bash for his wife.

In order to lure investors, Rees would serve the best champagne on rented luxury yachts; he was reported to have once spent over R300 000 on French bubbly for his guests to spray at each other.

Leigh, who retired as practising attorney, owned two Lamborghinis and two Mercedes-Benz cars.

By the time the investors woke up to the fact that the scam had run dry, Tannenbaum and his wife, Deborah, had fled South Africa for Sydney, Australia; ironically, their last known address was in Runaway Bay on Queensland's Gold Coast.

Soon before the scheme collapsed, Rees left South Africa for his Switzerland hideout by chartered private jet, with jewellery and watches, including a Blue Phantom watch valued at R1 million, to continue his high-flying lifestyle and drive around in a McLaren Mercedes sports car.[4]

How the scheme collapsed was entirely predictable: it ran out of new 'investors' and couldn't keep up the payments to existing 'investors'.

When the payments stopped, naturally some investors tried to contact Tannenbaum to find out what was going on. The first whispered hints that it may be a Ponzi scheme quickly turned into panic.

Rose broke the story in the media in June 2009.[5]

Within days of the story having gone public, SARS took the initiative, even though we knew very little about the scheme except that it had collapsed and that the duped 'investors' were crying for action by the State.[6] I was called by then deputy commissioner Ivan Pillay and asked what we should do first.

One of my suggestions was to form a joint task team with the Financial Intelligence Centre,[xiv] the South African Reserve Bank, the SAPS, the NPA and the Asset Forfeiture Unit. My reckoning was to create a means whereby all the agencies would be able to execute their statutory mandates in parallel, using the Financial Intelligence Centre as the information hub. And that's what we ultimately did.

We called the heads of all these institutions to a meeting at SARS to put the framework to them. All agreed on the way forward, and because SARS was best placed to quickly provide legal support in the form of external legal counsel and attorneys, all parties present agreed that, for the time being, and at least until SARS's own cases that would flow from this were concluded, SARS would assist in this manner. SARS thus effectively carried the legal bills for all the agencies for at least the next two years.

One thing that frustrated the hell out of me was the lack of pace of some of the officials from the other agencies – we started off by having weekly progress meetings, and sometimes found the various role-players to not have done what they'd undertaken to do within set and agreed time frames. We waited a day or two for the police to obtain search warrants to search the various premises, but to no avail. I knew from experience that once these scams went public, and those involved knew the game was up, minutes counted. The suspects would immediately go into overdrive to move assets and get rid of evidence, so the sooner law-enforcement agencies moved to conduct searches and seizures of suspects' premises and evidence, the better.

xiv The Financial Intelligence Centre is a statutory body that acts as an 'advance warning system' for money-laundering and corruption. Banks and other financial institutions report suspicious transactions to the Financial Intelligence Centre, which may direct law-enforcement agencies and SARS to investigate.

Exasperated, I decided to use something I'd noticed in some of the media articles and on the Frankel website: that the scheme claimed to be involved in the import and export of medicinal products. Citing the Customs and Excise Act, we decided to go to the premises and conduct our own inspections. I knew we at SARS were the best option to act immediately and secure whatever we could, before it could be destroyed or hidden. And once we had the evidence, we could use the Financial Intelligence Centre as a conduit to ensure that the other law-enforcement agencies were given access to it.

And that was how and why, late on a chilly Friday afternoon in 2009, our hastily put-together search team drove through from Pretoria to Joburg to conduct the inspection. We arrived as the sun was setting, and after what had already been a long day for most of those SARS officials on the team. But soon enough we were standing in the offices once occupied by Barry Tannebaum and company, where we found an administrative assistant, sitting in front of a paper-shredding machine, with boxes and boxes of documents strewn around.

The entire office space was in a mess; it looked like it had already been ransacked. But time would prove that we'd made the right call, and had arrived just in time to stop vital evidence and documents going through the shredder. The assistant, who had no inkling that her boss wasn't planning on returning to South Africa and that the business was a sham, was just doing what she'd been told; she was innocent.

We worked late into the night, going through documents, forensically sealing computers, and boxing whatever evidence we could lay our hands on. The assistant, who required some calming down once we'd told her what was actually going on, agreed to be present as we detained documents and computers, and to tell us everything that she'd been ordered to do by her boss.

We finished well after midnight, returning to our offices in Pretoria to safely secure and store the evidence.

The hard work lay ahead of us. Once we'd identified valuable evidence, we'd make copies of it and hand it over to the Financial Intelligence Centre. With the assistance of its counsel, advocate Andre Bezuidenhout, the Financial Intelligence Centre would in turn farm out the evidence to the various government agencies involved in the joint team.

The NPA team was led by the tough-as-nails, swears-like-a-sailor and very capable advocate Glynnis Breytenbach, who'd already moved to have arrest warrants issued for Barry Tannenbaum, Dean Rees and Darryl Leigh. At SARS we moved quickly to identify the 26 bank accounts used in the scheme, including those held at ABSA, Diner's Club, Discovery, First National Bank, Investec, Mercantile Bank, Nedbank, Rand Merchant Bank and Standard Bank.[7]

By then we'd worked out a systematic process whereby we would call in one investor at a time, with their lawyers, and put them through a series of questions. Most were extremely helpful and cooperated with SARS, and those who'd made money through the scheme and not declared it in prior years were taxed on the amounts and fined.

I also arranged for members of the joint agencies to travel to Australia and engage the authorities there, and we got brilliant international cooperation from them; the same went for the authorities in Switzerland and some other countries we'd identified, including the United States and the United Arab Emirates.

It was mainly the Central Projects Unit and National Projects Unit (another investigative unit that I managed at this time) that were involved in wrapping up the SARS leg of the joint team's work. The SARS investigators had to trawl through records at the deeds offices, the Natis vehicle-ownership database, and third-party information and evidence obtained from banks and investors. It was a mammoth task, executed by only a handful of people but done exceptionally well.

The SARS investigators looked at nine companies and close corporations connected to Tannenbaum (including a trust and five Australian entities), painstakingly auditing their books and records. Barry Tannenbaum himself was sequestrated and his companies liquidated.

Tannenbaum, from the safety of Australia, of which country he'd become a resident in 2007 and who therefore qualified for the full legal protections of the Australian judiciary system, issued a short statement: 'I have not amassed some fortune that I have spirited away, and in due course an audit will bear out this statement, if people are still interested in hearing the truth,' it said. Then he all but disappeared from the public eye.[8]

By July 2009, the Asset Forfeiture Unit had obtained preservation orders against Leigh's and Rees's remaining assets in South Africa, including four luxury cars, two properties and R43 million in cash held in bank accounts, including the Daryl Leigh Trust, which was subsequently liquidated.

The South African Reserve Bank appointed KPMG as inspectors for its own investigation, which led to the determination that the role-players were conducting the business of a bank in contravention of the banking laws of South Africa. In February 2010, the matter was referred to the Registrar of Banks.

In May 2011, Tannenbaum's liquidators for his insolvent estate received a comprehensive letter from Central Projects head Pieter Engelbrecht. It included 17 pages of detailed spreadsheets in support of the assessment of an underdeclaration of R444 770 202. The normal tax, additional tax, penalties and interest added to this brought it to a whopping R747 990 921. Interest at 15,5% was also levied.

The tax assessment made its way into the public domain as part of over 30 000 pages of evidence that the trustees of Tannenbaum's bankrupt estate were obliged to hand over to anyone against whom they were litigating.

In 2013, the South African trustees of Tannenbaum's estate tried to take over his Australian assets in an action brought in the Queensland Federal Court. During the proceedings, Tannenbaum declined to reveal his home address and said he didn't have a permanent home. The court case was unsuccessful but what it did do was make publicly known many aspects of the SARS investigation: Tannenbaum had raised US$390 million between 2004 and 2009. Of this amount, a mere 0,05% was on-loaned by Tannenbaum for the purpose of purchasing pharmaceutical ingredients.

According to the court documents, R44,8 million was used by Tannenbaum for personal transactions 'with a substantial portion being spent on gambling'.

The records showed that he'd transferred US$31,7 million into the bank account of the Bartan Group, an Australian incorporated company that was by then in liquidation. Of that amount, US$14 million was transferred into other entities controlled by Tannenbaum or to people associated with him.

'It may very well be that his decision to quit South Africa was inherently bound up with a desire not in the future to be dealt with under the law of that country in respect of his involvement in the scheme described, and a related desire to enjoy the benefits of proceeds repatriated to Australia,' the judge noted, and continued, 'It is not necessary in this proceeding conclusively to determine whether or not or to what extent he has enjoyed the proceeds but there is no doubt on the evidence that substantial funds sourced from South Africa were transferred to Australian entities controlled by him and his wife.'[9]

During 2008 and 2009, Dean Rees with his company had reportedly invested R1,5 million and received almost R69 million. By 2013, trustees had obtained a court order against Rees for R159 million.[10]

Darryl Leigh lost all his assets.

The SARS part of the case had gone as far as it could: assessments had been issued against the estates of Tannenbaum, Rees and Leigh; investors had been assessed, debts collected, and claims made against liquidated estates. Evidence that could help pursue criminal cases had been funnelled to the relevant agencies.

Under the hand of advocate Glynnis Breytenbach, warrants of arrests had been issued and the proceedings to apply for the extraditions of the kingpins had commenced.

SARS had done its bit and seen its statutory mandate through to its logical conclusion.

Despite criticism from some quarters, given the small team we had and the immense odds we faced, I think this case could make a good case study of a formula for how law-enforcement agencies and oversight bodies can work together on large and sophisticated white-collar-crime cases.

By 2013, we hadn't heard from the other state agencies for some time, and since our SARS investigations had reached maturity, I could no longer justify paying legal fees on their behalf. I was forced to pull the plug on costs being incurred by them, and this caused some unhappiness between them and myself.

In May 2013, 15 disciplinary charges brought the previous year against Glynnis Breytenbach, which had led to her suspension following an internal hearing, were dismissed. However, in an attempt to discredit her, Breytenbach also faced accusations of being a spy for Mossad, the Israeli secret service, which she naturally denied.[11]

She resigned from the NPA soon afterwards, to take up a position in the official opposition party, the Democratic Alliance, as its shadow Justice Minister. Not long after, she and her attorney, Gerhard Wagenaar, were both charged on almost the same matters of which she'd been cleared in her disciplinary hearing.

In early March 2018, they were both acquitted on all charges.

The paperwork and coordination of all the criminal cases in the Tannenbaum matter had been handled by Breytenbach, and following her resignation from the NPA, they all came to an immediate halt. To date, none of the scamsters have been arrested or extradited from any country, and the case docket seems to be gathering dust somewhere.

17

The tax 'fixer' – Glenn Agliotti

It's been alleged that I first met convicted drug trafficker and drug dealer Glenn Agliotti, also known as 'the Landlord', in 2001. This is false. My first meeting with him was actually in September 2008, when Leonard Radebe, then general manager: Customs and Excise at SARS, was implicated in a hoax tax settlement with businessman Dave King, as described in an earlier chapter.

I personally oversaw the registering of a criminal case against Agliotti – who in a court finding was once described as being among the 'snitches, pimps [and] rats who would sell their soul to evade a long prison term' – and others in respect of the Radebe matter.[1] And no sooner had we exposed Agliotti's shenanigans in the Radebe matter than I discovered that he was effectively running a ring of people from the veranda of his luxury pad who all acted as middlemen for those with tax problems: Agliotti had convinced people that he had influence in SARS that could make people's tax disputes go away – for a fee, of course.

Throughout August and September 2008, I, together with a handful of SARS investigators, followed the trails of these scams day after day. We travelled from one side of Johannesburg to the other, from suburbs to industrial areas to office parks. We encountered person after person who'd been led to believe that their tax issues would be cleared up if they paid a certain 'commission' to the middlemen and Agliotti.

What complicated these cases was the fact that the taxpayers in trouble had to admit to having at least considered paying a bribe, and in some cases actually done so, to have their tax matters disappear in an irregular manner. So most didn't really want to cooperate with us.

There were many of these instances but, by way of example, in late

2008, the *Mail & Guardian* reported that Brett Kebble's father, Roger, had paid at least R8 million through Agliotti on a promise to resolve his tax dispute with SARS. This didn't happen but what could Roger Kebble do? He could hardly complain that he'd been scammed after having paid a bribe.[2]

This was at exactly the same time that Agliotti was under the 'care' of the Scorpions as their star witness against Selebi.

In November 2008, it became public knowledge how there was a 'ring of tax fixers' around Agliotti. At the time, the *Mail & Guardian* reported that 'Agliotti and some of his associates have boasted, apparently falsely, of being able to solve tax problems – and appear to have wrung considerable sums out of other business people'.[3]

In the same period, an affidavit that Agliotti deposed and handed to the head of the then National Intelligence Agency (now the State Security Agency), Manala Manzini, basically contradicted the affidavit that he'd provided to the Scorpions which had implicated Selebi.

Nothing much came of this, except for the fact that he named businesswoman Tania Volschenk as having assisted him in typing up the affidavit on her laptop. Volschenk would later confirm knowing Agliotti but denied playing any part in typing the statement handed to Manzini. What was interesting about Volschenk, and what I believe demonstrated how close she was to Agliotti, was the fact that she'd purchased for R5,7-million the luxury pad that he and his family were living in in November 2007.

Then there was Jacques 'JJ' Nel, Leonard Radebe's friend who'd introduced Radebe and Glenn Agliotti to each other; and tax consultant Delville Whatley, who supposedly acted for SARS on occasion. All three of these people – Volschenk, Nel and Whatley – played a role to some extent in the hoax tax settlement of Dave King, and compromised Radebe in the process.

On a certain day, a foreign businessman, Jack Black (not his real name), who held assets and money in South Africa, decided to invest about R50 million in a venture in Zambia. His financial adviser, one

Rob Wurdeman, wasn't clued up on the legal and statutory technicalities about exchange rules and moving such sums out of South Africa, so he started looking around for a suitable professional to assist him.

Soon enough Wurdeman introduced the businessman to Tania Volschenk, who brought Delville Whatley along to the meeting. 'Not a problem,' Black was told; 'We can help.' For a fee, of course. A big fee.

Here's the thing. Jack Black wanted to move his South African investment legitimately, and if he'd asked SARS and the Reserve Bank for advice, he would've received guidance for free and the actual transaction would've cost him very little. But he was led to believe that it was extremely complicated and required all sorts of contacts and deals at SARS and the Reserve Bank – which would cost, you see?

Whatley, Volschenk and Agliotti scored big, fleecing Black of over R2 million in days, before he decided to cancel the arrangement and get proper advice.[4]

It was claimed that Nel had also benefited, but Wurdeman denied that Nel was involved.

Volschenk, Nel and Whatley declined to comment publicly on the matter.

I can't tell you how frustrated I was that no law-enforcement agency showed any interest in investigating this matter, or in taking forward any of the matters we uncovered, despite the very able SARS investigators already having concluded most of the work that needed to be done. Not a single one of these cases ever moved beyond our registering them with the police and notifying the Scorpions, and having a few meetings with senior officials there to try and get them to speed up the investigations. They all just died a quiet death.

I remain of the view that this lack of will on the part of the NPA to act against Agliotti was solely to protect him as a witness in the case against former national police commissioner Jackie Selebi. As I've already stated, had any of the criminal cases we registered that implicated Agliotti been properly investigated and dealt with, it would have demonstrated how

Agliotti had been involved in suspected offences under the watch of the Scorpions and would certainly have been a feature in the eventual trial where he testified against Selebi.

As it happened, none of this mattered anyway: the judge in the Selebi case, Meyer Joffey, wasn't impressed with Agliotti's testimony and denied him immunity from prosecution. The State was therefore free to charge him for any offence, including the corruption of Selebi. But he was never pursued for these cases at all.

What you need to keep in the back of your mind as you read this is the fact that the old Scorpions were heavily invested in a few highly politicised cases from the early 2000s onwards, most notably the corruption case against Schabir Shaik and then Deputy President Jacob Zuma, and the case against Selebi. They were fighting for their very existence as a result of this, at a cost that I believe may have been far too high.

I call these cases – the cases of the Scorpions against Zuma, Selebi and Shaik, using Agliotti as a witness – the 'seeds of discontent'. I firmly believe that these cases ultimately contributed to the motives of some who caused mayhem at SARS years later. The seeds of some of the motives, the anger, jealousy, misguided professional rivalry and plain stupidity of those who would later jump on the bandwagon to drive home the fake 'rogue unit' story, were germinating when these cases started unfolding. Of that I have no doubt.

In all these cases, different officials from the Scorpions and the NPA tried at various times to ask SARS to disclose taxpayer information to them in a manner that wasn't lawful. But we wouldn't bend the rules, and every time they approached us at SARS with these requests, we'd respectfully point them to the correct legal means. To be clear, it was never a case of SARS not wanting to provide information to law-enforcement agencies; rather, we simply wanted to do so following proper laws and procedures.

For reasons not known to me, the various law-enforcement agencies instead continued trying other avenues to access SARS information.

This played out rather publicly in the State's case against Schabir Shaik.[5] In December 2004, it was revealed during the trial how the Scorpions had approached a Durban-based SARS investigator, Rob Reid, asking him to provide them with Schabir Shaik's tax information together with an affidavit. Reid, under the mistaken belief that this had been approved at SARS's highest level, obliged. Bearing in mind that we'd by then already told the Scorpions to do things the right way, this, in my view, was a shocking abuse of office.

Reid was subpoenaed by the prosecuting authority to testify in the Shaik trial. We quickly briefed senior advocate Peter Olsen, who brought an application on behalf of SARS to ask the court to make a ruling on the matter. Olsen, representing SARS and Reid, put to the court that the Scorpions had not followed proper procedures when they'd sought to obtain the information, and that Reid had unwittingly breached the confidentiality laws.[6]

The reality of the matter was that an employee of SARS could reveal information only in the course of his duty or by order of a judge. Presiding judge Hillary Squires found that Reid's testifying in Shaik's trial would not be in the line of duty, and refused to issue an order for him to testify. Squires added that only SARS could determine whether a tax offence had been committed, and not the prosecuting authority, and that 'a revenue official is a witness of last resort'.[7]

In the Zuma case that commenced in 2003 and dragged on over many years, a very similar scenario played out, with a few prosecuting officials and Scorpions approaching SARS at various levels, asking for pretty much the same thing, and in the same untoward manner. As always, our response was 'do things the right way or not at all'. I have no doubt that this, too, caused some people to view us as enemies; and when Zuma filed his appeal application in 2008 and it became public knowledge that he'd been working with SARS to resolve his tax affairs and was compliant by then, the amount of vitriol that some of us had to face was immense – not just from people in the law-enforcement agencies, but also from within the ranks of SARS.[8]

The Selebi case produced similar behaviour, with similar results, but by then we were being openly accused of being obstructive and not wanting to 'help' the NPA. I was told to provide an affidavit stating that Agliotti was present during a meeting I'd attended on behalf of SARS in 2001, when he hadn't been, and when I declined, the same pattern of recriminations and accusations followed.

It was a living hell to have to negotiate doing our jobs at SARS, and in a manner that wouldn't make life difficult for the Scorpions or prosecuting authority, while being constantly undermined and faced with threats, instead of calmly sitting around a table and working together on how best to navigate around each of our statutory mandates.

Because Agliotti had been offered indemnity from prosecution for tax evasion, as SARS, we had to wait for the Selebi trial to come to an end before we could do anything on the criminal case. The details of the SARS case against Agliotti would see daylight in 2013, when it was revealed that SARS had conducted a tax inquiry into his tax affairs during 2009 and 2010.

Court papers filed by the Central Projects Unit that resorted under me would later in 2013 reveal that we'd found evidence that Agliotti had received about R40 million from the mining company JCI around the time of Brett Kebble's murder in September 2005.[9]

It was also revealed in our complaint to the police that Agliotti had admitted during a tax inquiry that Kebble had paid money into Agliotti's Clariden Bank account in Geneva, Switzerland, which might well have amounted to money-laundering.

More revelations at this time emanating from our criminal case included Agliotti's use of an account called Springs Lights as a mechanism to receive R39 million from JCI, of which R18 million was for 'consulting fees'. A company of which Agliotti's wife was a director had supposedly 'borrowed' R16 million from a JCI subsidiary, and Agliotti was confronted with a receipt showing that R11 million had been paid into the Springs Lights account between 2004 and 2006. Agliotti admitted the money came from JCI but claimed that it was for 'projects like counterintelligence operations' and had been paid out to a variety of security companies.

Glenn Agliotti was found to owe SARS almost R78 million in unpaid taxes and penalties incurred between 2003 and 2008. We showed that he drove around in a Rolls-Royce and boasted how he had use of a yacht in the Mediterranean; that he gave money to his former fiancée, Dianne Muller, and paid her bond; that he'd bought her (and others) extravagant jewellery; and that he'd bought a BMW for Muller's daughter, settled her university fees and paid for overseas trips. We argued that he deliberately got divorced from his wife of three years, Lelani, while still living in the same house as her – a luxurious villa on an exclusive golf estate – in order to hold assets through her and out of the way of SARS. We showed how he'd failed to disclose a family trust and a host of companies in which he had interests, and that he had at least two overseas bank accounts, one in Geneva and one in Guernsey in the Channel Islands.

In 2010 we seized all his movable assets; and in 2012 we applied to the North Gauteng High Court for his provisional sequestration.

You may have noticed that SARS had begun investigating Agliotti in 2005, and that the tax inquiry was therefore on the go prior to the Selebi trial, which took place in 2010. But back in 2009 and 2010, when the Scorpions realised the value in offering Agliotti immunity from prosecution in exchange for Selebi's head, whatever we at SARS had done, however advanced our audit and investigations may have been, and whatever the tax inquiry may have revealed, mattered not.

In 2013, I was given a memory stick containing two recordings; the person who gave it to me said I could use the recordings as I wished.[10] The first recording was of a meeting between Agliotti, tobacco manufacturer

Yusuf Kajee, transport magnate Paul de Robillard, and someone called Warren;[11] in the second, Warren seems to be absent. The recordings appear to have been made in 2013.

Although both recordings contain plenty of astonishing information, the parts I'd like to focus on here are extracts that illustrate how Agliotti continued to con unsuspecting people who owed money to SARS – both Kajee and De Robillard were under investigation by SARS at the time. (Also, although at one stage during the first meeting Agliotti told Kajee and De Robillard that he and I 'are like this' – very close – keep in mind that I only ever physically met with and talked to Agliotti once, in 2008.)

Kajee: *How is JvL? Is he a guy you can talk to?*

Agliotti: *He seems a nice guy. And then he will fuck you up ... Don't think they have nothing on you. ... They will arrest you. They will take you to Pretoria, Silverton. Johan van Loggerenberg, Ronel* [SARS head of criminal investigations, Ronel van Wyk], *their whole team. ... Pieter Engelbrecht* [then head of the SARS Central Projects Unit that I oversaw] *from SARS. He did my case. They sequestrated me. They said 90 million from me. The sheriff came, I said, sit down relax. ... He* [me] *is my best mate.*

Then Agliotti switched into overdrive: *Understand one thing. SARS will run you. For ten years. They will kill you. Keep it going. Don't go that road. My experience. I'm your protection. Nobody will extort from you. I've been there. 'Speak to my partner Glenn Agliotti if anybody approaches you. Give me my number.'*

Kajee: *But does Johann want something?*

Agliotti: *You can't talk to Johann.*

Kajee: *How much does he want?*

Agliotti: *Who?*

Kajee: *Johann.*

Agliotti: *Don't let him meet you. I will sit with Johann on Sunday. How do we let it go away? How much will it cost?*

Obviously, Agliotti couldn't allow Kajee to have direct access to me, as then Kajee would immediately have realised that Agliotti was lying about his influence; Agliotti went to a great deal of trouble to ensure that he was perceived to be the go-between, because in this way he could demand a fee – a bribe – to broker any deal.

Kajee: *They have done an audit. They have nothing.*

Agliotti: *Don't kid yourself. They will not play their hand. Van Loggerenberg is not a cunt. And the team around him is brilliant.*

Agliotti then mentioned the one and only meeting that I really did have with him – a tactic of all experienced scammers, weaving in a bit of fact in case someone tries to check their story.

Agliotti: *First time he came to my house. When I was under house arrest. The Scorpions put cameras up. I said to him, 'You are now on Candid Camera.'*

Kajee: *What did he come for?*

Agliotti: *He wanted information on Antonio.*[xv] *I said, I can't give you information ... and ... do the Scorpions know that you came to see me? ... He and Ronel van Wyk, that fucking blonde bitch, came and sat there. She was just writing and writing.*

Agliotti now began really spinning a yarn about knowing me: *I am trying to turn this thing around. I am going to find out from Johann. I will meet with him. Johann knows me. I don't take his shit. ... 'Don't waste your time. What do you have on these guys? What do you want to achieve?' And then I will [ask] him, 'What do you want, personally?' And then I am going to say to him, 'Is that the best you've got?' And he will play open cards with me. And then I will go to my guys to run this operation and tell them what they've got on my guy. And I am going to tell them that you are my guy. 'This is who I want to run my operation with. But I want this thing sorted out.'*

De Robillard: *Glenn, before you take the settlement, will you know what the settlement is? Come with the information?*

Agliotti: *No, I am going to hear what they have and then we sit and I will give you the story. Understand it. They did it with me. They*

xv A tobacco trader whose name he got wrong.

fabricated half the shit against me. Do you think there is a judge in this country that will go against SARS?

De Robillard: *No.*

Agliotti: *You are onto a hiding to nothing. They do this, they do that … There is no judge in this country that will go against them.*

Kajee: *Johann van Loggerenberg – I heard his job was on the line.*

Agliotti: *Ag, bullshit. Johann is most probably the most honest guy in SARS besides the DG [or] whatever they call him in SARS.*

Kajee: *Ivan Pillay?*

To this day I wonder what Kajee was referring to here, since at that time there was not yet any clear indication of any direct attack on SARS and myself.

The following part of the recording revealed Agliotti trying to recruit the others for some sort of harebrained scheme to smuggle tobacco in order to combat tobacco smuggling, which he claimed was authorised by the Presidency. The idea seemed to have been to create a smuggling network so large that it would effectively push other smugglers out of the market. 'Phase one' was supposedly how Agliotti intended to 'fix' the cases against Kajee and De Robillard and bribe me, while 'phase two' was the smuggling scheme.

De Robillard: *This 'phase two' – what do you want me to do?*

Agliotti: *I will come back to you and say, 'This is what it is going to cost.'*

Kajee: *But if I understand correctly, phase two doesn't include Johann van Loggerenberg?*

Agliotti: *I am going to come to you and say, 'This is what they have on you.' Both of you. You have to … this thing. If you don't, you're fucked.*

Kajee: *The way you explained it, the first part is to sort Johann and them out, get them out of the way. The other one is coming from Zuma's office.*

Agliotti: *No, no, no. I am talking about your shit. Johann will say to me, 'Glenn, this is what we've got. This is what it's gonna take to make this thing go away.' And that's what they want. And then I can come and say, 'Guys, this is the situation. They're going to take you to Hollywood or they're going to arrest you or the helicopters are going to land,' whatever the situation is. Then you know. Then you decide. The second operation is the smuggling operation. That's a different operation, because there we are going to make money.*

De Robillard: *So what's the deal?*

Agliotti: *I gonna come back to you. I'm meeting Johann on Sunday. Whatever we discuss stays here. It is in nobody's interest if it gets out. Sunday night I will phone. And then we will meet Monday, Tuesday. As soon as I've got everything. This is what they think they have. We will not even fight that. How can we counter that, that's the first step.*

The second meeting took place some time later.

Kajee: *How was Johann van Loggerenberg?*

Agliotti: *Waiting to set a deal. But I'm playing hard ... Johann is on our side. Listen, they're gonna come clean with everything. They've got you, which is understandable. They will run the process.*

Here, because Agliotti was obviously lying about being able to 'fix' the investigation, he had to create the impression for Kajee and De Robillard that the investigation would be run in a way to make them 'seem legitimate' – in other words, that it would continue as usual.

Agliotti: *The bottom line is, Johann is on our side. Whatever you do, you've got to tell me who you are going to appoint as counsel, which lawyers you are going to use. Do you want me to appoint for you guys? I don't know who you are going to use. Who do you use?*

At this point, Agliotti really laid it thick on by pretending to know exactly what SARS was investigating and expanding on why the case would appear to be going against the victims.

Agliotti: *Thirteen of your companies are being investigated right now.*

Kajee: *What do they have? Is he just stressing us out, or does he want something for his pocket, or what does he want?*

Agliotti: *The thing is too big to just let it run by. I'm not going to lie to you. They're going to investigate. They're going to run it as a project. It is a project. Okay. But Johann will be on board with us. Pieter Engelbrecht ...*

Kajee: *Pieter Engelbrecht – where did I hear the name before?*

Agliotti: *He is from SARS. Special Investigating Unit. ... Because they are going to pull a profile on you. Have you got any previous criminal conviction?*

De Robillard: *No.*

Agliotti: *And you? Because within ten days they get a High Court judge ... If you've got [one], tell me because prevention is better than cure. ... By tomorrow we've gotta decide which counsel we are going to use. I'd rather go with, because* [name redacted] *and* [name redacted] *know Johann. There is* [name redacted], *there is* [name redacted] *... there is a lot of guys. For my money ... and also how do you pay them. You've got to be careful ... Let me do this. I come to you tomorrow. I wanna ... the parcel* [referring to the bribe] *and say, 'Listen, I don't want arrests ... arrests, no fucking way.'*

Kajee: *If it hits the news, all the businesses ...*

Agliotti: *Already in the news.* Carte Blanche *... 'I told you this is going to happen. Why are you in the limelight?' It is a fuckup. I can say to Johann. And Pieter Engelbrecht is the guy who has to sign. I can say to him, 'Listen, cunt, this is not going to happen. You must tell me what you want.' ... I will go to Johann and say, 'In reality this is what is happening.' As long as I give him something ... and I say to Johann, 'There is your parcel, fuck off,' but I will turn it around ... Leave Johann van Loggerenberg to me ...*

Despite all Agliotti's bluster, in the end Yusuf Kajee and Paul de Robillard didn't buy the story and didn't pay him a cent. What became of their cases I can't tell you, however, because by the time I left SARS, they were still ongoing.

But perhaps the most fascinating thing for me about these conversations is the fact that nobody ever referred to them in any of the later reports against me, and no law-enforcement agency ever bothered to investigate or follow up on the illegal extortion and smuggling schemes mooted by Agliotti.

When I resigned from SARS in February 2015, I never imagined I would ever hear from, far less meet, Glenn Agliotti again. But one day in November 2016, I received a phonecall from a prominent Johannesburg advocate who invited me to a meeting at his office but indicated that he didn't want to mention the names of people on the phone. I'd only ever had good interactions with this particular advocate, so agreed.

On the agreed day, I was at his chambers promptly on time. Shown into the advocate's office, I came face to face with the advocate, an attorney, a SARS whistleblower I'd met back in 2013... and Glenn Agliotti.[12] I immediately but surreptitiously switched on my phone's recording device, so that I could back up anything that was misconstrued or twisted at a later stage.[13]

We all sat around a table, and Agliotti gave me his proposal. He wanted to 'go into business' with me. I would become the owner – 'the face' – of a tobacco-manufacturing company, and I would run the business, which would include applying to SARS for the licence to import and export tobacco and manufacture cigarettes, and ensure that taxes were paid. Agliotti wouldn't feature at all; he would be a 'silent partner'.

The bottom line? The company would be used to smuggle tobacco.

'No, thank you,' I told them. 'I won't front for anybody, and you should know this of me. No, I won't go into such a business. And no, I won't go into tobacco manufacturing. You guys want to smuggle. I don't smuggle. I won't get involved in something like this and you should know better.'

18

Document '02'

The role of a revenue and tax authority is key to any functioning democracy, but especially a fledgling one such as South Africa. It's the lifeblood of the State's entire machinery, enabling Government to fund its services to citizens, provide for programmes to develop the country, pay grants to the underprivileged and maintain its sovereignty.

This is why it's so important that such an authority be free from any interference and bias. It has to treat each and every taxpayer in exactly the same manner.

In my career at SARS, I've had to 'walk the talk' of this principle of no bias in a few instances, but none was more memorable than in the case concerning former President Jacob Zuma.

Despite the fact that in 2005 he'd been dismissed as deputy president after being implicated in corruption during the Durban High Court trial of his former financial adviser Schabir Shaik, on 18 December 2007, Jacob Gedleyihlekisa Zuma was elected as the new president of the ruling African National Congress (ANC) at the party's national conference in Polokwane.

Just ten days after his election, a criminal indictment was served on Zuma at his home in Forest Town, Johannesburg, in his absence. The charges included various counts of racketeering, money-laundering, corruption and fraud, in contravention of the provisions of the Income Tax Act.

Michael Hulley, Zuma's lawyer, said that the timing of the indictment was 'peculiar' and that it 'proved the Scorpions were being influenced and their prosecution informed by political considerations'.[1]

This was not the first time that the NPA had tried to prosecute Zuma: it had brought a number of charges against him in 2006 but they'd been dismissed on the basis that there wasn't enough evidence to prove the case.

In September 2008, Thabo Mbeki was asked to step down as president of the country. A caretaker president in the form of ANC stalwart Kgalema Motlanthe took the reins.

In April 2009, advocate Mokotedi Mpshe, then head of the NPA, decided to discontinue the case against Zuma after recordings of conversations between various senior NPA officials concerning the timing of the charges came to the fore.

In May 2009, Jacob Gedleyihlekisa Zuma was sworn in as the president of the Republic of South Africa.

In November 2009 and again in February 2010, then ANC Youth League president Julius Malema – at the time an ardent supporter of Zuma – told the media that he was in possession of a dossier listing people who were close associates of Zuma (the 'Friends of Zuma') who were allegedly being targeted by a SARS unit known as the Special Projects Unit (later renamed the National Research Group). Malema was pointing a finger directly at SARS and a unit that I managed, saying in no uncertain terms that we were 'anti-Zuma'. As a loyal SARS employee who'd always done things by the book and who prided himself on treating all people equally, I took great umbrage at these claims, but I kept my thoughts to myself.

On 12 October 2014, the *Sunday Times* ran a front-page article entitled 'SARS bugged Zuma'. The article stated as established fact that a 'former spymaster blackmailed the South African Revenue Service into paying him R3 million to keep silent about how its rogue intelligence unit broke into Jacob Zuma's private home in Forest Town, Johannesburg, and planted listening devices at the time Zuma was unemployed after he had been fired as deputy president'.

Next to this screaming headline, above the fold, was a photograph of me. The article claimed that I'd been involved in breaking into Zuma's home and planting a listening device there, or at least had allowed officials who worked with me to do so. 'The unit's existence and alleged targeting of politicians aligned to Zuma in the run-up to [the] Polokwane [conference in 2007] has been reported on before,' the article read.[2]

So, according to Malema, the author of his 'dossier' and the *Sunday Times* and its 'sources', I – and by extension the units working under me at SARS – had been 'anti-Zuma' as far back as at least 2007. The fact that the SARS unit mentioned in the *Sunday Times* story didn't even exist then is another story altogether.

Now consider the following. In June 2008, in a review application brought by Jacob Zuma against the 2007 decision by the NPA to charge him on a variety of corruption charges, he presented an affidavit to the High Court in KwaZulu-Natal (see Addendum 1) in which he made some noteworthy revelations concerning SARS.[3]

Zuma's affidavit was stated under oath, before a High Court. It referred to matters dating from 2003 to 2008. The annexures were placed on public record by Zuma himself. The affidavit was also published online by none other than the Friends of Zuma.

An important part of the affidavit reads: 'It was wholly improper and unlawful of the NPA to institute such prosecutions under the Income Tax Act, without the necessary consultations and go-ahead from SARS.' In this Zuma and his lawyers were correct. This was confirmed in an earlier court case in the Durban High Court, in which the court affirmed the position that only the commissioner of SARS may institute criminal prosecutions against taxpayers.

Then, '[The NPA] was well aware of the fact that I had been in discussions with SARS in connection with my tax affairs,' Zuma states. 'It was well aware that SARS would not have agreed to such prosecution and would indeed in all probability have been opposed to this.'

Zuma and his legal team were correct. In fact, I was the one who coordinated discussions with his lawyers, following a number of earlier engagements with Ivan Pillay and Gene Ravele. What's more, I personally informed the NPA about the discussions by way of a formal letter.

Then, '[T]he truth of the matter is that my legal representatives, and particularly my attorney, Mr Michael Hulley, have for some years now had discussions and negotiations to regularise my income tax affairs vis-à-vis SARS.'

Again, Zuma and his team were correct.

'In the end the dispute between myself and SARS was resolved, with a large amount being paid to settle the amount of SARS's assessment,' Zuma's affidavit continued. 'I can thus gratefully testify that the entire dispute between SARS and myself has been resolved, and SARS's claim has been settled in full. In this regard I point out that I had always, in the discussions with SARS, indicated my acceptance of any duly estimated amount of income tax. I point out that the amount assessed did not invoke any tax amnesty such as had been extended in the past to thousands of South Africans.'

Indeed, I can assure you, we did Zuma no favours, and we treated him exactly like any other taxpayer. In fact, it became public knowledge at the time that SARS had prosecuted Zuma for failing to submit information on time, and he paid an admission of guilt fine in 2007.[4] Soon afterwards his lawyers provided what we needed, and a splendid team of tax experts from various units – Sibusiso Tshikovi, Azam Khan and Casper Visser – worked closely with me to go through mounds of paper in order to reconstruct years of Zuma's financials to determine his tax liability.[5]

Zuma's affidavit continued, 'I annex, however, a letter from Mr Hulley's office ('01') and the reply from SARS ('02') which confirms receipt of the payment of the amount assessed, and the existence and basic outline of the agreement. The settlement was reached without any admission of criminal conduct on my part and on the basis that it disposes of and resolves all liability in respect of the said tax issues – both criminal and civil liability.'

Again, this was perfectly accurate.

So, if indeed I, or any other person or group or unit within SARS, was so 'anti-Zuma' in the period between the years 2003 and 2008 (or at any other time, before or since) to the extent that we would do anything to bring him down, why did this supposedly occur at the very same time as perfectly civilised 'discussions and negotiations to regularise [Zuma's] income tax affairs vis-à-vis SARS' were taking place?

Since we'd been accused so many times of scheming and plotting against Zuma, think about it: wouldn't it have been the easiest thing for us just to lay a complaint of tax evasion or tax fraud with the NPA, and let matters take their course? Or, even easier, what if we'd unlawfully passed Zuma's tax information to the NPA? Or, easier still, what if we'd simply done nothing at all?

Had the consequences of the slanderous allegations that we were anti-Zuma not turned out to be so traumatising and serious, it would have been one big joke.

And here's more little-known insight into what happened to me and others at that point in time.

The volume of cruel accusations, verbal abuse and vitriol that I and others suffered at the hands of colleagues who were clearly anti-Zuma, and people in law-enforcement agencies who truly were anti-Zuma, was incredible. And what was expected of us, according to them was, well, as one put it to me, to 'bend the law a bit', because they 'don't want him to be president'. The expectation was apparently that we should help out the NPA by looking the other way. And when we said no, that we did things by the book, the response was, 'Well, you're either with us or against us.'

When the review-application affidavit was filed by Zuma and became public, ill feeling against us took a turn for the worse, because then I was told, 'You could have "helped" the NPA, and look what's happening to our country because you didn't: now he's president and it's all your fault.'

Then, conversely, at the same time, according to other people, we at SARS were in fact 'pro-Zuma' and supposedly protecting him.

Despite these slings and arrows, I, on behalf of SARS, with the guidance and oversight of my bosses and the assistance of my colleagues at the time – and regardless of what others may have said to us, irrespective of how they tried to cajole us and convince us to do otherwise, and regardless of what others might have thought we should or shouldn't do – did what the law said we should do: we treated each taxpayer, including Jacob Zuma, equally before the law. I swallowed all the abuse and just focused on my job. The words of hatred, the denigrations, the vilifications and arguments directed at me and ultimately at SARS and senior managers there – we just took it all on the chin and carried on.

Meanwhile, there were a number of very significant tax and customs fraud cases in the hands of the NPA which weren't moving at the pace that they should've been. It was around this time that the attention span of the NPA on the cases concerning (among others) Dave King, Billy Rautenbach and Glenn Agliotti started slipping.

One day I asked one of the managers who reported to me to make a call to the NPA and insist that one of the largest-ever tax-fraud cases in the history of our country please be expedited. The guy came back to me saying that the people at the NPA didn't want to take his call; instead, they'd sent him a text message telling him that they were fighting for their political lives and didn't have time for our concerns.

19

The Young Man

As noted in the previous chapter, in late 2009 and again in early 2010, Julius Malema was provided with a document, which he referred to as an 'intelligence dossier',[1] by a disgruntled former SARS employee named Michael Peega.

Peega had been dismissed from SARS for the possession of illegal firearms and ammunition, and for his involvement in rhino-poaching, following his arrest by the police on Christmas Day in 2008. Before he left SARS, Peega threatened me and others that he'd get back at us – and in due time he did just that, claiming ownership of the 'intelligence dossier', which he called Operation Snowman.

Malema would, then, claim that the dossier was 'proof' that SARS was 'anti-ANC', and was targeting the Friends of Zuma and others, including himself, Fikile Mbalula, who was deputy Minister of Police at the time, ANC spokesperson Zizi Kodwa, and businessman Fana Hlongwana.

Peega claimed that the unit was conducting lifestyle audits on these people as a part of a grand conspiracy against President Jacob Zuma. It was a ridiculous allegation: if these people had indeed been subjected to lifestyle audits, they would each have received a formal questionnaire and notification by SARS, asking specific questions, and providing details of the SARS department, office and auditor involved.

Ironically, as it would later turn out, Malema took a decidedly different approach when it came to the crunch concerning his own tax affairs.

In response to Malema's announcement about the dossier, SARS did a number of things. First, the tax authority issued to the media a line-by-line refutation of the dossier, attaching to it as annexures Peega's confession to the police about how he'd colluded with a syndicate to poach rhinos, his disciplinary-hearing records, and details of the unit he'd worked in and about which he'd made allegations.[2] We did this to demonstrate the fallacy of the 'intelligence dossier' and to show Peega's real motives.

We also wrote to various law-enforcement agencies and a parliamentary committee, providing them with a more detailed line-by-line refutation of the dossier, and included additional aspects, such as how others had reported to SARS that Peega was trying to recruit people in SARS and among former disgruntled officials to build a dossier to discredit (mainly) then Finance Minister Pravin Gordhan, deputy SARS commissioner Ivan Pillay and me. One reported how Peega had had several meetings with former and current SARS officials, claiming that he was working for 'the Old Man' (Zuma) on something called Project Broken Arrow aimed at discrediting Pravin Gordhan, Ivan Pillay and me, and with the intent to cause 'chaos and mayhem at SARS'.

SARS also briefed the chairperson of the standing committee on public accounts and some members of Parliament, and cooperated in several investigations that were conducted mainly by the then National Intelligence Agency (now State Security Agency), allowing them to interview staff in the unit and providing them with whatever documentation they required.

And SARS went to the extent of sitting down with Malema to take him through the entire 'dossier' in order to demonstrate to him the fictitious nature of its contents. In fact, I was the person who met with him in January 2010, at the Sheraton Hotel in Pretoria, at a time and date of his convenience.

My own impressions of the man? He was as sharp as a razor, quick-witted and extremely focused. He had a natural charm, and I was astounded at how, while we were sitting in a relatively out-of-the-way area of the hotel, people would come over to shake his hand and say hi to him – and he took the time to say hello to every single person, continually interrupting our interaction. He made each person who came to him feel special.

I immediately recognised that he wasn't one to be easily fooled, and I felt comforted by this. I could see that as I took him through the details, he immediately recognised the 'dossier' for what it was: pure nonsense.

When we concluded the conversation, Malema said that he accepted SARS's explanations insofar as the 'dossier' was concerned, and undertook to brief President Zuma about it.[3]

The 'dossier' stories were looked at countless times, including at least twice by State intelligence agencies, and SARS wrote letter after letter to the national police commissioner and State intelligence seeking closure on the matter.[4]

A second, far more detailed refutation of the 'dossier' was compiled and provided to many media houses in February 2010.

In spite of all these efforts, the stories continued circulating, never being refuted or meaningfully denied because none of the agencies that investigated the allegations or to whom we wrote ever brought matters to a conclusion. And I believe that it's because these things were left unattended that the 'rogue unit' narrative picked up steam in late 2014, and was used as a basis to advance the very same type of allegations, even relying on Peega as source again.

Once a rising star in the ANC, Julius Malema – also known as 'Juju' or the 'Young Man' – is a firebrand politician who'd been an activist from a very young age. At one time an ardent supporter of the 'Old Man', Malema even once stated that he would 'kill for Zuma', while Zuma noted in October 2009 that 'one day (Malema will) become a good leader worthy of inheriting the ANC'.[5]

Malema served as the ANC Youth League president from 2008 to 2012, until he was expelled from the party. He promptly formed his own political party, the Economic Freedom Fighters (EFF), and quickly became a fierce opponent of Zuma.

In 2013 Malema stated that SARS was 'a mere branch of ZANC (Zuma-ANC)' and accused the tax authority of being used by an

Indian cabal led by a 'vindictive' Pravin Gordhan. So where, according to Malema, we'd once been 'anti-Zuma and friends', we were now apparently 'pro-Zuma and friends'.

Malema later, in 2015, stated publicly that he was being pursued by SARS because of his strong stance against Zuma, and at Zuma's behest.

As SARS spokesperson Adrian Lackay put it, 'In January 2010, Mr Malema claimed to be in possession of an "intelligence dossier" which, in his view, proved SARS had a special unit focusing on him and other persons because of their association and support for president Zuma. It is ironic that Mr Malema is now claiming the exact opposite.'[6]

In 2013, court records and a statement by SARS revealed the truth: SARS had started to audit Malema, and others related to him, as far back as early 2009. And the unit involved in the audit wasn't the unit that Malema had sought to implicate; in fact, the only thing the two units had in common was that I managed both.

At the time, many people and media houses were shining a light on what appeared to be the lavish lifestyle of Malema, including his expensive home and his penchant for very expensive watches. Opposition parties were questioning his ability to live such a high life on the income he earned as president of the Youth League, and calling on SARS to conduct an audit of his tax affairs.

Malema retorted in July 2011 by publicly inviting SARS to audit him. He claimed – inaccurately – that his tax affairs were in order.

Court records show that during my meeting with Malema in January 2010, I'd raised his non-compliance with him insofar as his outstanding tax returns. I asked him to please ensure that he complied with tax laws, and he undertook to ensure that his auditors would do so. He and they did not.

Later in 2010 SARS again made contact with Malema, and, in accordance with the tax authority's general procedures, he was afforded a reasonable opportunity to submit his outstanding returns. He undertook to do so within a month, and asked SARS to conclude the matter in the same period.

The promised month came and went; I can't tell you how many times I emailed and called Malema's accountant, pleading with him to hurry up and finish the job.

In the end, it took Malema more than 18 months to file his outstanding returns, and even then, he failed to comply with various aspects – a basic analysis showed that he'd submitted inaccurate information for the tax years 2005 to 2011, with the Ratanang Trust, held by him, not even registered for tax purposes at that late stage.

In the meantime, in 2011, the then Public Protector, advocate Thuli Madonsela, had received complaints that implicated Julius Malema in tender fraud, and she commenced investigations into these. Her report, 'On the Point of Tenders', was published in October 2012. The report read, 'The investigation followed three complaints lodged in July 2011 in which it was alleged that the former president of the African National Congress Youth League, Mr Julius Malema, used his political position to influence the awarding of tenders by the Limpopo Department of Roads and Transport and other departments of the Limpopo Provincial government to certain companies where he is involved. It was further alleged that Mr Malema benefited improperly from corrupt kickbacks paid to him by the companies involved via the Ratanang Family Trust, set up by him.'

The report also revealed how a Mr M Mthwalo had emailed the commissioner of SARS on 25 July 2011, copying in the Public Protector, alleging that Malema might be using a trust fund to avoid tax; and that the income received by the fund might itself be 'ill gotten'.[7] In his email, Mthwalo referenced two *City Press* articles about the Ratanang Trust, which revealed how 'a seasoned businessman who moves in Malema's circle of friends and associates told how he deposited R200 000 into the trust's bank account after Malema facilitated a government tender for his benefit. According to him, there are at least 20 other business people who do the same.'[8]

Malema admitted in 2011 to owning shares in a company called On-Point Engineers through the Ratanang Family Trust, but denied that he'd influenced any of On-Point's tenders, adding, 'I just queue when the dividends are due.'

One of the Public Protector's findings was that due 'to the fact that the awarding of the contract to On-Point was based on deliberate misrepresentation and non-compliance with procurement prescripts, its shareholders, including the Ratanang Family Trust and the Gwangwa Family Trust that eventually became the shareholders of Guilder Investments (the sole shareholder of On-Point), benefited improperly by means of the payments of "dividends" and other payments made to it by On-Point. As a Trustee of the Ratanang Family Trust, Mr J Malema was therefore also put in an advantageous position as his family was supposed to benefit from it.'

The report further found that 'On-Point paid more than R2 million directly to the Ratanang Family Trust from November 2010 to May 2012 in the form of "dividends" and loans. The amount of R1 million, withdrawn five days after one of the kickbacks was paid under the back-to-back agreements, is further accounted for in the bank statements as having been paid towards the Ratanang Farm.

Further amounts of R160 000 and R100 000 are reflected as having been paid in respect of the "Sandton Property" and "Sandowns Property", respectively. Payments were also made to Tshiamo Dichabe, the Makatele Family Trust, Guilder Investments and the Gwangwa Family Trust (former and current shareholders of Guilder Investments, which is the sole shareholder of On-Point).

'The evidence of Mr Gwangwa in respect of how and by whom it was decided that On-Point should pay (monthly) dividends to the Ratanang Family Trust and make payments to the Gwangwa Family Trust (via Guilder Investments) furthermore supported the allegation that the Trusts were probably used as vehicles for the transfer of funds obtained through an unlawful process.'

This appears to be the basis of later criminal charges brought against Malema and others by the Hawks and the NPA.[9]

If it hadn't been for Lesiba Gwangwa, the founder and owner of On-Point, going to court in May 2012 to try and set aside a tax inquiry instituted by SARS in 2012, the public would've been none the wiser about the entire saga. Gwangwa effectively placed a whole lot of facts in the public domain when he asked the North Gauteng High Court to set aside an application by a unit under me, Financial Investigations (later called Centralised Projects), to conduct a tax inquiry into the tax affairs of On-Point and related entities and persons, which naturally included Malema.

Around this time, it was reported that the Hawks and the NPA were pursuing fraud and money-laundering charges against Malema and several others. Like in days gone by when the Scorpions had tried to get SARS to pass information under the table to them on then Deputy President Jacob Zuma, it was the same old story.

Every now and then, a Hawks investigator would come by my office, sometimes announced and sometimes not, to try to get me to slip them something. And just as we'd done in the matter of Zuma in the years between 2003 and 2007, my answer was always the same: 'Do it the legal way or not at all.'

This all culminated in a meeting in 2012 between the Hawks, NPA prosecutor Glynnis Breytenbach and myself, during which I stated in no uncertain terms how we at SARS were approaching matters, and what was expected of them if they wished to access evidence from us. After that meeting, I think we all clearly understood the various frameworks within which we were working.

The tax inquiry subpoenaed a number of senior government officials from Limpopo and businesspeople close to Malema to appear before it, and Malema himself was expected to appear to answer questions about alleged tax evasion.[10]

I attended the inquiry a few times and assisted in some instances with tactical approaches and questions; it was a less complex case than many others in which the unit had been involved. I found Lesiba Gwangwa – a qualified engineer and genuine entrepreneur – to be a soft-spoken man and very sharp. My sense was that he wanted to do the right thing, and I believe that the fact that he discarded his court challenge of the tax inquiry soon afterwards, in August 2012, speaks volumes.

Judge Ferdi Preller, who heard the court challenge, said that he was surprised that Gwangwa had settled the matter out of court and had agreed to testify at the inquiry. 'I didn't think this matter was capable of being settled,' he noted.[11]

The tax inquiry continued to the end but – as was the case with so many other SARS cases concerning prominent taxpayers – Malema used every public platform possible to attack and insult SARS, and in particular me and the team of people involved in the case, accusing us of being racists and investigating his tax affairs with an ulterior motive in mind.

On 2 August 2013, using a clause in the new Tax Administration Act, SARS took the unprecedented step of releasing to the public facts about Malema's tax matters.[12] SARS reported that on 27 June 2013 counsel for SARS had addressed a letter to Malema and his legal representative, cautioning him to refrain from making false public statements about the state of his tax affairs and his engagements with SARS. Malema was given 48 hours to rectify a number of false allegations, including his claims that there was an agreement in principle between him and SARS to repay outstanding tax liabilities, and that the agreement had been breached by SARS due to political interference; that a request for a compromise had been declined by SARS due to political interference; and that SARS was part of a 'concerted effort' to discredit Malema and remove all means for him to generate an income.

Malema not only refused to correct his lies, but repeated these allegations in various news interviews.

In later media interviews Malema would suggest that he'd approached SARS at the start of the process that ultimately led to his predicament.

This wasn't true. During 2010 SARS had made contact, of its own accord, with Malema after he'd failed to submit his tax returns for a number of years. In accordance with SARS's general procedures, Malema had been afforded a reasonable opportunity to make good on his tax obligations and submit outstanding returns.

On the insistence of Malema, SARS attempted to resolve the matter within a month. But, as I've already indicated, the month came and went, and the matter wasn't resolved. In fact, far from complying within the promised month, Malema repeatedly delayed matters. Responses in respect of his outstanding returns were only received when we repeatedly requested the information over the many months that followed. At no stage were any responses to SARS initiated by Malema or his representatives. It took him more than 18 months to file his outstanding returns and, ultimately, he failed to regularise his tax affairs as promised.

As far as his Ratanang Trust was concerned, even after a number of requests from SARS, Malema had still not registered it for tax purposes – a situation that certainly wasn't helpful in demonstrating his willingness to comply with his tax obligations.

After eventually receiving the outstanding tax returns, all indications were that Malema was attempting to restructure his asset holdings without informing SARS. This situation left SARS with no alternative but to launch an in-depth investigation into his tax affairs.

As for Malema's allegations of racism, the matter was assigned to the Financial Investigations team, of which the senior manager was an African man.[13] Since then, even though line managers have changed over time, the new senior manager responsible for the unit was also an African male. The project leader, a white male, reported to these managers throughout. Two lawyers were designated by SARS to participate in the case, of which one was a white female and the other an African male. The primary financial investigator in the case was a white female.

The outcome of the financial investigations led to SARS finding that Malema had failed to register for tax in 2005, had under-declared and misdeclared his income in the years 2005 to 2011, had failed to register the Ratanang Trust for tax purposes, and had not submitted tax returns for the Ratanang Trust. We also found that while Malema was engaging with SARS, he was transferring assets he owned to third parties in a clear attempt to shift assets outside the reach of the tax authority.[14]

And even after he'd been assessed, Malema failed to pay the tax due by the required date, and was unresponsive to several attempts from SARS to get him to pay. This left SARS with no alternative but to obtain a default judgement for debt against him. Malema, despite being given an opportunity to do so, didn't challenge this judgement, and the Sheriff of the Court ended up attaching property in his name. Only then did Malema finally contact SARS with an offer to settle.[15]

The SARS investigation also resulted in Gwangwa signing over his luxury properties and assets to SARS in lieu of his tax debt.

Malema's outstanding tax due to SARS was calculated at R16 million plus interest, pushing it to near R20 million. We immediately started collecting against his assets. In May 2013 we sold his incomplete mansion in Sandton on auction for R5,9 million, and the following month his farm in Limpopo plus some of his household goods were also auctioned, for R2,5 million.[16]

In early February 2014, the Central Projects Unit obtained a provisional order to initiate sequestration proceedings against Malema.

In May that year, Malema's newly formed political party, the EFF, contested the general election and was one of 13 political parties that won seats in the National Assembly. With the backing of 1 169 259 voters (of a total of 18 654 771 people who voted), Malema, the 'Young Man', was headed for Parliament.[17]

Suddenly, our provisional sequestration order against Malema became the talk of the town – National Assembly rules state that a sequestrated individual may not serve as a member of Parliament.

Malema knew this, other political parties knew this, law-enforcement officials knew this, SARS officials knew this and the country knew this.

In the media, article after article analysed the scenario; radio shows and television panels discussed it; it was on everybody's lips: would Juju go to Parliament or not?

On 21 May 2014, Malema was one of the many new members of Parliament who swore an oath to uphold the Constitution in the interests of South Africa. Now the question became: would Juju remain a member of Parliament or would SARS take him down?

It was a time of enormous pressure for me, both professionally and personally. I was at the tail-end of a tumultuous relationship with a person who'd lied to me about her involvement in crime; I'd just come to discover the extent of her dishonesty and had begun to extricate myself from the relationship (this story is recorded in my previous book, *Rogue: The Inside Story of SARS's Elite Crime-busting Unit*.) My father, who was in poor health, became very ill; he would pass away in mid-2014. My mother, who lived next door to me, began suffering heart pains.

I was up to my eyeballs in cases at the time, overseeing 87 different projects, some involving very important people and very influential politicians. I have no doubt that we'd been stepping on some seriously powerful toes.

Reports started coming in that members of several units I was managing were under surveillance or that their homes had been broken into and work-related documents and hardware stolen. An attorney told me that he'd been approached by members of State intelligence and the Hawks looking for dirt on me, and he gave me a written statement to this effect. (These officials were part of a multi-agency tobacco task team who had come to discover that I had evidence implicating them in corruption, racketeering, running interference in SARS cases and money-laundering.) Fake dossiers were being emailed to the media and smear campaigns were starting to unfold all around me. An official working with me told me that he'd been told by State intelligence officials to warn me that they were 'coming for me'.

I had a feeling something terrible was about to happen to us at SARS.

Whenever I went outside to have a cigarette, or in corridors in passing, those opposed to Julius Malema would try and pump me for information on the case and determine how it was going to unfold. The media kept asking questions.

Although I never received any direct instruction to the effect – it was all very 'nudge, nudge, wink, wink' – it became clear to me that the vast majority of people who did this wanted me to somehow ensure that Malema didn't settle with SARS and was ultimately sequestrated. It seemed that I was expected to 'save' us from Malema.

In hindsight, there was irony in the similarities in circumstances between the 'Old Man's' case of years before and this one – that of his arch-rival, the 'Young Man', the last big case of my career at SARS. If anything defined my life as a tax official, it was these two cases. In both, I was hated and reprimanded and falsely accused of treating them too leniently, while at the same time (depending on who was making the allegations) I was accused of racism and having conspired and having had a political agenda and vendetta against them.

The two people I trusted most, Ivan Pillay and Gene Ravele, kept reassuring me and saying I should just stick to the law; we do things the right way, regardless of who the taxpayer may be. It was the same message from long ago in the Zuma matter: we remain independent, we stick to the rules, we let the system work by itself.

Tax settlements are described and provided for in tax law. Reaching a settlement isn't an easy procedure and taxpayers have to jump through many hoops in order to qualify.

The system requires a taxpayer to, first, accept and own up to the tax bill assessed. Then the taxpayer has to make full disclosure of their financial and tax affairs, including assets and liabilities. An offer to settle could then be submitted to a committee (or, depending on the amount, several committees) of SARS officials, after which it would be submitted to a chief officer for sign-off. Annually, the Auditor-General of South Africa also casts a keen eye over these settlements.

Malema tried three times to pass these stringent tests. Although the settlement was only required to pass scrutiny by two committees, based on the value, I insisted that the team take it through four committees for approval, right up to SARS executive level, and I didn't personally participate in the presentations to any of the committees.

The settlement offer was finally agreed to on 26 May 2014. Malema's lawyer, Tumi Mokwena, confirmed it in the media on the same day.

The provisional sequestration process was extended, and the matter postponed to August 2014 after a draft order was handed to court in order for Malema to comply with the settlement agreement. The sequestration application would later be withdrawn by SARS provided Malema complied with his side of the agreement.

At the time, Malema was rather magnanimous, apologising for his previous statements directed at us at SARS and promising to comply with tax laws in future. He apologised unreservedly for his conduct during the SARS audit, and sent what I considered to be a valuable message to all South Africans by calling on all to honour their tax obligations.

Nonetheless, I had a sinking feeling that the Malema matter was going to come back to haunt us.

At the end of 2014, in a move that apparently reversed its own position, SARS, now under commissioner Tom Moyane, called off the tax settlement with Malema, and sought to have him finally sequestrated. This would have meant that Malema would no longer be able to serve as a parliamentarian.

When I learned of this through the media, it was clear of me that the intention probably had little to do with whether Malema complied with the settlement or not, but rather sought to have him removed as a member of Parliament. The judge would have none of it, however, and SARS had to withdraw the application.[18]

I've studied the records of the case, and the suggestion in the court application that I somehow influenced SARS official Pieter Engelbrecht of the Central Projects Unit some time late in 2014 to reverse SARS's position on the matter is complete nonsense. I hadn't had a say in cases at SARS since 1 June 2014, when I'd asked to be put on special leave, and I hadn't spoken to Engelbrecht since that time. (It was Engelbrecht who deposed an affidavit for SARS in a later attempt, in 2015, to finally sequestrate Malema.)

For this reason, one thing I'm quite sure of – and I think in the fullness of time I shall be proven to be correct – the day SARS settled with the 'Young Man' was perhaps the last straw for some politicians when it came to SARS's independence, because I have no doubt that some wished for us not to settle with him and had hoped that we would sequestrate him and prevent him from remaining in Parliament.

I resigned from the tax authority in February 2015, thinking that I would never have anything more to do with Malema or, in fact, any of the old SARS cases. But some months after my departure, I received a phonecall from Malema's lawyer, Tumi Mokwena, asking to meet with me privately. I'd come to know him somewhat from the days when Malema sought settlement with SARS in early 2014, and found him to be attentive and genuinely trying to assist his client.

I met with Mokwena on three occasions after I'd left SARS, at his request. I made sure that the relevant authorities, such as the State Security Agency with whom I had been liaising on the 'rogue' allegations, and SARS remained abreast of these interactions.

The first meeting was at a hospital in Pretoria, where Mokwena was visiting someone who was ill. During the relatively short meeting, he effectively asked me if I'd ever received any improper instructions relating to his client, Julius Malema. I told him, truthfully, no, that we did things by the book, and he seemed to accept this – a friendly guy, all smiles, no problem. I think he was basically trying to determine if the case against Malema was in any way politically driven.

During the second interaction, which occurred soon after, and after the strange turnaround by SARS on the Malema case already mentioned, Mokwena asked me to consult for them on their case against SARS; I was offered a lot of money to do so, which I declined. After that, there was one more meeting, for much the same reason. I'd only attended these latter two meetings because the State Security Agency man assigned to liaise with me said I should continue meeting with the lawyer and see where things went.

The outcome of all this was an understanding between all concerned, including the State Security Agency, that I couldn't and wouldn't be able to help Julius Malema or the State Security Agency in any meaningful manner.

In late 2017, Julius Malema was a guest speaker at The Gathering, an annual event hosted by online media site *Daily Maverick* which brings together big names in South African business, media and politics to discuss topics of the day.

Questioned by a member of the audience about his failure to pay his tax bill prior to his original settlement with SARS, and accused of hypocrisy because of it, Malema became very defensive. He first claimed ignorance, saying, 'I had very little knowledge on how taxes were dealt with – I thought the employer dealt with it.' Then he fell back on his old conspiracy theory, claiming he was a victim of a politically motivated vendetta by SARS. A SARS 'rogue unit' followed him around, he said, supposedly in the hope of destroying him. He claimed that SARS wanted to sequestrate him in order to drive him out of Parliament and referred to me specifically as a 'racist of note'.[19]

He also expanded on the responsibility of SARS to ensure that taxpayers were educated about their tax obligations and on how, when found wanting, they should be assisted by the tax authority. Of course, he was right in this respect. But my, oh my, how short memories are!

Back in May 2014, when SARS and Malema had come to an agreement, I'd played a significant role from a service perspective, assisting his attorney, Tumi Mokwena, in preparing responses for SARS, always staying well within the law, in the very same way as I'd done so many times with other taxpayers. Had Malema forgotten about this? And when I was assisting his lawyer, even after hours and on weekends, was I being racist in doing so?

In fact, on 26 May 2014, in a public statement, Malema had said, 'I can confirm that I was informed by SARS today that it has accepted an offer of compromise I submitted in respect of my outstanding tax. This followed my making such an offer to SARS as provided for in the Tax Administration Act. I was informed that a governance committee considered my submission and found it to have complied with the requirements for such an offer ... I can further confirm that the offer was conditional on a number of aspects, including that I accept that I failed in my past tax obligations that resulted in me owing the fiscus outstanding tax. ... It was also a requirement that my tax affairs be brought up to date at the time of the offer which I have done ...'

In the statement, Malema said that he accepted that he hadn't attended to his tax affairs 'in the manner that I was required to by law in the past, and in certain instances I left my financial affairs in the hands of others without making sure that my obligations were complied with. When my difficulty with SARS became public knowledge, I accepted and acted on advice from persons, which in hindsight, I should not have.'

His statement concluded, 'It is so that at times I was very frustrated with the process and I may have said things publicly that reflected negatively on the reputation of SARS and some of its officials. Where I may have made public utterances that may have suggested bias or wrongdoing on the side of SARS, I unreservedly apologise. I accept the bona fides of SARS and its officials who have dealt with the matter ...'[20]

PART 4
RAPID DESCENT

'In time, the full measure of the damage caused to the South African Revenue Service arising from false news coverage will manifest itself in a tarnished reputation, questionable independence and lower levels of compliance with tax and customs law. Make no mistake. This is about far more than us losing our jobs.'

– *Ivan Pillay, writing in the 'Opinion and Analysis' section of the* Sunday Times, *3 April 2016*[1]

20

Walking quietly and carrying a big stick

I oversaw and was involved in literally thousands of cases during my 16 years at SARS. Working these cases was always a team effort, requiring not only coordination and cooperation within the tax authority and its various units, but also close workings with the police, the NPA, specialised units and the State's intelligence agencies. It wasn't always easy, with a state machinery inherited from the apartheid regime and a constitutional order at different levels of development.

We at SARS were lucky in being a relatively small institution; and the part of SARS engaged with law enforcement and crime combating was even smaller. We were almost as close as a family would be; we trusted each other with our lives.

We were also lucky in having the kind of stability and predictability that I believe institutions in a developing state require. Trevor Manuel, the Minister of Finance in 1998 when I began my tenure at the tax authority, would go on to become longest-serving finance minister in the world, replaced in 2009 by the equally trusted and respected Pravin Gordhan, who'd served as the commissioner of SARS from 1999. In that year, Oupa Magashula was a natural replacement as commissioner for Gordhan, having been at SARS in charge of corporate services for some years by then.

In this stable environment, modernisation, business and strategic plans were formulated in the early 2000s and came to fruition a few years later.

This continuity was maintained when, in 2014, Gordhan was replaced by Nhlanhla Nene as finance minister; Nene had been overseeing SARS as deputy finance minister since 2008.

This stability provided us as individuals with the ability to remain focused on our cases, dedicating our time and resources to them, and maintaining the pressure on those that spanned many years. There were no interruptions or dislodging of people as a result of a new boss coming in with ideas of restructuring or drastic changes. From an enforcement perspective, this allowed us as investigators and managers to grow and develop skills and institutional memories that in turn enabled us to tackle more cases of a similar nature, becoming more skilled and experienced as we went along.

Behind each of the big cases reported on in the media were countless people, seldom publicly acknowledged, slaving away, often until late at night and on weekends, trying to make our country a better place for all. These men and women – far too many to list individually – were from different backgrounds, language groups, racial and class groups, and had different sexual orientations, ages and skill sets. From the most highly trained and experienced auditors, the doctors of mathematics, the senior specialists and unit managers, the external lawyers and advocates, to the junior investigators, the graduate trainees, the administrative staff, the human resources and finance support staff, the administrators and personal assistants – we all made up a collective producing results because everyone pulled their weight, and then some.

I met many of these people as strangers, and they became like family to me. We suffered defeats and celebrated victories together, had hilarious moments together, and broke bread together: we lost our hair or watched it go grey (like mine), remained single, got married; some went through divorces; I saw some of their kids grow into young adults; and some, sadly, passed away.

We had our differences, sometimes vehemently so, and sometimes we argued and disagreed, but in the end, we shared the same concerns and worries whenever our big cases were before court, and we always found our 'higher purpose' and buckled down to get the job done.

They were, and are, all my heroes.

When disaster struck SARS, first with the obscure 'complaint' by someone I'd dated briefly, in May 2014, and then from around October

2014 onwards, when it metamorphosed into the 'rogue unit' propaganda campaign, many people began to disengage from me and the others who would ultimately leave SARS; and I disengaged from them. For the most part, this wasn't for any underhand reason. The reality was that some of us were being bullied, vilified and purged, and I completely understood the fears and concerns they had for their careers and their families by mere association with us.

I was once asked whether I believed that SARS had been 'captured' after I left, and my answer was 'no'. I still do not believe so. SARS consists of almost 15 000 people, the vast majority of whom have been there for many years. Even the suggestion that they've all been captured would be a personal affront to them.

Certainly, some in the higher echelons of SARS were indeed part of state capture, but by and large, the bulk of officials at SARS would just keep on trying to do their best under the circumstances. There may be some people in management with dastardly agendas causing the system to serve the wrong ends, but in my opinion most of those at SARS wouldn't be happy with this and would, in their own way, resist such things.

Indeed, both our law-enforcement agencies and financial-regulatory authorities are staffed by many thousands of good and honest civil servants. While there's a lot of evidence in the public domain that suggests that certain board members of state-owned enterprises and senior state officials (and even some junior officials) may well have been 'captured', and seem to be doing the nefarious bidding of the few, our institutions are so much more than just heads and senior managers.

Do not give up hope in the many. The fight against state capture is taking place not only openly in courts and parliamentary committees, but also through public protests, via various civil-societies taking action, and thanks to the media's exposure of the rot. It's also playing out in various institutions where unseen and unsung heroes refuse to do what's wrong, and steadfastly play by the rules.

Managers come and go; it's the systems, and the people who make up those systems, that ultimately see to it that an institution survives. SARS may be going through difficult times now, but the tax authority has been there before.

In the long run, provided that the majority of officials maintain the 'higher purpose', South Africans have nothing to worry about. The bulk of SARS people are exactly what we need – hardworking, honest and caring employees, always serving the higher purpose of maintaining the contract between State and society.

In the early 2000s SARS did tremendous work in conjunction with the police and the NPA to bring a famous Cape Town gang boss, Colin Stansfield, to book for, among other things, tax evasion. At that time, SARS received little to no public acknowledgement for its work.

Another Cape gang leader, Quinton 'Mr Big' Marinus, also ended up having to pay SARS millions of rands attributable to his undeclared income; ultimately, he was sequestrated, SARS selling off most of the assets he owned in 2013.

A couple of years later the media reported on a meeting Marinus had supposedly attended with a number of other gang leaders and then President Jacob Zuma, wherein he allegedly complained about SARS and got assurance from the president that he would 'look into it'.[1]

Such was our life at SARS. There were always attempts to strong-arm, cajole or threaten us, or to try to manipulate the system to make us back down. But we never did. This had the unfortunate consequence of making us enemies beyond those we were investigating; we became the enemies of those they knew, too, and had influence over and access to.

The same SARS crew that were under my management and had delivered on Stansfield and Marinus, had by 2013 tackled enigmatic businessman Mark Roy Lifman and his associate, Cape gang leader Jerome 'Donkey' Booysen, raising tax assessments exceeding R380 million.

I can't for the life of me understand why these particular cases have been dragging on for years, with no end in sight. I often wonder how much money and effort have gone down the drain because these cases have been left in limbo. It isn't in the interests of SARS, nor of the taxpayers concerned and their employees, to leave matters in this way.

Another famous case focused on murdered striptease-club boss Lolly Jackson and his empire. In that matter, we seized control of all his clubs in lieu of outstanding debts. For a time, technically speaking, SARS did own strip clubs.

Then there was the widely reported case against international fugitive and convicted murderer, fraudster and drug dealer, Radovan Krejcir, and people and businesses related to him. In that case, by 2013 we'd obtained a preservation order against him exceeding R100 million; in the end, all his assets were auctioned off and the proceeds paid to SARS.

An investigation into Pan African Refineries and its primary shareholder, Juan Meyer (also a former business partner of Krejcir), got plenty of media coverage, not least because Meyer himself made a noise wherever he went.[2]

So if I made enemies along the way, all would later jump on the 'rogue unit' bandwagon because it suited their own cases and litigation with SARS. I was once rather bemused by Meyer going on a local radio show, for instance, and making all sorts of allegations against me, and later also complaining about me to several journalists. Meyer claimed that he'd met with me (I'd never met him in my life) and that I'd 'instructed' him to sell his refinery to Krejcir; he claimed that I said that if he didn't, I would investigate him. He was basically suggesting that I was working for Krejcir – in spite of the fact that it was, in fact, units under me that brought down Krejcir.[3]

South African-based Taiwanese businessman Jen Chih 'Robert' Huang once publicly boasted about his access to former President Zuma, whose nephew, Khulubuse Zuma, was on the board of Huang's company Mpisi Trading 74. A dispute over import duties and undeclared taxes implicated the company in reported tax losses of almost a billion rands. Who knows where that case is these days: it could've been settled years ago in the interests of the fiscus, but at this rate, given the delays in the preservation order, SARS will be lucky to collect a cent when the matter is ultimately resolved; and who knows how many jobs will have been lost as a result.

Another significant case for SARS concerned the Krok brothers, who inherited a massive fortune from their parents, who'd made huge fortunes in skin-lightening creams during the apartheid years. The brothers relocated to Australia, where they quickly fell out with the taxman there. The Australian tax authorities asked us to assist them in obtaining a freeze order for the Kroks' assets in South Africa, pending the finalisation of their tax audit in Australia. In another first in South African tax history, after lengthy court battles, SARS obtained the order, which was eventually rescinded in 2016 when the brothers reached a tax settlement with the Australian tax authorities.

Then there's the case of well-known businessman Gary van der Merwe, who fought SARS tooth and nail in one court battle after another, ultimately to lose when the court dismissed his arguments against us.

The role of SARS in the Fidentia investment fraud scandal and the later Sharemax investment cartel case was well covered in the media. In the case of Fidentia, one lone investigator in Cape Town shouldered the workload of at least four people and never once complained. He simply slogged on, producing his required targets every year, and persevering with the Fidentia matter until it reached its logical conclusion, with the main culprit, J Arthur Brown, convicted following a criminal trial.

Project Honey Badger consisted of 15 separate criminal cases against various tobacco manufacturers and importers. I've maintained my contacts in the tobacco industry, and based on what they've told me, it seems that they all got off with little or nothing to pay to SARS. What I estimated to be potential tax, customs and excise duties of over R3 billion due to the fiscus, and which we aimed to retrieve through that project, all seemed to have come to naught.

Common to several of these cases is how, since 2015, they seem to have lost steam: money due to the taxpayer remains uncollected, and criminal cases simply die quiet deaths.

Most of these stories I shared in *Rogue: The Inside Story of SARS's Elite Crime-busting Unit*, to the extent that I was able to.

One matter – the very existence of which I was unable to confirm or deny at the time – concerned the infamous Gupta family and their associates.

The Guptas rose to prominence following their brazen abuse of our national air-force base at Waterkloof, Pretoria for the landing of a private plane conveying guests to a family wedding at Sun City that reportedly cost in excess of R30 million. We were later to learn that much of that money apparently came from a State-funded dairy-farming project in the Free State intended to uplift local previously disadvantaged farmers.

Back in May 2017, a massive cache of emails concerning the doings of the Guptas was leaked to the media, with scandal after scandal involving them then emerging on a regular basis – but with seemingly very little or no action by our law-enforcement agencies. At the time of writing, there had been little to no attempt by any of our agencies to search and seize computers and documents from any of their myriad companies, in particular their Sahara Group and Oakbay.

There were some indications, following a changing of the guard within the governing ANC in December 2017, that some energy had been injected into our law-enforcement agencies, but how far these will ultimately go, time will have to tell.

A rather belated raid was carried out by the Hawks on the Gupta home in Saxonwold, Johannesburg in early 2018, but given the passage of time, and the exposé after exposé based on the leaked emails, I suspect it was a case of too little, too late, and that any evidence was long gone.

A few Gupta-related people and companies were, in 2018, charged by the NPA for the alleged dairy-farm fraud. An asset-forfeiture order was obtained by the NPA in what appeared to me to have been some haste; within a month, Atul Gupta, one of the brothers, had approached the court and had a R10-million preservation order set aside, freeing him to claim back this money.

SARS was and remains conspicuously absent from all these events.

Since then, a welter of criminal charges has been registered with the police by various civil-society groupings, implicating the Guptas, past and current ministers, politicians, senior government officials and people who served in our state-owned enterprises in a wide range of alleged offences, including treason, racketeering, fraud and corruption. However, apart from the dairy-farm matter, our law-enforcement agencies seem to have been seized with pursuing matters other than these, and none has advanced to any significant level of investigation or prosecution. One can only conclude that the appetite to pursue these cases is, shall we say, limited.

But it certainly came as no surprise when, some time in 2017, I was approached by a journalist asking for comment about an email they'd found in the leaked cache. Dated 15 November 2013, it was correspondence between the Gupta brothers and one Gary Naidoo, managing editor of then Gupta-owned *The New Age* newspaper and frequent Gupta family spokesperson, warning the Guptas that SARS was investigating people 'close to' then President Zuma and the Guptas. It names me at the top of the list of SARS officials doing the investigations. (See Addendum 2.)

The 'Guptaleaks' emails were acknowledged by SARS commissioner Tom Moyane in July 2017 – but apparently dismissed as hearsay.[4] Replying to a question posed to him by journalist Karyn Maughan, he said, 'We hear about them, and as I've said, we are not run by the media. I am run by what is factually available at our disposal. Because once we do that, we are going to be distracted by the core business, which is the efficient and effective collection of revenue. But where we feel there is merit and prima-facie evidence on issues that are brought to us, not what we hear, then we deal with the matter.'

When asked whether the thousands of emails couldn't be considered 'prima-facie evidence', Moyane said, 'Hearing about them does not necessarily mean that I have to move there. Because, bear in mind, the world has moved to what is called fake news ... but I as a commissioner must work on factual information at my disposal.'[5]

In January 2018, shortly before his resignation as president of the country, Jacob Zuma finally announced a Commission of Inquiry into 'state capture', in spite of having apparently resisted this following a recommendation by the Public Protector for such commission back in early 2017. After Cyril Ramaphosa took over as president, the very credible Judge Raymond Zondo was appointed to head this commission, and Zondo has since established an able team of experts to assist him. Aspects of the terms of reference have since been amended, and I hope that the scope of the commission will be widened further still.

If this happens, I will most certainly be making submissions to the commission regarding the happenings at SARS back in 2014 and 2015.

21
Tigon

The so-called Tigon case is probably the biggest and longest-running white-collar-fraud case in the history of our country.

It started late one afternoon in 2001, when I was 32 years old. I'd just established the SARS Special Compliance Unit, intended to enable SARS to assist the State and its law-enforcement agencies to curb the rising levels of crime in our young democracy. We'd started growing the unit by appointing additional investigators, auditors and lawyers, and we'd moved to new offices in Hatfield, Pretoria. It was early days for us.

At first glance it seemed like just another case. Its details would only be revealed many years later, in 2010, in an affidavit that I compiled at the request of the then Scorpions.[1]

In November 2002, a search-and-seizure warrant was executed jointly by the police and SARS at the premises of businessman Grant Hugh Ramsay and auditing firm Galahad. Ramsay was arrested at Galahad's offices in Randburg, Johannesburg by members of the police's Serious Economic Offences unit, accompanied by officials of the SARS Special Compliance Unit.

In April 2003, Ramsay appeared in the Pretoria Commercial Crimes Court on 16 charges of contravening the Income Tax Act. The evidence and charges stated that Ramsay had created fictitious tax losses and financial statements for a wide range of companies between 1988 and 2001 to the detriment of SARS amounting to at least R177 million as calculated at that time. Ramsay also faced charges of fraud relating to the expropriation of R638 529 in VAT cheques for SARS entrusted to him by the company Europoint Cellular, and to the submission of false

VAT returns to SARS that had enabled Europoint Cellular to reclaim refunds totalling R1,14 million.

At the time, police spokesperson Ronnie Naidoo said, 'We believe there are about 300 investment companies involved and we are possibly looking at a figure of about R3 billion.'[2]

But Ramsay also rendered taxation and financial advisory services to the financial-services company Tigon and telecommunications company Shawcell. A year before, Tigon chief executive and Shawcell chairperson Gary Porritt, Galahad director Shirin Ismail and former senior SARS manager Jacobus 'Kobus' Viljoen had been arrested for alleged fraud and income-tax contraventions; and a month prior, Sue Bennett, a director of Tigon, and Tony Hodgkinson, the financial director of Shawcell, had been arrested on similar charges of fraud. The Johannesburg Securities Exchange had suspended Tigon and Shawcell.

In 2003, Ramsay struck a plea-bargain agreement with the prosecutors and was sentenced to an effective five years in prison. As part of the agreement, he undertook to assist SARS and the State to pursue the civil and criminal cases against Tigon. Significantly, in his plea-bargain agreement, he admitted that he'd been involved in and assisted Tigon and Shawcell and their officials in various offences, including contraventions of the Income Tax Act, exchange-control regulations and various other statutory offences.

In October 2010, Viljoen was sentenced to nine years' imprisonment, four suspended, after pleading guilty on corruption charges. In his plea-bargain agreement, he admitted to having received more than R395 000 to assist two companies of which Gary Porritt was the chief executive officer, Shawcell and Synergy Management & Finance, allowing them to claim back expenditure for income-tax purposes to which they were not lawfully entitled. He also pledged to assist SARS in its civil and criminal cases against some of the companies and individuals involved.

The heavy lifting in this case was (and is) being carried primarily by one SARS official. Deon Boshoff (ably assisted by outside counsel, advocate Etienne Coetzee and prosecutor advocate Jan Ferreira of the NPA) has been slogging away through all these years, in much the same way as Mr Chipps stuck to the Dave King case.

Gary Porritt and Sue Bennett, who face over 3 000 charges of fraud, tax evasion and racketeering amounting to over R160 million, have fought this case at virtually every level of our court system for over a decade, on every imaginable technical point. In 2011, the legal filibustering took the form of a High Court application on the basis that private prosecutor Etienne Coetzee didn't have legal title to prosecute on behalf of the State. Their case was upheld, which was a bit of a blow for all of us.

Soon enough, however, the matter was taken to the Supreme Court of Appeal, which overturned the decision in 2012 and ruled that the trial should continue.

At the time, a SARS statement read, 'As the [Supreme Court of Appeal] explained in an earlier judgment, Mr Porritt and Ms Bennett "intend to employ every stratagem available to them in order to delay the commencement and thereafter continuation of the trial for as long as they possibly can".'[3]

Porritt and Bennett responded by launching a bid to the highest court in the land, the Constitutional Court, trying to upset this decision. They have consistently failed in their efforts.

This saga has an interesting back story, which I reveal here for the first time – partly to clear my name of the slanderous, false and malicious allegations contained in a so-called 'documentary review' conducted by audit firm KPMG ordered by SARS commissioner Tom Moyane between December 2014 and January 2016 for a consideration of R23 million. The KPMG process followed three prior 'panels', all with the same hallmarks: all conducted 'probes' into vague allegations; none allowed those making the allegations to be cross-examined or required them to go under oath; none afforded those being 'investigated' a hearing; and none heard any persons they judged before finalising their 'findings'. All the reports were found to be controversial in one way or another, and faulty in fact and law, as all were contradictory, quashed evidence of very serious offences that implicated the very 'star witnesses' they sought to rely on, and all were ultimately proven to have omitted material facts. And all the reports were deliberately leaked to the media to bolster the 'rogue unit' narrative.

All this said, I believe it was the KPMG process that caused the most damage.

Had any KPMG representative bothered to ask me a single question during their efforts, the truth would've been obvious. Their report, which included the disclaimer that it couldn't be used for any 'controversy or proceedings' and 'may not be referred to in part or in full' by its paymaster, SARS, stated (among other things) that I'd had an improper relationship of some kind with philanthropist and businessman Gavin Varejes and convicted drug dealer Glenn Agliotti, stemming from a certain day in 2001; and that I'd lied about having met Agliotti on that day.[4] In truth, I didn't even know of Agliotti's existence in 2001, and only met him for the first time in September 2008 for official purposes.

I'd been asked by the Scorpions about this alleged 2001 meeting with Agliotti: on 20 September 2009, at a formal meeting at SARS, the Scorpions set out for me what they wanted me to say in my affidavit, including that Glenn Agliotti had arranged a meeting back in 2001 at which both he and I were present. This was nonsense, so I declined to cooperate.

On 9 October 2009 I received a legal demand from the Scorpions asking me the same questions and requesting me to submit my answers in an affidavit.

I always kept a diary and notes of meetings and, referring to those, I drafted a factually accurate affidavit. It told how I, together with Ivan Pillay, then general manager: Special Investigations at SARS, had travelled, at Pillay's request, to a house in Johannesburg late on the afternoon of Tuesday 13 November 2001, because the newly appointed police commissioner needed SARS's help. We travelled in an official SARS vehicle, driven by a SARS driver.

On our arrival, we were met by some bodyguard-type people and shown into the very large house. There were quite a few people present in one part of the house, but Pillay and I were immediately shown to an outside area with seating, so we only saw them from a distance and did not interact with them at all. There, we met with the then commissioner of police, Jackie Selebi, a man introduced to me as Gavin Varejes, and a third person I may not identify for his own safety as he's a whistleblower.

Selebi opened the meeting, telling us that Varejes and the other man knew about a massive tax-evasion scheme and share fraud. Selebi, whom I distinctly remember noting that he 'did not understand tax anyway', suggested that the best way forward would be for us to hear it straight from the horse's mouth. He then sat back and didn't participate further in the meeting in any meaningful manner; he was mostly on his cellphone.

Pillay and Varejes, similarly, didn't participate, and mainly just observed. After this meeting, I wouldn't hear from or interact with Varejes in any way for 11 years.

The whistleblower and I spoke, and he elaborated on the details of a listed company and how different forms of fraud were being perpetrated there. It was a complex story, and I realised that we'd have to have a longer sit-down meeting with the man to debrief him properly.

The entire meeting, from beginning to end, lasted no more than an hour, and Pillay and I left immediately afterwards.

The very next day, on Wednesday 14 November 2001, I sent an instruction to Avinash Parbhoo and Deon Boshoff, both chartered accountants in the old Special Compliance Unit, to register 'Project 32',[5] and asked them to meet with the whistleblower without delay to debrief him. They did so the following Monday, 19 November 2001.

Project 32 would later become the well-publicised prosecution battle against Gary Porritt, Sue Bennett, Tigon and a range of other entities; over time it simply became known as 'the Tigon case'.

My self-drafted affidavit of 2009, setting out the basics of these event, didn't sit well with the Scorpions and the KPMG team conducting the forensic audit of Selebi's finances, and – informally – I was told so in no uncertain terms. It goes without saying that I stand by my affidavit to this day.

In May 2010 I took the stand as a witness for the defence in the much-publicised Jackie Selebi case.

This curious state of affairs had begun two months before, when I'd insisted that the Scorpions subpoena me in my official capacity as a State witness against Selebi, on the basis that I may have to testify about tax-related matters, and the subpoena would relieve me of my duty of taxpayer confidentiality.

On the day I was set to testify, in accordance with the subpoena, I arrived at the High Court in Johannesburg, willing to take the stand. Before this could happen, however, I was asked to meet with NPA prosecutor Gerrie Nel, key Scorpions investigator Andrew Leask and my lawyers in an office next door to the High Court. It was during a period of load-shedding (intermittent interruptions of the electricity supply), and we sat in an office some floors up, in the weak morning light shining through a window.

In a very short exchange of words, Nel said that he had good news and bad news for me. The bad news, he said, was that I'd travelled to Johannesburg for no purpose at all; the good news, according to him, was that I didn't have to testify.

Just the week before, Nel had told the court that I didn't want to testify or was being difficult or couldn't be traced, none of which was true.

Now, if the State subpoenas a witness, and complains about him, and then all of a sudden goes back to the court and tells the judge that the witness is no longer needed, that shoots off a bright-red flare for any criminal lawyer, who would naturally wonder what it was that this witness might or might not say that was so important at first, and then suddenly so unimportant. As a result, I was promptly subpoenaed by the defence counsel for Selebi, advocate Jaap Cilliers.

This is why I took the stand in May 2010. My testimony was very brief. I was asked only a few basic questions by Cilliers, and I told the court that I'd occasionally worked with commissioner Selebi on tax and crime issues over the years. I stated that, for legal reasons, I wasn't allowed to disclose certain details of information Selebi had shared with me. I noted that most of the cases about which Selebi had tipped SARS off had resulted in successful prosecutions and the confiscation of hundreds of millions of rands' worth of contraband goods. I also explained that I'd once assisted Selebi with his own tax matters pertaining to his military veterans' pension.

Then it was over to Gerrie Nel, on behalf of the State, for cross-examination – but after some consultation with his team, he told the judge that he had no questions for me, and I was excused.

I would come to learn some days later, through news articles, that the Scorpions had alleged in their case docket that Selebi had used his connections with SARS officials (presumably Pillay and me) to 'help his friend Gavin Varejes in organising a tax-evasion sting on Tigon', a company owned by one Gary Porritt, a KwaZulu-Natal farmer-accountant. Apparently, the prosecution had advanced the notion that Varejes had a score to settle with Porritt, so had supposedly 'used Selebi to set SARS on Porritt's company'.

How I wished I'd been asked questions about this, and that my affidavit had been the subject of cross-examination that day, because it would've shown something quite different.

This case was most certainly not a 'sting' – an undercover operation. SARS had simply interviewed a whistleblower introduced to us by the police, taken the evidence he gave us, and then commenced with a tax audit in a manner no different to countless others. Porritt had known from day one that SARS was auditing Tigon because SARS had to notify him and request records from Tigon.

Much later, as I was doing research for this book, I would also come to learn that Varejes (who went on to head Richmark Holdings, with interests in information technology, communications, property and security) confirmed that he was close to Selebi but insisted that he'd never used this friendship for any improper purpose.

Selebi's version at the time was that his relationship with Varejes concerned an initiative by Selebi to rehabilitate street children. I would learn years later, again as part of research for this book, that Varejes was a benefactor of many charitable organisations, including being the largest contributor and fundraiser for the police's Widows and Orphans fund for many years. Selebi and Varejes had attended a fundraising event in June 2007, the latter in his capacity as president of the South African Rugby Legends Association, a non-profit company that aimed to develop rugby at grassroots level, and which supported the street-children initiative. At the time, Varejes told the media that his company, Richmark, had also made donations to police rugby and police athletics.[6]

To recap (as covered in a previous chapter), Jackie Selebi was convicted for having received a bribe of just under R170 000 and sentenced to 15 years' imprisonment, almost immediately hospitalised for an incurable kidney disease, and released on compassionate parole, and dying soon after. The Asset Forfeiture Unit later pursued his estate for around R230 000.

Glenn Agliotti was found to have been an unreliable witness and failed to receive indemnity; to date, he hasn't been prosecuted for having bribed Selebi or in any of the other cases we implicated him in, including a massive tax-evasion case. Dianne Muller, Agliotti's ex-fiancée, also a State witness, did receive indemnity from prosecution, and her testimony formed the primary basis of Selebi's conviction.

In the final court judgement, my testimony wasn't even referred to – I was simply listed among the witnesses.

I've always believed, and have stated so on many occasions, that Selebi's bribe of less than R170 000 was unjustly weighed in the scales of justice against what the trial cost the State, the number of criminals who got off the hook as a result (among them, Agliotti, Muller, the shooters of Brett Kebble, and Kebble's right-hand man John Stratton, who's been living large in Australia ever since) and the never-to-be-pursued amount of at least R3 billion lost at the listed company JCI.

Fast-forward five years, and guess who KPMG relied on as a star witness in its 2015 'documentary review' of the 'rogue unit'? None other than Gary Porritt – uncritically so, and after having been approached by Porritt personally. KPMG didn't want to hear anything from me, but Porritt was most welcome to meet with them, sit down, have a chat and advance whatever he wished.

In their report, KPMG made no mention of the fact that Porritt was, at that very time, being investigated and prosecuted for one of the largest share and tax fraud schemes in our country's history, following investigations by SARS by persons managed by me. If ever I've come across a conflict of interest, and serious ethically and legally challengeable behaviour by an audit firm, this would be it.

The background to KPMG's deceit in this respect has its origins in October 2012, when a few of my friends (none from SARS) and I decided to participate the following year in a well-known annual social rally event through southern Africa, to showcase this part of Africa to the world as a tourist destination, and at the same time collect money for a charitable organisation that buys school shoes for underprivileged children.

I promptly declared to SARS my participation in this effort in detail in October 2012, and again in 2013 and 2014. At no stage did any of my managers, the Ethics officer, the head of Integrity or the Anti-corruption and Security Unit dealing with such declarations deny or query my participation. To the contrary, it featured large in an internal SARS newsletter in 2013.

My friends and I were among 60-odd such 'crews' of people from all over the world who came to South Africa to participate in the rally that year. All the rallies over the years have functioned in exactly the same way: to qualify to participate, a crew must collect a certain amount of money for the charitable cause that buys and gifts brand-new leather school shoes to underprivileged kids. Once a certain target has been reached, crews are allowed to add additional charitable causes to their efforts, and causes ranging from animal-protection societies to educational trusts have benefited in this way over the years.

By 2013, the fundraiser consisted of hundreds of people from all over the world, and had extended its scope to raise funds for an education trust for underprivileged children in Alexandra township, and for 40 children in Zambia in pre-primary, primary and secondary schools.

In addition, many projects were being funded from supporters' own pockets; in my case, I'd built a four-bedroom brick home for my housekeeper, who'd been living in a shack for most of her adult life. We were genuinely changing lives in ways few of us could ever have imagined.[7]

One day in November 2012, I received a call from my old colleague and friend Shirish Soni, who by then was South African ambassador in Kazakhstan. Soni was the fundraiser's special ambassador, and he recruited political ambassadors from all over the world to assist in the fundraising drive.[8] A truly special person on so many levels, he'd also been collecting donations for the charities,[9] and he told me about a friend of his, a businessman, who'd expressed his desire to help. The man, whose name Soni told me was 'Gavin', was willing to donate money to the shoes charity, Soni said, but he wanted some form of documentary proof of its authenticity. Soni asked me to deliver official documents for this purpose – he couldn't do it himself because he was in Kazakhstan – and gave me the address of Gavin's company.

So, on an afternoon late in 2012, I travelled to the address given to me by Soni, armed with a briefing pack containing the material provided by the rally organisers for crews to present to people who wished to donate to their cause. I asked for Gavin at reception, and it was only when he came to meet me that I recognised him as Gavin Varejes, the man I'd met back in 2001 with Pillay, Selebi and the whistleblower.

Varejes was in a rush, as most successful businessmen normally are, but he invited me in to his office and we sat on a big couch. The walls and shelves were full of sports paraphernalia and it was clear to me that he truly loved rugby. I quickly took him through the briefing pack and he loved the idea. He noted how a former Springbok rugby captain was one of the founders of the annual rally and the shoes charity, and he particularly enjoyed the fact that this dovetailed with his own charitable organisation, the South African Rugby Legends Association, which did much good for development in sports, for underprivileged children, and for former rugby heroes who were struggling financially or otherwise, such as Tinus Linee and Joost van der Westhuizen, both of whom suffered from motor-neuron disease.

Varejes then accompanied me out of his office. He had to go, he said, as he had other business engagements, but his administrative assistant would do the necessary.

I showed her the online donation link to the shoes charity, then left.

Some days later, it was confirmed that the South African Rugby Legends Association had donated a record R100 000 directly to the charitable cause concerned; and they did the same the following year. On each occasion, the shoes charity acknowledged this publicly on its own website and social-media platforms for the world to see.

KPMG's 2015 documentary review reported that there was something untoward about this very generous donation – just because I'd met Gavin Varejes once very briefly in 2001, and then again over 11 years later under totally different circumstances and at the request of someone else. KPMG falsely reported that Varejes, or 'entities associated with him', had donated money directly to me or the fundraiser when none of this was true. Varejes never donated anything: the South African Rugby Legends Association made donations directly online to the shoes charity; and the fundraiser, Wachizungu, was something else entirely.

Innocent people and companies with pure intentions who had of their own accord donated directly to other independent charitable organisations, were projected falsely as having donated to me or the fundraiser of which I was part. Some, including a large audit firm and a journalist, hadn't donated at all – they were simply named and included as 'donors', for reasons unknown to me. It was pure smoke and mirrors.

The report also contained an unattributed – and false – allegation that the fundraiser had a bank account in the European country of Liechtenstein. The report conceded that no evidence of such a bank account could be found, but noted that this didn't mean that such a bank account didn't exist – an astounding statement by chartered accountants and forensic experts.

Amazingly, the authors of the KPMG report conceded that I'd offered to provide any information, records and assistance they required regarding this fundraising effort, but that they'd thought it unnecessary. Confusing the issue further, there was another person also called Gavin involved in the fundraising efforts, and KPMG erroneously assumed this was Gavin Varejes.

In 2015, and into 2016, I took on KPMG directly in several letters, pointing out the facts to them. I even wrote to KPMG's chief executive officer at the time, Trevor Hoole, asking for access to the report and for the underlying basis for its having come to the conclusions it had. I wanted them to hear me, and to correct the facts publicly.

They stonewalled me, then put their – expensive – lawyers onto me. Norton Rose Fulbright stepped in, interrupting the correspondence between myself, Hoole, KPMG's lead auditor, Johan van der Walt, and legal officer Oloff van Niekerk.

I tried to be nice, but I was as angry as hell. I pointed out to them that they had responsibilities as professionals, and as members of professional bodies, that required them to operate within certain bounds of ethics, morals and standards. I asked nicely, then I begged, to be able to see on what they'd based their 'findings'.

Eventually, I resorted to asking them who their designated Promotion of Access to Information officer was and where I could find their manual and application forms – but they ignored this too.

I finally sent them a generic 'access to information' application but it drew a predictable answer from the KPMG lawyers: no, you may not see the report.

I pointed out that the report had a material impact on my human rights, and on my rights as a citizen of South Africa; that it had caused immeasurable harm; and that they'd made errors, and statements that were false and incorrect. I pointed them to their own codes of ethics and rules, and reminded them that once they'd been made aware of certain facts that could have a material effect on any of their findings, they were duty bound either to distance themselves from the report or to alter the report to reflect the truth. They simply ignored me.

In 2015 I commissioned and personally paid for a forensic line-by-line audit, the results of which were made available online to KPMG and anybody else who bothered to check the website, Twitter or Facebook pages. The audit examined each and every donation, ensuring that it was correctly accounted for and publicly reflected on the website and social-media pages of the organisations that had received donations, and that all donations had gone to the charitable organisations for which they were intended. Just to be sure, I then asked the auditors to assign another independent auditor to double-check their work.[10]

Finally, in 2017, I did what SARS and KPMG should and could have done in the first place: I simply emailed Gavin Varejes' lawyers and asked them to confirm or deny whether he, or any entity associated with him, had ever donated any money to me or any charitable organisation of which I was a director or member or beneficiary.

I received a response, hand-delivered to me on the same day, wherein they unequivocally confirmed that the donations about which KPMG had made such a fuss had accrued no benefit of any kind whatsoever to me, and that neither Varejes nor the South African Rugby Legends Association had ever donated a cent to me or any organisation of which

I'd ever been part. They also confirmed that the said donations were made directly to the shoes charity online.[11]

KPMG could have asked the same question of Varejes or Varejes' lawyers at any time over the preceding few years, and no doubt would have received the same answer. After all, KPMG had been happy to talk to Porritt; why on earth had they not spoken to Varejes? The only conclusion I can come to is that they knew the answer all along and didn't want to have it on record; it didn't suit KPMG and those behind the 'rogue unit' smear campaign to publish the truth.

I've publicly condemned the KPMG report as a mix of speculation, unsubstantiated allegations, fiction, material omissions and misrepresentations. A shocking piece of work, it caused enormous reputational harm to the charitable organisations we supported, as well as to many others, including SARS, the economy, the country and its citizens.

What KPMG did in compiling this report is a crying shame. I don't know how they sleep at night.

It was this KPMG report that came to serve a nefarious purpose in one of Gary Porritt's endless attempts to delay the case against him – and this perhaps explains why Porritt had sought the audience with KPMG in the first place, planting a seed to germinate for a future date and purpose.

In 2016 (after many people, including me, had left SARS), Porritt complained in court that the KPMG report supposedly included evidence suggesting that SARS had been biased against him. He further alleged that the State had acted with ulterior motives and obtained false evidence from witnesses, and he demanded disclosure of all relevant information, including the KPMG report.

Tom Moyane, while denying me and all others affected by the report access to it, was quite happy to provide it to the court and, by extension, to Porritt. It became Porritt's self-fulfilling prophecy, and the seed he'd planted with KPMG back in 2015 came to fruition.

The 2001 meeting cited in the report between 'former SARS officials

Ivan Pillay and Johann van Loggerenberg' and a one-time business associate of Porritt named as 'Mr X' – Gavin Varejes – was the issue Porritt raised. Porritt claimed that this meeting was the start of SARS's 'unlawful' pursuit of Tigon on tax-related offences, and that SARS had caused the collapse of Tigon by pursuing considerable tax assessments against it while ignoring evidence Porritt claimed he'd uncovered against Varejes.[12]

At the time, Pillay naturally denied all the charges of impropriety or improper conduct that the applicants put before court. 'In my view, it is untenable and, indeed, undesirable, in law and in practice, that taxpayers who command substantial financial resources can apply any legal obfuscation to avoid, for more than a decade, their day in court to answer serious criminal charges,' he noted.

The media reported my view too: 'My role and significance in the matter has been greatly exaggerated,' I said. The 2001 meeting with Varejes had been quite brief, and covered only basic aspects of allegations of tax evasion. It was immediately allocated to another investigator. 'I played no further operational part in the case,' I said.[13]

Judge Brian Spilg's ruling made no bones about the fact that Porritt's strategy didn't wash with the court: 'None of the grounds on which a permanent stay is sought prior to the accused actually pleading to the indictment and evidence being presented at trial are extraordinary or can be said to constitute trial prejudice,' he said.[14]

By pure coincidence, also in 2016, while these events played out in court, news broke of the 'Panama Papers', a massive data leak detailing thousands of accounts used to hide money offshore by various people and companies worldwide. It caused a huge fuss, because many formerly unknown tax evaders and fraudsters were suddenly outed.

The Panama Papers made up over 11,5 million documents detailing financial and attorney-client information about 214 488 offshore entities. Belonging to Panamanian law firm and corporate service provider Mossack Fonseca, the documents were leaked to the International

Consortium of Investigative Journalists by an anonymous source.

Among the documents, journalists identified those that proved that some Mossack Fonseca shell corporations were being used for illegal purposes, including fraud, tax evasion and evading international sanctions. And guess who featured? Gary Porritt. Some of the shell companies registered in offshore jurisdictions were instrumental in transactions for which Porritt had been charged.

By this time, 15 years had gone by, with no fewer than 47 judgements by various courts, without Porritt or Bennett having even pleaded to any of them.

In September 2016, the Tigon criminal trial eventually took off. The first witness was Jack Milne, the former managing director of Progressive Systems College, who'd earlier pleaded guilty as part of a plea agreement relating to the collapse of Progressive Systems College Guaranteed Growth, an investment fund underwritten by Tigon, and served 11 months of an effective five-year sentence. Under oath, Milne admitted that he, together with Porritt and Bennett (also a director of Progressive Systems College Guaranteed Growth) had committed deliberate fraud by making misrepresentations in a company prospectus.

The prosecutor entered into evidence the plea agreement into which Milne had entered with the NPA – but because the original had been lost, the prosecutor presented to the court Milne's personal copy, with one page and four attachments missing.

Predictably, Sue Bennett brought an application for the court to investigate the authenticity of the copy, advancing that the document was a forgery and that the authenticity of the signatures was in doubt. She asked the court to subpoena witnesses to testify as to the authenticity of the document.

Porritt supported this application, of course, using the opportunity to complain about 'collusive fraud by prosecutors in two courts'.

Judge Spilg wasn't amused. There was an uncomfortable exchange of words between him and Porritt during which Spilg noted that Porritt might have seen how trials were conducted elsewhere, like in the USA, but that wasn't what happened in his court. 'This is not a show,' the judge said.[15]

Milne was ultimately allowed to continue with his testimony, revealing many misrepresentations in the Progressive Systems College Guaranteed Growth prospectus – in the production of which Bennett was involved, and of which she was a signatory – aimed at encouraging the public to buy shares in the company. He told how representations claiming that a team under his leadership would invest money raised from investors, using a method promoted by him and taught by Progressive Systems College, were false; the real plan was to invest only in Tigon and Porritt's other company, Shawcell. And even before the prospectus was produced, Milne said, he, Porritt and Bennett had planned on transferring the money raised by selling the shares in Progressive Systems College Guaranteed Growth immediately to an account under Porritt's control.[16]

Milne spent days on the stand, providing many details, and was finally released as a witness on 17 October 2016.

The trial was set to resume on 31 January 2017, but Sue Bennett – who, like Porritt, was out on bail – failed to appear. She claimed ill health. On 6 March, Judge Spilg ordered that Bennett make her medical records available for examination by several doctors and medical experts.

Spilg found that the evidence presented by advocate Annelene van den Heever on Bennett's behalf, as well as a supporting affidavit by Porritt, failed to give a good enough explanation for Bennett's absence from court, and ordered that several medical practitioners from KwaZulu-Natal and the Western Cape report to him by 31 March to testify and be cross-examined about Bennett's health and ability to stand trial. There were contradictory expert and medical opinions submitted on the issues of Bennett's health and ability to stand trial.

At the time of writing, the court has yet to consider these medical reports and expert evidence, and make a ruling on Bennett's failure to appear in court on the fraud charges. It has also yet to determine whether Bennett will be able to participate in future court proceedings and, if not, whether any such inability would be temporary or permanent. Should Bennett not be able to attend the trial, the court will then have to decide whether to separate her trial from that of Porritt or resume the case in her absence.

The execution of an arrest warrant for Bennett was suspended, and Porritt's bail was extended in March 2017.

The trial recommenced in June 2017, only to be halted again – when Porritt claimed to be too sick to come to court. Judge Spilg, apparently fed up to the back teeth with this lot, ordered Porritt's arrest, and Porritt was put in jail. The trail then proceeded.

In September 2017 it was again postponed for a month, when Porritt brought a fresh bail application, and an application for Spilg to recuse himself from the case. This failed too.

In February 2018, Porritt was reported to have been forced by Judge Spilg to apologise to him or face a contempt-of-court ruling. Both Bennett and Porritt had accused Spilg of having 'already made up [his] mind'. Porritt also said to Spilg that his 'eyes, ears and mind [were] closed to the accused's arguments'.

Porritt apologised[17] but it didn't end there.

In March 2018 Porritt appeared before Judge Ramarumo Monama and made a new application for bail. Monama stated that Porritt was acting like former President Jacob Zuma by delaying his criminal trial 'even when there [was] manifestly no prospect (of success)'. Monama dismissed Porritt's bail application, referring to the endless delays and legal filibustering, and noting that the trial had the hallmark of the 'Zuma Principle'.[18]

According to the media, the trial is expected to run for a further two and a half years.

I'm not holding my breath.

22

It's a system, you see?

On 16 March 2016, the then director of the Financial Intelligence Centre, Murray Michell, informed Parliament that an estimated R60 billion had left the country illicitly during the 2015/16 financial year, and that almost nine million suspect transactions had been reported. He noted that 'about 2 490 products to the value of nearly R58,94 billion' were representative of possible illicit financial outflows. 'Products' here refer to financial reports, analysis, investigations and referrals from the Financial Intelligence Centre.

'Illicit financial outflows' may refer to anything from straightforward money-laundering (such as through loop structures,[xvi] front companies and concealed foreign-exchange transactions) and smuggling (carrying or transporting bags of cash or items of value such as gold or precious stones to other countries), to their distant cousins, 'aggressive tax structuring' and transfer pricing[xvii] (for example, multinational non-arm's-length transactions and thin-capitalisation[xviii] schemes), to legitimate businesses circumventing exchange-control and customs regulations through false invoicing, undervaluation-import scams, mispricing and over-invoicing schemes, which unlawfully shift profits across borders.

xvi A 'loop structure' describes paying money to an offshore entity for valid reasons, when no such reasons exist, and then, in another set of transactions, repeating the same to bring the money back into the country, so that it seems a distinct and legitimate transaction.

xvii 'Transfer pricing' refers to the rules and methods for pricing transactions within and between enterprises under common ownership. Because of the potential for cross-border transactions to distort taxable income, SARS can adjust intragroup transfer prices that differ from what would have been charged by unrelated enterprises dealing at arm's length.

xviii Where a company has debt from a related party that is a tax resident outside South Africa, and such debt exceeds a certain level, the company is considered to be thinly capitalised. The effect is that SARS will contend that too much interest is being claimed as an income-tax deduction.

Members of Parliament were apparently astounded by Michell's revelation, and reportedly concerned that neither the police nor our elite Directorate of Priority Crimes Investigations, the Hawks, were able to confirm whether they were investigating these dodgy transactions or not.

In May 2017, our National Director of Public Prosecutions, advocate Shaun Abrahams, said, 'The challenges that we face today as a country in our ability to combat money-laundering, illicit financial flows and terror financing is [as a] direct result, and I say this respectfully, of various Finance Ministers failing to constitute or have constituted the counter-money-laundering advisory council.'[1]

The concerns expressed by the honourable members of Parliament, and that of Abrahams, may well be fair comment, but – and I say this respectfully – these responses are an oversimplification of what we face as a developing nation when it comes to illicit financial outflows. Space in this book is inadequate to allow for a detailed analysis of the issue, but I believe that there are six cardinal aspects to bear in mind when our Government considers how best to deal with the challenge.

First, let's accept that illicit financial outflows are a global phenomenon, affecting both the developing and developed world. Determining the actual value, identifying and meaningfully addressing illicit financial outflows is a 'holy grail' for governments and law-enforcement agencies worldwide. There's no simple solution, no silver bullet.

The formation in late 1989 of the intergovernmental Financial Action Task Force to combat money-laundering (and, after the attacks on the twin towers of the World Trade Center in New York in 2001, terrorism financing) led to the formation of financial intelligence centres or agencies all over the world. We in South Africa established our Financial Intelligence Centre in 2001, and it seems to be working well, to the extent that it's capable of having produced 2 490 products to the value of over R58 million in just one year.

Our Financial Intelligence Centre has adopted every single recommendation emanating from the Financial Action Task Force, including the now newly amended Financial Intelligence Centre Act (FICA), No 38 of 2001, and gazetted standards in respect of measures on foreign 'politically exposed persons',[2] beneficial owners and record keeping. It has also passed its peer reviews and oversight audits every year since its establishment. We can be proud of them.

But identifying and trying to understand suspicious transactions is all they do. The Financial Intelligence Centre isn't a complete solution to deal with every instance of illicit financial outflows from our shores, and it has no real investigative, prosecuting or executive functions in the true sense of the word. That's not what it was designed for.

Second, we must realise that illicit financial outflows are made up of a range of income-generating activities that are not limited to pure criminal activities. It's a complex subject that requires a deep understanding of what the term 'illicit financial outflows' really means, and the expertise to understand how each of these materialisations comes about, and, perhaps more importantly, why. This is why a knee-jerk reaction that expects law-enforcement agencies to investigate whenever we come to learn of such instances isn't the right one; rather, a measured attempt to understand the root causes underpinning the problem and its manifestations should come first. If we could find a clear view of those, seeking the best solutions to combat illicit financial outflows would be a lot easier.

Third, our Government deals with illicit financial outflows largely via a combination of the criminal-justice system and, to an extent, the financial-regulatory system.[3] But, as engineers will tell you, for any system to work, all the parts that make up the system need to work together – and I'm afraid that following our 'honeymoon years' of the mid-1990s to the mid-2000s (when there appeared to be great prospects of getting the criminal-justice and financial-regulatory systems to work as one), evidence suggests that some of the parts appear to be failing.

Fourth (and very closely related to the two points above), preventing illicit financial outflows is as much about identifying those involved and holding them accountable as it is about putting measures in place. The

State must be seen to prevent and react at the same time, all the time. Given the high volumes of illicit financial outflows identified, and the lack of sufficient capability and capacity of our developing nation's law-enforcement agencies, part of the solution rests in the prioritisation of cases in terms of value, frequency and prominence. As the saying goes, this is an elephant that must be eaten piece by piece – and we must start with the biggest ones that are right in front of our noses.

Fifth, there's the state of our economy. Naturally, the worse an economy performs, the higher the levels of normal, legitimate capital outflow, as investors look elsewhere for better returns with less risk. The same applies to illicit financial outflows: when times are tough, crooks move into overdrive.

And last, there's a lack of 'compliance culture' in our society, which has its roots in the horrible apartheid regime that encouraged and facilitated illicit financial outflows on a grand scale, at a systemic level, in order to prop up the economy and enrich a few. Old habits die hard, and the new learn from the old: since 1994, we've seen many examples that suggest that this lack of compliance culture has continued and even become more sophisticated as time has gone by. When our Government isn't seen to be acting on significant crimes that lead to illicit financial outflows, this affects the general compliance culture in society; when powerful and influential people are seen to be getting away with it over and over again, others think they can get away with it too. And many do. The nine million suspected transactions reported to the Financial Intelligence Centre in the 2015/16 year speak for themselves.

Some of the parts of our financial regulatory system do seem to be working well. As noted, based on the volumes of the reports produced by our (relatively small) Financial Intelligence Centre, we can't really fault them much. But, clearly, they're producing more referrals than those who receive them for further investigations can cope with – the police, the Hawks and SARS.

Our commercial banks, too, seem to mostly be doing the right thing when it comes to reporting suspicious transactions, since these make up most of the Financial Intelligence Centre reports and products. We've learned that they've even closed a few bank accounts because of risky transactions attributed to the infamous Gupta family and friends – not that these are being investigated by our criminal-justice system, but hey, who's to blame for that?

We have an even smaller outfit situated within our Reserve Bank, the Financial Surveillance Department, which also seems to have done rather well over the years in some prominent cases – the Tannenbaum Ponzi scheme and Dave King's tax-evasion case, for instance.

Then there's the Financial Services Board, an independent institution overseeing the non-banking financial-services industry,[4] and the Johannesburg Stock Exchange's investigations department. (By the time of writing, the Financial Services Board had changed its name to the Financial Sector Conduct Authority (FSCA) and had a host of new legal powers.)

These are the rule-makers, the early-warning mechanisms and the overseers. They design statutes and rules to combat illicit financial outflows, and their role is to ensure that these are implemented. The logic of this system is sound: it's intended to put in place proactive measures that should, theoretically, deter or at least make it difficult for those involved in illicit financial outflows.[5]

But, as with most things in life, it's not that simple: proactive measures impose rules and obligations on us on the premise that if we break them, punitive consequences will certainly follow. And this is where the other part, our criminal-justice system, comes into play.

Ultimately, the financial-regulatory system assumes that where people are up to mischief, a fully functional criminal-justice system will come in and do its job without fail. It's this system that's required to do the heavy lifting: the detecting, investigating and collecting evidence that enables the State to hold people to account, refer matters for prosecution and recoup lost funds. And therein lies the rub.

It's a fallacy to say that if there are nine million suspicious transactions reported to the Financial Intelligence Centre, and if SARS, the police and these Hawks investigate all of these, the problem of illicit financial outflows will be solved. It's simply a question of volumes and complexity.

The average investigation into a commercial crime takes 494 hours (about 62 eight-hour work days) to complete to a level where the matter can be handed to the NPA for a decision whether to prosecute or not.[6] And even then, it may be passed back to the investigator for further evidence-gathering. And this doesn't factor in any additional work required to freeze, repatriate or recoup monies, and the legal actions that follow on these types of investigations.

Furthermore, not all detectives and investigators in State agencies can do these types of investigations, which require a certain skill set that's rather rare.

In South Africa we have a work year of about 208 days (factoring in leave and weekends). Even if each and every one of our State investigators worked every single day of the year, for 12 hours a day, they wouldn't even scratch the surface of the 2015/16 nine million suspicious transactions or 2 490 products. And bear in mind that the new inflow of Financial Intelligence Centre reports, those for 2016/17 and 2017/18, would also have to be factored in.

Another way of putting this is that the Financial Intelligence Centre sits at the front of what amounts to a value chain, together with whistleblowers, complainants and victims, and self-detection by our law-enforcement agencies. In the middle sit the investigative arms of the criminal-justice system. And at the back is the NPA.

It's the NPA that obtains court orders to freeze bank accounts and forfeit assets. They're the ones who can, through mutual legal-assistance agreements, reach across the globe and get a hold on shifted funds. It's the NPA that must ultimately prove that the outflows were illicit in the first place, because if they're unable to do so, nothing that preceded the process will matter and the State will have wasted time, resources and energy.

But the NPA, like all our state departments, is resource constrained – there are only so many prosecutors. And standing in the same queue, case files under their arms, competing for attention from the same limited number of NPA prosecutors, are members of the police, the Asset Forfeiture Unit, the Special Investigations Unit, and other government-department investigative units.

And even if the NPA could somehow conjure up the means to increase the number of prosecutors to the extent that there were enough to deal with the volumes of incoming completed investigations, it still wouldn't help much, unless our Department of Justice provided for more courts, magistrates, judges, scribes, interpreters and support staff.

When you consider all this, there's little wonder that while we have nine million Financial Intelligence Centre reports and estimated illicit outflows valued at over R58 billion, we have no significant numbers of money-laundering or Financial Intelligence Centre-related criminal convictions to brag about in the same year.

This point was amplified in June 2017, when the standing committee on public accounts in Parliament heard how, over the three previous financial years, our country's highest-level multi-agency anti-corruption task team could claim only 42 successful prosecutions, of which 41 were as a result of plea-bargains. These numbers tell a story, and it's not a good one.

Coupled to these complexities is the fact that our criminal-justice system is dependent on skills and resources it increasingly no longer possesses. This is usually compensated for by outsourcing key aspects of core investigative processes.

As long ago as the early 2000s we saw law-enforcement agencies outsourcing to the private sector core aspects of their investigations relating to accounting, auditing and financial functions. Even what should be a very basic audit of a senior manager's income streams over a period of five or six years may be contracted out to a law firm, which can take a year or so to complete the job. And then there are the huge projects, an example being the investigation into mining giant JCI and the alleged missing R3 billion referred to earlier in this book. This matter, along with the highly publicised cases against senior managers of the collapsed Saambou bank, Schabir Shaik, former police commissioner Jackie Selebi, and even the case against former President Jacob Zuma, all share the same audit firm – KPMG. These outsourced investigations come with a massive price tag to the State.

Many of the auditors and investigators within these private-sector audit and law firms began their professional careers in our State law-enforcement agencies. It's therefore important not only to develop but also to retain a skills base within the criminal-justice system that's able and capable to deal with complex financial crimes and illicit financial outflows. It takes time to develop the necessary skills and capability to deal with complicated financial crimes, and it's imperative that our law-enforcement agencies invest in creating and retaining these.

Unfortunately, there are far too many white-collar-crime cases that remain somewhere in an in-tray or that fall by the wayside because prosecutors and investigators leave their agencies, are transferred or move on elsewhere. Two examples of large, complex commercial-crime cases before the courts that have collectively been dragging on for over ten years are *The State v G Porritt (Tigon) and Others* and *The State v Hennie Delport and Others.*[7] Both share one advantage for the State: the same prosecutors and investigators that started these cases are still working them – but who knows for how long.

Finally, organised criminals adapt very quickly, and they watch our criminal-justice system closely. For this reason, our law-enforcement agencies need to be equally adept. This requires stability and a cycle of continuous improvement within those specialised capabilities. As soon as the criminals try something new, our officials must be on to them, and be prepared to run the course to bring the criminals to book and bring back the money.

SARS is a unique role-player that straddles both the financial-regulatory and criminal-justice systems. Basically, the tax authority is an all-in-one agency with some serious legislative teeth with which to audit, apply civil punitive measures, freeze and seize assets, and conduct criminal investigations. It's a regulator, licensee, administrator and enforcement agency rolled into one.

Of all the bodies in the financial regulatory system, SARS has the greatest executive powers to access third-party information, and to obtain information from most other countries worldwide through international treaties and agreements.[8] For example, when the Panama Papers were made public, SARS announced within months that it had identified over 1 700 implicated South Africans.

SARS is also the only part of the government system legally able to investigate aggressive transfer pricing and thin-capitalisation schemes.

From a criminal-justice-system perspective, and by virtue of the construct of its relationship with banks and taxpayers, SARS is a potentially formidable force to combat illicit financial outflows in whatever form they may manifest. There can be no doubt that SARS's enforcement component has the necessary skill sets, it certainly has the right kind of legal powers, and its customs component is situated at every commercial port of entry around the country.

For both the financial-regulatory and criminal-justice systems, there's also the issue of prioritisation of investigations and prosecutions. We need stable law-enforcement agencies that aren't distracted by political noise and disruptions or perceived and real 'capture' at any level, and they should guard against being seen to be selective in their investigations and prosecutions.

Not a week goes by these days without the media reporting massive fraud, and incredible tales of corruption and greed, some involving our state departments and parastatals, at great expense to our economy and a taxpayer population that's already under severe stress. Just think of the public allegations affecting South African Airways, the Passenger Rail Agency of South Africa, the rail, port and pipeline company Transnet, our State arms company Denel, and the South African Broadcasting Corporation – to name but a few.

Other evidence of big crimes has come directly from our Public Protectors' office. We continue to be bombarded with credible and prima-facie evidence (which is what NPA prosecutors would require to proceed with a case) of monies looted on a scale not seen since the apartheid regime's fiscal shenanigans.

The Guptaleaks leaked cache of emails, mentioned earlier in this book, was reported on by our media weekly, if not daily, through most of 2017 and into 2018, and all pointed to very serious criminal offences and massive amounts of lost money. Yet very few, if any, of these priority-type crimes appeared to receive the kind of attention that we as citizens would (and should) expected of our criminal-justice system.

Only at the beginning of 2018, following a change of guard within the ANC ruling party, did we start seeing some signs of our law-enforcement agencies beginning to act. But could it be too little, too late? How much evidence that could have been seized back when the revelations first saw the light of day has since disappeared? How much money has since left our shores and where is it now?

To act so long after the exposure of such complex fraud and corruption cases creates a massive impediment for investigators and prosecutors, who are forced to work back in time and against suspects who know what's out there, and who would very likely have used the opportunity of the delay to get rid of as much evidence as possible.

We can't have a situation where the Guptas land a private jet at one of our military bases unchecked by our customs, or at private airports, and leave this unchallenged by our criminal-justice system.

We can't have a situation where a Gupta associate takes a bag through customs, and then when its contents are considered fishy and a request is made to inspect them, the person is allowed to take the bag away unchecked.

Thanks to our Financial Intelligence Centre and a 2017 court action brought by the then Minister of Finance Pravin Gordhan, asking the courts to order the Guptas not to interfere with his duties to impose on private banks, we've come to know that at least 72 Financial Intelligence Centre suspicious-transaction reports to the value of almost R7 billion exist somewhere in the criminal-justice system. The court ultimately ruled these reports inadmissible for the purposes of the court action, but that doesn't negate their existence, and the need for some sort of action by our police. Our criminal-justice system can't just pretend not to know of them.

It's the system, you see? It's not working as it should.

In the early days of our democracy, the ability of the criminal-justice system and other agencies to function in tandem with and support each other showed great promise. Now, they aren't being managed as a single system; some parts are unstable, and others operate in isolation. The operational agreements and common work teams and methodologies seem to have been consigned to the dustbin.

One result of a system that doesn't work is that people look for scapegoats, such as blaming the ministers of finance when things go wrong.

The anti-corruption task team I mentioned earlier, a multi-agency body made up of most of the heads of institutions in our criminal-justice system, has been around for some years now, since about 2010. In 2015, our then president, Jacob Zuma, told us that 'South Africa has a strong anti-corruption architecture' and assured us that the anti-corruption task team 'was fully operational and had been strengthened under the leadership of an anti-corruption interministerial committee led by

Minister in the Presidency for Planning Monitoring and Evaluation Jeff Radebe.'[9]

So how has this been working for us?

In mid-2017, we learned from our finance ministry in Parliament that only 733 of more than 5 200 cases that the Financial Intelligence Centre had passed on to law-enforcement agencies had been investigated over the previous six years. This translates to about 14% of such cases receiving any reaction from our law-enforcement agencies.

The envisaged counter-money-laundering FICA advisory council, which the ministers of finance were blamed for not constituting, sees as its participants virtually all the agencies that make up the core of the anti-corruption task team. Given the track record of the anti-corruption task team, I'm not convinced that the mere existence of a council would be much use in dealing with illicit financial outflows. The heads of the Hawks, the NPA, the police, SARS, the Financial Intelligence Centre and other agencies would simply have more added to their already heavy work burdens by having to participate in yet another committee.

Committees and councils abound. We need to start looking at substance rather than form. What I'm advocating is that we should be looking anew at, on the one hand, how these crimes manifest, why they occur and what makes it easy for people to commit them; and, on the other, combine this with an understanding of our government systems as a single system, upskilling them, keeping them stable, and continuously improving their abilities and capabilities.

We would need to understand how long it takes to investigate these sorts of cases and what skills are required, and begin to regard our criminal-justice system as a single system.

The mere reporting of seizures of money on its own, or arrests, would mean very little if the prosecutions and recoupment of proceeds aren't coupled to these. To do this, the way our criminal-justice system needs to go about prioritising cases is key.

Justice must be seen to be done, and criminals must fear our criminal-justice system, regardless of who they are and who they may know. As things stand now, many criminals appear to scoff at the system.

The values and behaviours of our leaders, politicians and senior officials are also key. We tend to look up to them, and their displayed values and behaviours often give direction to ours. What they do and why they do things are critical to guiding our fragile and young society. If they misbehave, some of us will too; and what they fail to do will be seen through the same prism.

Massive crimes are regularly committed in our country, most of which we learn about through the media. Many people are getting away with daylight robbery, right in front of our eyes, and our agencies aren't seen to be acting decisively against them. Ministers don't arrive at parliamentary oversight committees when called on, leading to subpoenas being issued against them. The Guptas and former President Zuma's son, Duduzane Zuma, face arrest warrants, but months have gone by with no sign of any arrests. Criminal cases opened against the politically connected, current and former ministers, and senior government officials by civil-society bodies are gathering dust somewhere in our criminal-justice system.

These cases collectively amount to hundreds of billions of rands that our Government desperately needs to develop our nation.

Seeing and knowing about these very obvious weaknesses in the criminal-justice system, bold crooks would be unlikely to have any qualms in trying to move funds offshore illegally. After all, what are the chances of getting caught? And even if they are, what will happen to them then?

23

Fall from grace

With the exception of one fiscal year during the worldwide financial meltdown, in the period 1998 to 2014 – the time that I worked at the tax authority – SARS consistently collected the amount of revenue required by the State to implement its service-delivery programmes and other initiatives, fund development and pay social grants, often collecting more than its target. Other revenue and customs authorities came to South Africa to study the successes of our tax authority, and SARS was invited to go and assist other governments with their programmes and with the modernisation of their own tax and customs authorities.

All this changed in 2014.

Tom Moyane commenced his duties as the new SARS commissioner on 1 October 2014. The executive committee was disbanded in November 2014, and within months, 55 senior managers had left.

The existence of a totally fictitious 'rogue unit' began to feature prominently – and deliberately, I would add – in the media from 12 October 2014. From that date, too, SARS's name started popping up with increasing frequency in one scandal after another.

In my research for this book, I collected over a hundred media articles about SARS published in the three years between January 2015 and April 2018. Re-reading them broke my heart.

In early 2015, much fuss was made about SARS having collected R1 trillion 'for the first time ever', for the fiscal years 2014/15. The tax authority's media statements about this suggested that it wouldn't have collected this amount had it not been for Tom Moyane. The reality is that, first, I firmly believe that SARS would have collected that amount with or without the presence of Moyane (who'd been appointed fairly late in that fiscal year, by which time the SARS team had already collected the bulk of the revenue); and, second, I know of at least R3 billion due to SARS by tobacco manufacturers which was not collected that fiscal year for reasons unknown to me. I can only conclude that these cases were politically laden and sensitive – which may have had a lot to do with the unfortunate events that started unfolding at SARS in late 2014.

I was sad to read in a press report how a relatively insignificant case brought before the Gauteng High Court in 2015 had an effect on the 'pay now, argue later' precedent that SARS had set so many years before: as a result, now (at the time of writing) there's a technical loophole using which unscrupulous tax dodgers can delay having to pay their dues.

The botched attempt in 2015 to reverse the tax settlement with Julius Malema was simply embarrassing.

A criminal trial in Durban in 2016 demonstrated that the standards of criminal investigation at SARS had dropped precipitously, when a High Court judge rebuked the tax authority for using information obtained during a tax inquiry as evidence in a criminal prosecution. This was tax 101 and should never have happened: tax legislation is very clear on the fact that SARS may not rely on self-incriminating evidence given at a tax inquiry to prosecute a taxpayer.

In February 2016, senior SARS insiders accused a group 'close to Moyane' of having become embroiled in a power grab which saw the alleged dismantling of the once-effective Large Business Centre. How did SARS deal with this? Moyane and his close confidant and executive committee member Jonas Makwakwa sued the *Mail & Guardian* in both their official and private capacities.[1]

And the scandals engulfing a once-proud SARS continued unabated.

In April 2016, Ivan Pillay wrote in his right of reply following the retractions of the 'rogue unit' stories in the *Sunday Times*: 'In time, the full measure of the damage caused to the South African Revenue Service arising from false news coverage will manifest itself in a tarnished reputation, questionable independence and lower levels of compliance with tax and customs law.'[2]

In February 2017, during his last days as finance minister, Pravin Gordhan noted that 'it takes many years to build an institution, to build confidence and trust, to build skills, culture, effectiveness, resilience. But it's very easy to break it down.'[3]

Every time I read about the massive fraud and corruption at state-owned enterprises, I expected SARS to leap onto the cases and within days bring preservation orders and other enforcement actions. But nothing happened.

I was particularly incensed when I was asked for comment by the media following the massive 2017 leak of emails from the infamous Gupta family, wherein it was shown how the Guptas had used one of their lieutenants, with the help of someone inside SARS, to unlawfully access and obtain details about investigations concerning them and others; their reach into the tax authority was so deep that they knew of me by name by the end 2013, well before the drama started at SARS.

Yet, when asked about this, Moyane kept quiet and did nothing.

And when the Guptaleaks resulted in news article after news article exposing allegations of massive corruption and money-laundering, Moyane responded to a media question by saying that SARS didn't consider the emails of value in the pursuit of any tax investigations. I couldn't believe what I was hearing – the Dave King case, one of the largest in the history of modern tax audits in South Africa, had been instigated after SARS auditor Charles Chipps read about the sale of a painting in a relatively obscure magazine.

In September 2017, Gordhan, by then unceremoniously removed as finance minister, was reported to say that 'SARS became a political project and it is now run by people who have no idea how to manage a tax administration system. They don't know what skills are needed and how to use them'. It was part of 'the whole conspiracy theory of replacing good people with bad to facilitate state capture', he noted.[4]

In October 2016, it was revealed how Moyane's nephew, Nhlamulo Ndhlela, had secured a debt-collection contract from SARS estimated at a value of R220 million.[5] Only after this saw daylight in the media did SARS approach the Gauteng High Court to have the contract set aside, with the explanation that Moyane had never been aware of this conflict of interest. Of course, the taxpayer had to pay for this court challenge.

By the end of 2016, more than 500 employees had left the tax authority in that fiscal year alone.[6] SARS noted that this number wasn't a big deal and was comparable to staff turnover in prior years – which may be so, but I know virtually every single one of those who left SARS, and they were mostly super-stars.

In my years at SARS, I learned that we could divide any working group into three broad categories: the lazy ones who were carried by work done by everyone else; the majority of staff who did their job well; and then that small percentage who could always be counted on to go the extra mile, who worked day and night, who were willing to learn and study while working – the super-stars.

If the super-star group was strong, the balance of people would try to emulate them, and the result would be a higher-performing group in totality. But once those at the high end were no longer operating at full tilt, then the greater group of people moved towards the negative lot.

The hypocrisy displayed by those who rode the 'rogue unit' bandwagon was astounding. Back in 2014, many had been quick to perpetuate nonsense stories about Zuma being bugged, the existence of a brothel and millions in slush funds, politicians being illegally spied on and taxpayer communications being unlawfully intercepted.

It was all hogwash, but this malicious propaganda campaign, which ran for over two years, tarnished the institution that formed one of the pillars of the contract between State and citizenry. It affected honourable, innocent and hardworking civil servants on levels both personal and professional. Families and friendships were indiscriminately and forever harmed as a result of these actions. Former Minister of Intelligence Ronnie Kasrils, former SARS boss Oupa Magashula and former Finance Ministers Trevor Manuel and Pravin Gordhan were dragged into the mess for a variety of reasons. And let me not even begin to talk about the suspicious break-ins, theft of laptops and IT equipment, surveillance, efforts to discredit us, how our investigations were undermined, and the threats – all which were reported formally and are on record, but all of which were ignored.

These bogus stories were used to instigate no fewer than four 'panels' – made up of senior State officials, lawyers, accountants, advocates, a retired judge, and so on; and which came with a final price tag of over R26 million – to investigate the 'rogue unit' allegations.

A quick recap. The Kanyane panel operated from June to August 2014. I wasn't invited to address it, but it nonetheless found the original allegations against me (made by a woman I'd dated briefly) to be wholly unsubstantiated. There were at this stage no allegations of a 'rogue unit'.

I wasn't given the report or an opportunity to reply to its findings, but it was leaked to the media by someone from within SARS. Its negative observations about a fundraiser I'd been involved in (detailed in a previous chapter) were so flawed that they'd be laughable if they weren't so serious. And even this allegation morphed over time, from the false claim that service providers of SARS, notably an unnamed audit firm, had donated money directly to the fundraiser, to 'taxpayers under investigation by SARS donated to the charity'; and later this would change yet again.

The Sikhakhane panel followed, from September to November 2014, comprising three advocates and the law firm Hogan Lovells. Its terms of reference expanded – following escalations in the media and *after* having 'interviewed' me in a rush job – to suddenly include a 'rogue unit'.[7] Reneging on an undertaking to afford me my right of reply, I was once again judged unheard. The Sikhakhane report also, by its own admission, ignored the first panel's report and all the evidence provided by me.

Again, the findings were denied to me; when my lawyer requested a copy, he didn't even get the courtesy of a reply. Again, the report was leaked to the media. And, again, the 'findings' were so flawed – and so contradictory – that they weren't worth the paper they were written on. Despite this, and despite not even being named in the report, SARS deputy commissioner Ivan Pillay and group executive Peter Richer were suspended by Moyane.

I asked for an opportunity to address the third panel, in 2015 – the Kroon advisory board, which comprised retired judge Frank Kroon and some external advocates and accountants – but my request, again, didn't even earn the courtesy of a reply. All this board did, in effect, was 'endorse' the prior report and okay it for publication.

The fourth 'panel' was the supposed 'forensic investigation' by audit firm KPMG; it would later emerge that the authors of the report had been instructed, in writing, by SARS, what to find and how to reflect these findings – and they did just that, typos and all. The investigation functioned throughout 2015 until January 2016 and, again, I wasn't heard by them.

In October 2015, KPMG compiled a 'summary of findings'. Naturally, and predictably, this report was also leaked to the media.

I've since read the entire report – which, tellingly, included the disclaimer that it couldn't be used for any 'proceedings' or 'referred to in part or in full' by SARS – and it's worse than the earlier ones: it not only misrepresents facts, twists truths, misleads and lies, but it omits material facts and evidence. As with the other reports, the people most directly affected were denied a hearing and their basic right to a reply.

All this time, a relentless campaign was being waged via the media, with ongoing leaks attributed to 'former [and] current SARS officials, and intelligence officials' feeding the 'rogue unit' saga. The very first approaches to the media, in June 2014, were by people who'd worked for State intelligence – I have proof of this.

The panels and their reports and the media smear campaign operated in tandem. A false story would be leaked and published by the media, which in turn would inform one or other aspect of any of the panels' scope, whose findings would then be leaked to the media, with each seemingly confirming the other. At no time were any of those affected allowed to defend themselves in the media, and Moyane said not one public word in defence of SARS or about the relentless attack on the reputations of SARS and many officials there.

In hindsight, and a red flag for me, was how former SARS commissioner Oupa Magashula was subjected to the same treatment. Not long before, in 2013, on the strength of a single media report, he was also subjected to a panel; he ultimately resigned from SARS. The media report was based on a leaked portion of an intercepted telephone conversation between him and a chartered accountant – State intelligence was, for some reason, spying on the commissioner of SARS.

Nobody batted an eyelid about this. The intelligence officials involved in the illegal procurement and unlawful leaking of the snippet of intercepted communication are known to the authorities (in 2016, when I went searching for them, I found their names with great ease), but they've never been held to account.

What's more, a member of the Kroon advisory board had advised the media to speak to Magashula, who was supposedly now 'ready to talk' – someone had convinced Magashula that it was the 'rogue unit' that had intercepted his phonecall and offered it to the media back in 2013, and were behind his fall. He was led to believe that I and another had met with the very same duo of journalists of the *Sunday Times* newspaper who'd run the 'rogue unit' stories, and offered the snippet to them.

This was pure nonsense. I'd never met the one journalist, and had only bumped into the other a couple of times late in 2013 or early in 2014 at official meetings. The fact is that the leak originated from three State intelligence officials.

In August 2017, KPMG announced an internal review of its SARS report, noting that the lead partner who'd headed the initial process had resigned from the company in March 2017.

In September, KPMG International came to South Africa to conduct a 'comprehensive investigation', and as a result withdrew the report's conclusions, recommendations and legal opinions, effectively ripping out its heart. The message was clear: the report was bogus and couldn't be relied on. KPMG repaid SARS its R23 million fee.

Unsurprisingly, following KPMG's withdrawal of the essence of its report in 2017, Moyane's response was to call a press conference to announce to the public that he refused to accept the withdrawal and stood by the contents of the report.

By late 2017, both the South African Institute for Chartered Accountants, under a panel led by the able and respected advocate Dumisa Ntsebeza, and the statutory Independent Regulatory Board for Auditors had announced separate investigations into the conduct of KPMG and its employees in relation to its SARS report and oversight of the Guptas' companies. Both investigations were still underway at the time of writing.

In early 2018, KPMG made the astounding admission before Parliament that parts of its supposedly independent report had been dictated to them by lawyers for SARS, Mashiane, Moodley and Monama, and incorporated verbatim, and that as such KPMG could not stand by its report.

The scandals from within SARS continued throughout 2016.

By November 2016, reports surfaced that there was a real rogue unit within SARS – one that had been set up to dig up dirt on then Finance Minister Pravin Gordhan and former employees linked to the entirely fictitious 'old rogue unit'.

News24 revealed that the team, which included senior SARS employees Gobi Makhanya (who had previously headed investigations in KwaZulu-Natal) and Yegan Mundie (who had worked at the anti-corruption unit in Pretoria), had allegedly been tasked with conducting an undercover investigation into Gordhan and the by-then-defunct National Research Group, and former employees such as Ivan Pillay, his special adviser Yolisa Pikie and me. 'Their task is to look at anything and everything humanly possible to make the former employees look bad,' an unnamed source said at the time.[8]

Ironically, the new unit was accused of illegally using undercover methods to gather evidence – the same complaint levelled at the fictitious 'rogue unit'.[9]

Also, in 2016, it was publicly revealed that the selfsame Yegan Mundie was linked to Zuma family associate Jen Chih 'Robert' Huang. Mundie's wife, *News24* reported, had been employed by Huang's Mpisi Trading 74 while SARS was investigating the company. 'Huang is a business partner of President Jacob Zuma's nephew Khulubuse, and has used Zuma's legal adviser and lawyer, Michael Hulley, to defend him in cases brought against him by SARS,' the report noted.

It was further reported in an affidavit that Mpisi Trading 74 had requested quotes to fix Mundie's BMW 3-series car, which was involved in an accident early in 2013. Apparently, in an email attached to the affidavit with the subject line 'Quote for Mundie', the panel beater, in La Rochelle south of Johannesburg, was asked for a second quote for the car.

SARS said they were unaware of any corruption charges laid against Mundie, but would 'cooperate with any investigation launched by any law-enforcement agency'.[10] Predictably, nothing came of this either.

Then Moyane's trusted deputy, Jonas Makwakwa, and his SARS-employed lover, Kelly-Anne Elskie, were exposed in the media as having been identified by the Financial Intelligence Centre for a series of suspicious transactions worth over R1,3 million in the years preceding 2016. Makwakwa was only finally suspended by Moyane months later, after this was exposed in the media.

While on suspension, Makwakwa was accused of improperly intervening in a politically laden case concerning Durban-based businesswoman Shauwn Mpisane. He was apparently disciplined as a result, although nobody seems to know exactly how.[11]

Almost a year later, Makwakwa and Elskie were cleared of any wrongdoing by an investigation that looked only at 'labour contraventions', and he returned to work at SARS. It would later transpire that they were still being investigated by the Hawks for alleged corruption and money-laundering but, at the time of writing, nothing had come of this.

In December 2016 civil-rights body Corruption Watch laid criminal charges against Moyane, Makwakwa and Elskie for various matters relating to having contravened the Financial Intelligence Centre Act and corruption allegations. Again, not much seems to have come of this.[12]

And in between all this, media reports told of multiple spats between then Finance Minister Pravin Gordhan and SARS commissioner Tom Moyane, culminating in a press conference during which Moyane complained about how badly the media were treating him.[13] Yet, while the media had been running story after story about the 'rogue unit' for over two years, Moyane's reaction was to express 'shock and awe' at the 'revelations', suspending whomever he chose to.

In late 2016, out of the blue, the then Minister of Finance Pravin Gordhan, former SARS commissioner Oupa Magashula and former deputy SARS commissioner Ivan Pillay were criminally charged by the NPA for an early pension payout dating back to 2013. This was announced with great fanfare by the newly appointed National Director of Public Prosecutions, advocate Shaun Abrahams. Abrahams was adamant that day, and with much indignation, in a much-publicised press conference, expressed how the 'days of disrespecting the decisions of the NPA are over'.

Within days there was a 'hostage drama' at SARS, in which legal adviser Vlok Symington was allegedly held against his will and documents forcibly taken from him by the Hawks. Symington had previously given legal advice on the pension issue, saying the request was proper, and didn't contravene any statute, regulation, SARS rule or provision. He was in possession of the opinion itself – a legal document that was exculpatory evidence in the charges against Gordhan, Pillay and Magashula, and which, if it saw the light of day, would ensure that there was no prospect of convicting any of the three men.

Just 20 days later, NPA boss Abrahams was forced to review the decision and withdraw the case against them.

Soon after, when civil-society bodies Freedom Under Law and the Helen Suzman Foundation decided to ask for the removal of several senior NPA officials because of this mess at the NPA and SARS, Abrahams submitted an affidavit in reply, in which he pointed out that the then head of the Hawks, Berning Ntlemeza, had deliberately withheld material evidence from the NPA, with specific reference to Symington's legal opinion – evidence that, in his view, would've had a dramatic effect on the decision whether to prosecute or not in the first place. This, by the way, is a crime: it's called obstruction of justice. Of course, nothing came of that either.

And the bad news out of SARS kept coming. We came to learn that Kgabo Hlahla, a new acting chief officer at SARS in charge of all IT systems, including e-filing and system refunds, had been dismissed in 2015 for misconduct from his previous job at the Limpopo Department of Health. Later, in early 2018, he was quietly dismissed from the tax authority.[14]

In late 2016, it was reported that the experienced Vusi Ngquluna, the group executive for debt collection, had handed in his resignation. Ngquluna's decision was apparently related to the outsourcing of debt collection to third parties, of which one was a company belonging to Moyane's nephew, Nhlamulo Ndhlela. Insiders with direct knowledge of machinations at SARS reported that some senior staff felt demoralised, sidelined and 'fed up' with the state of affairs at the tax authority.[15]

There was a reported increase in taxpayer complaints regarding the alleged improper delay of refunds, but, in 2017, we learned that the infamous Guptas had no such problem. In fact, it would seem that Moyane had personally intervened to facilitate a massive R70-million VAT refund for the family, despite legal advice against doing so. 'Moyane allegedly intervened and secured the payment to the Guptas. According to sources, the refund was made begrudgingly by SARS staff and left tax employees feeling despondent and angry,' a report noted at the time. [16]

And, indeed, in September 2017, the Tax Ombud found that SARS was delaying paying taxpayers their refunds, calling this a 'serious' problem. The Tax Ombud noted that while the 630 credits from the sample provided by SARS 'may indeed constitute less than 0,01% in terms of numbers, their monetary value is ... a whopping R25,86 billion'.[17]

And yet more experienced staff bled from SARS, with the head of strategic portfolio management George Frost and the head of enterprise quality management James Matthews resigning in 2017.[18]

By this time, SARS and Moyane had come under fire publicly for the loss of critical staff, allegations they denied. But just days later a senior staffer with more than 20 years of experience and who was in charge of cases involving assessments in excess of R3 billion, senior audit manager Lorraine van Esch, resigned. According to media reports, part of the reason for her resignation was 'that managers at the Enforcement Audit Unit[19] wanted auditors to do smaller, more limited-scope audits, and to reduce the complex audits, some of which she was doing'.

It was also reported that in the wake of Van Esch's resignation, one of the most experienced customs investigators at SARS, Kumaren Moodley, had been suspended. Moodley had headed a unit that was busy with numerous investigations into the tobacco industry, among others.[20]

Towards the end 2017, the list of people leaving the institution continued to grow. The head of criminal investigations, Ronel van Wyk, left, and SARS insiders reported that she, too, was a victim of what was now being called 'the Mundie unit'.

The list included Kosie Louw, the longest-serving member of the SARS executive and an internationally renowned tax expert; Matsobane

Matlwa, the chief financial officer; Elle-Sarah Rossato, who'd been in charge of a specialised legal and debt-management team within the enforcement unit; and top tax investigator Azam Khan.[21]

By December 2017, SARS was reported to be behind in its annual target by tens of billions. Moyane nonetheless promised the nation that the target would be met. It wasn't.

By the end of the 2017/18 fiscal year, Treasury had revised the revenue target for SARS downwards by R42 billion, and even then SARS missed the new target by R700 million. (For the fiscal year 2015/16, Treasury had to adjust the revenue target for SARS downwards by a massive R11 billion, and in 2016/17 it was downwardly adjusted by a staggering R22 billion.)

It hardly needs stating that the loss of highly skilled staff and the continued downgrading of revenue targets – among many other signals – weren't indicative of a healthy and fully functioning tax and customs agency. What it came down to was that our Government was growing poorer, meaning it had less money to spend on building new schools, hospitals, infrastructure and housing, funding services, growing the economy, creating jobs and assisting the poor.

I took no pleasure in this bad news: if SARS failed, the country suffered – and it was the poorest of the poor who bore the biggest brunt.

In December 2017, the ANC elected a new president and national executive committee. The deputy president of the ANC and of the country, Cyril Ramaphosa, won by a narrow margin. He and the newly elected party leadership ushered in what quickly came to be known as a 'new dawn' of hope for South Africa.

Following a tense week of speculation and a high-stakes game of political chess between various role players, in February 2018 Jacob Zuma announced his resignation as president of the country with immediate effect. With this, the 'Zuma era' began to draw to a close.

Within days, Ramaphosa was elected the country's new president and sworn in on the same day; a week later he delivered the State of the

Nation address. Overall it was well received. I personally pricked my ears up at a comment in the speech: 'We will … take steps to stabilise and strengthen vital institutions like the South African Revenue Service. … I will shortly appoint a commission of inquiry into tax administration and governance at SARS, to ensure that we restore the credibility of the service and strengthen its capacity to meet its revenue targets.'[22]

Days later, the country's annual and much anticipated Budget Speech was delivered by then Finance Minister Malusi Gigaba. It wasn't good news for the nation. Taxes went up, including VAT for the first time in democratic South Africa.

In his budget speech, Gigaba echoed the new president: 'Tax morality is a crucial component of a healthy democracy. It has taken many years and lots of effort to build the foundation of trust that supports our tax morality. We have seen how quickly that citizens' trust can be eroded by perceptions of poor public governance. … The president has announced his intention to establish a commission of inquiry into tax administration and governance at SARS.'

In early 2018, several media outlets revealed a link between Moyane's nephew's company, Lekgotla Trifecta Collections, which was awarded the botched debt-collection tender, and a company known as Terbium Financial Services, which had apparently acted as a pay agent for the Gupta family (a pay agent is a third party that receives money and pays money on behalf of a person or business). Curiously, it seems Terbium Financial Services, which was never registered as a pay agent as it should have been in law (something SARS should have checked as a rule),[23] had also been the recipient of the questionable Gupta tax refunds from SARS.

There was much protestation from SARS at the time, claiming that the entire Gupta refund process was above board and done properly and in accordance with the law. But as the media began to dig and expose more shenanigans related to this, SARS finally capitulated and bizarrely changed its story. By April 2018, SARS was accusing 'Gupta holding company Oakbay Investments of lying about its banking affairs when it demanded – and controversially received – an unprecedented third-party VAT refund of R70 million last year'.[24]

Within days, more bad news revealed that Makwakwa, Moyane's right-hand man, freshly back from suspension, had sat on a tender bidding committee in which a debt-collection tender had been awarded to a company implicated in the very same Financial Intelligence Centre report that had implicated him (Makwakwa) and Elskie. Parliament jumped in and asked for the records of Makwakwa's disciplinary inquiry, the internal SARS investigation and his tax affairs – a request that Moyane had been resisting for over a year.

SARS ultimately gave in and undertook to provide the information to Parliament, but just a day later, Moyane announced Makwakwa's resignation from the tax authority. Moyane appointed SARS 'old hand' Mark Kingon as Makwakwa's acting replacement.

On 19 March 2018 President Cyril Ramaphosa announced Tom Moyane's immediate suspension, pending a disciplinary inquiry. Ironically, Ramaphosa appointed Kingon, chosen just days earlier by Moyane to be his new number two, as acting commissioner.

In March 2018, it was revealed that Moyane had allegedly instructed a SARS official to commit fraud by feigning illness when called on back in 2015 by KPMG for an interview and thereby avoiding giving testimony. Neither Moyane nor KPMG denied this allegation.[25]

A further R89-million VAT refund to the Guptas, alleged once again to have been made via a third party, was also exposed.[26]

In April 2018, it was reported that the Gupta company Oakbay was allegedly implicated in a R100-million VAT-fraud case, with the State taking action against several people, except Oakbay and the Guptas.[27]

It also emerged that some legal practitioners who'd been acting for SARS had allegedly been having a devil of a time getting paid by the tax authority. Notably, these were lawyers, advocates and curators involved in several high-profile cases, such as those concerning Julius Malema, billionaires Shauwn Mpisane and her husband S'bu, and tobacco magnate Martin Wingate-Pearse. Apparently, SARS had not been paying its bills between 2014 to 2018, which had resulted in these cases being removed from the court rolls and preservation actions being halted.

The cases in question added up to hundreds of millions in lost taxes, and one former SARS official suggested that the payment delays were deliberate, in order to 'sabotage' the cases.[28]

Not a single one of any of these very serious allegations, and many more that I haven't mentioned here, resulted in the types of 'panels' that Magashula, Pillay, others and I had to endure. On the contrary, in many instances, SARS would acknowledge cases being registered with the Hawks but do nothing, or simply keep quiet.

Compare this to the single 'complaint' that caused such a fracas at SARS that it led to no fewer than four questionable 'panels', whose findings were always leaked to the media, and with those affected prohibited from being heard or defending themselves; and the single newspaper article that resulted in a 'panel' looking at Magashula.

Surely, even the most uninformed among us must see these stark contrasts for what they are.

24

Ivan's rugby ball

I've known Ivan Pillay for the greater part of my adult life, from the days before we both worked at SARS. No other person has influenced my personal values and approach to life more than this man. I have the utmost respect for him. He's softly spoken, a deep thinker and a real leader.

His struggle credentials are unquestionable: he's not only dedicated his entire adult life but also sacrificed a significant part of his youth – often under threat of torture and death – to achieving freedom for all and building the future of our nation. He was a part of the ANC and its structures that brought political freedom to all who live in our country.[xix]

Pillay played a pivotal role in post-1994 democratic South Africa, and has also been a loyal and dedicated civil servant in the new dispensation. He ably led us from the beginning of the 'new' SARS back in 1999, until December 2014 when he was forced out.

If credit for the development and ultimate successes of SARS's enforcement capability should go to anyone, it should be him. He gave us direction and guidance, and was always there for all of us. Whether in meetings or in private discussions, he was a tough taskmaster, but he always backed us up when needed.

This incredibly smart man has always been very willing and able to ask for advice from others who might know better. And if someone was out of line, he didn't hesitate to challenge them.

Pillay made a difference as part of the broad collective of the ANC

xix From 1985 to 1991, Pillay was based in Zambia. A member of the central committee of the South African Communist Party and project manager of Operation Vula – the main objectives of which were to smuggle freedom fighters into South Africa and maintain open communication links between the ANC leaders in exile, at home and in prison – he reported directly to ANC president Oliver Tambo.

Government, and as a SARS executive, but he also touched lives at an individual level; he's a much loved and respected person. He's open, honest and straightforward, regardless of who you are or your standing in life. Above all, he's nonjudgemental and humble.

In Pillay's smallish top-floor corner office in A Block, Lehae la SARS, was a picture of a young man. It looked like a passport picture that had been enlarged. It was neatly framed and hung behind the door. The photo was of Krishna Rabilal.

Pillay grew up in Merebank outside Durban, a poverty-stricken area to which Indians were relocated during apartheid. The local high school became a terrain of struggle for the young men of the area, and the first slogans in the area – 'ban apartheid' – were painted there.

In 1974, Pillay, then in his early 20s, was recruited, along with several of his closest friends, including Rabilal, a brilliant student and community activist, into an underground cell. Three years later, Pillay crossed into Swaziland to begin 34 years in exile.[1]

At the same time, Rabilal went to Botswana, where he joined MK, and after undergoing military training in Angola and East Germany, was deployed to Swaziland and Mozambique.

In January 1981 the South African Defence Force of the then apartheid government raided ANC safe houses serving as transit points for MK cadres in Matola, about 15 kilometres from Maputo in Mozambique. During the raid twelve MK members, including Krishna Rabilal, were killed.

Another feature of Pillay's office at Lehae la SARS was a diagram stuck on the wall. Some of us called it 'the rugby ball' on account its appearance: it consisted of two ovals, a larger one, with a smaller one inside it.

The larger 'rugby ball' represented SARS as an institution. Labelled 'higher purpose' – a term that became a common feature of our meetings, planning documents, deliberations and everything else we did at SARS – within it were listed elements such as 'values', 'purpose' and 'integrity'.

The smaller 'rugby ball' represented the individuals working for SARS.

The diagram sought to demonstrate that when an individual's values and integrity were aligned with those of the institution, the institution would function optimally, and the individual would be content.

Pillay is a very forgiving person: he advanced the careers of many, selflessly, even of some who would later turn on him, spreading rumours about him and advancing the 'rogue unit' narrative, but he's never been bitter or vengeful about this. I've often wondered how many of those people who came and went through his office over the years noticed the photo of Rabilal and the 'rugby ball', and understood their significance.

The much-loved and revered Nhlanhla Nene has been reappointed to the Finance Ministry, and I'm certain that the SARS staff cheered at this, as Nene knows SARS well and has walked with many SARS people over the years. He understands the business of SARS and will no doubt be making all the right moves to return the institution to its former glory.

In the days preceding Tom Moyane's suspension in March 2018, rumours made the rounds that Pillay was also going to go back to SARS, to help fix things at the tax authority. There's no doubt that this would have done wonders for SARS, and that he would've been able to help make a difference at a time when it was most needed.

But, of course, the rumours of Pillay's possible return to SARS reached other ears, too – the ears of people who greatly fear such a move. Why? Well, it has to do with the values that Pillay espouses; it's about Ivan's rugby ball.

Pillay would waste no time in reinstituting the true values of SARS. This would mean reviewing the cases that seemed to have dropped off the radar, including those involving the Guptas, politically exposed people, and a host of others. It would cause some internal reflection at SARS, and a reconsideration and investigation of events at the tax authority after Moyane took over. And there are some people who just can't allow that to happen.

It's little wonder, then, that on 9 March 2018, 18 months after we'd been called by the Hawks to make 'warning statements', summonses were served on the former head of the old Special Projects Unit, Andries Janse van Rensburg, Ivan Pillay and me, for alleged events dating back to over ten years ago.

At the time of writing, we've all appeared in the Tshwane Regional Magistrate's Court, where we were released on warning. We're due back in court in June 2018, when the matter will probably be remanded again.

The net effect? Pillay can't go back to SARS until the matter is resolved.

Epilogue

Flashback

On 28 May 2014, two days after the SARS tax settlement with Malema became public, I emailed a woman I'd dated for a few months, warning her of media enquiries about her and me, and letting her know how I intended to respond.

In her reply, this woman – a lawyer – effectively accused me of unlawfully sharing taxpayer information with her about Julius Malema, Jacob Zuma and British American Tobacco, the largest publicly traded tobacco company in the world, which operates its eighth-largest factory globally in Heidelberg, south of Johannesburg; she also accused me of using her to gain unlawful access to her clients' confidential affairs. She copied in various senior managers at SARS.

In doing this, she cracked ajar a door at the tax authority that would soon be kicked wide open by a range of people who had axes to grind and scores to settle.

I've always maintained, and presented clear evidence in support, that the reasons why she reacted in this manner were quite simple. First, she needed to discredit me, SARS and a few people there, and specifically evidence that implicated her, a number of high-ranking State officials in law enforcement and intelligence agencies, and the tobacco industry in acts of racketeering, bribery, fraud, corruption, derailing SARS investigations and money-laundering, to name a few.

Second, on the day before her 'complaint', she tried to extort money from me, suggesting I should somehow get SARS to pay her for information. In a threatening tone, she texted this to me, stating that if I didn't 'seriously consider' it, she would go public with all our text exchanges from prior months. I told her to do what she wanted, and said I wouldn't be blackmailed by her.

At the time and at my insistence via a lawyer's letter, she undertook to provide her allegations to SARS under oath, and to supply SARS with copies of all emails and text exchanges between us, although she never did this.

I wish to be very clear here, because many people, including her and some at SARS, would later suggest that on that day, she 'exposed' the 'rogue unit'. She did no such thing: in that email, she made absolutely no mention of any unit at SARS. She only climbed onto that bandwagon months later, during August and September 2014, when she and others (including Michael Peega) began to collaborate in attacking SARS and me.

In June 2014, she was afforded another opportunity to add to her 'complaint' and she didn't hold back. The list of accusations against me grew, but she made absolutely no allegation against the High-risk Investigations Unit – she didn't even mention it and most certainly said no word of a 'rogue unit'. When asked to place her allegations under oath at this time, she refused.

By then it had become public knowledge that she'd been an agent of the State Security Agency before I met her, and that she'd been instructed to infiltrate me, and had even surreptitiously recorded me from the very first day we met. Some people in the tobacco industry and media had known that she was a spy, and that she was secretly recording me, since at least February 2014, when she confessed to them about this. None said a word of this, either at the time or when her 'complaint' landed at SARS.

The woman's allegations against me were false and defamatory. She never did describe precisely what 'taxpayer information' I'd supposedly unlawfully shared with her, and in the four processes that were subsequently instituted as a result of her allegations, she never went under oath or allowed herself to be subjected to cross-examination.

I asked SARS to treat the matter as a domestic dispute, and leave it to the woman and me to resolve between ourselves. However, probably because some of those copied in on the email happened to have their own beef with me, on the insistence of one manager at SARS, they decided to consider it a formal complaint.

As soon as her 'complaint' gained traction, there was no stopping the many others waiting in the wings who saw this as a great opportunity for their own nefarious agendas. And with other enemies joining the fray, the allegations grew lives of their own, continuously adapting and changing as people began to collaborate with each other.

During the period in which the first of the ensuing SARS 'panels' functioned, from June to August 2014, this woman suddenly 'remembered' a whole lot more information: I was a spy (she lied about having a secret recording, which she claimed was of me boasting that I'd used her as a 'source for SARS'); I owned secret shares in a wine farm; I'd conspired to assault her (an allegation that dated back to a time before I'd even met her); I was likened to a paedophile; I was mentally ill; I was an alcoholic; and I was unfit to hold my position at SARS.

Others joined in with new stories of their own, using these platforms to hammer away at me and others at SARS. Some of those who began to participate in this propaganda were SARS officials; others had already left SARS, several under a cloud; and yet others came from law-enforcement agencies, the intelligence fraternity and (predictably) from within the tobacco industry.

And still more allegations followed: I'd conspired with local cigarette-manufacturing company Amalgamated Tobacco Manufacturing to bring criminal complaints against a member of a multi-agency illicit-tobacco task team; a fundraising club with which I was associated had received irregular donations; I'd conspired with a State Security Agency member to threaten her and her family, and had illegally intercepted and monitored her communications; and I'd conspired with tobacco manufacturer Carnilinx to bring an interdict application against her and British American Tobacco in exchange for tax leniency.

The list was endless, and her 'complaint' morphed and adapted over time to such an extent that her original allegations finally fell by the wayside.

She sued both SARS and me, for R10 million and R2 million, respectively, in 2014.

Although the Kanyane panel found this woman's allegations against me to be without foundation and unsupported by evidence, soon enough, in August 2014, following exchanges between the woman and the *Sunday Times*, the allegations grew even more outrageous. She now 'recalled' how I'd advanced criminal activities and the agendas of criminals, and caused criminals to contact her and threaten her; I was an apartheid-era spy; my promotions at SARS hadn't been earned; and I'd unlawfully shared confidential SARS information with certain journalists. Even at this point, however, she still had made no mention of a 'rogue unit'.

Soon enough, with various parties attacking SARS and me, some in open collaboration with each other and others joining in the bullying for their own ends, it became the pretext for what I believe was a much larger political campaign.

Remember, it was also around this time that the Hawks and the Independent Police Investigative Directorate (an oversight body that conducts investigations of identified criminal offences allegedly committed by members of the SAPS and the Municipal Police Services, and makes appropriate recommendations) were also under a siege that carried the same hallmarks as that besetting SARS. There'd be an 'allegation', which would feature prominently in the media; a 'probe' or 'panel' would follow; 'findings' would result; and soon enough the heads and senior staff would be suspended or leave. Quietly, over at the State Security Agency, directors-general were replaced, and at the boards of our state-owned enterprises, the coffers were thrown open wide with the appointments of new and 'compliant' board members.

It was from around October 2014 that the screaming *Sunday Times* headlines became progressively more ludicrous, and that more people joined forces to smear me and, ultimately, SARS as an institution, Gordhan, Pillay, Richer and a host of other innocent people. The media always quoted 'former and current SARS officials' and 'intelligence officers' as their sources.

By then, SARS had supposedly run a 'rogue intelligence unit', which had broken into then President Zuma's home and planted listening devices there; the former head of this unit was blackmailing SARS about this bugging and was supposedly paid over R6 million to keep quiet about it; the unit had spent hundreds of millions of rands buying new homes and cars, as well as expensive spying equipment used to illegally intercept taxpayers' communications and unlawfully spy on politicians and other top State personnel; the unit was involved in the deaths of former colleagues; we used a brothel as a front company ... This list, too, was endless.

The Sikhakhane panel made startling findings against me without even bothering to hear from me on these false allegations.

And the allegations kept piling up. By February 2015, the woman had miraculously recalled yet more fantastical 'information' – including that I'd conspired to manipulate elections in South Africa, and that the fundraising club was a 'front' for the 'rogue unit'. She had no qualms in openly accusing Pravin Gordhan of acting unlawfully.

The Kroon advisory board and the KPMG 'investigation' functioned for the entirety of 2015. Neither bothered to hear me before judging me.

By 2016, I was being accused by the woman of having stolen documents from SARS and sold them to the media to embarrass State agencies; of causing people to lay false criminal complaints with the police; of having done work for giant audit firm PricewaterhouseCoopers; of owning property in Cape Town which was somehow untoward; and of receiving payments totalling R600 000 from someone being investigated by SARS.

All hocus pocus.

In the meantime, the civil suit brought by the woman in 2014 dragged on. Every now and then it would flare up, with the plaintiff threatening my lawyers, and, of course, resulting in further legal costs to me.

In a rather fascinating turn of events, which seems to have gone largely unnoticed and which I publicly reveal here for the first time, this woman went under oath in 2015 before a High Court, pointing out several factual errors made by the Sikhakhane panel in its report, for instance, its finding that I met with her alone at our first meeting in September 2013, which was against SARS policy.[1] She pointed out, correctly, that I had, in fact, been accompanied by another senior manager from SARS.

She also admitted to having lied to SARS about having a recording on which I boasted that she was a source for me.

And, shockingly, she claimed under oath to have acted as the attorney of record for tobacco magnate Martin Wingate-Pearse in an old tax dispute with SARS, when she hadn't; she hadn't even been a candidate or admitted attorney at the time. She only started representing tobacco manufacturer Carnilinx, of which he was a director, to a very limited extent, several years later.[2]

Another shocking affidavit compiled by her, dated April 2015, also surfaced. In this one, she admitted to having breached her fiduciary duties to her clients, including Wingate-Pearse, unlawfully selling their confidential information to British American Tobacco for thousands of pounds, and participating in corruption, fraud and money-laundering.

It didn't stop there. Even SARS would claim as fact that in early 2015 she made fraudulent representations on behalf of then London-based listed company Lonrho and subsidiary Rollex to the NPA concerning tobacco smugglers; created a paper trail showing that Carnilinx 'owed R20m less in tax than was truly due'; suggested to Crime Intelligence officer Hennie Niemann that imported tobacco should be recorded as 'waste' to defraud SARS for a scheme to gather intelligence; corrupted a SARS official in Alberton in order to obtain a confidential SARS report setting out why licences granted to Carnilinx should be withdrawn; and participated in a proposed scheme named Project Robin to dupe the State Security Agency into accepting that a smuggling ring was a front for collecting intelligence. But, aside from saying so, neither SARS nor any other law-enforcement agency has ever done anything about this.

And it gets even more interesting. It turns out that between 2008, when she was still a candidate attorney, and until at least 2014, she acted as legal counsel in another tobacco-manufacturers' matter for the very forensic-investigative department of KPMG that compiled the SARS report, and was paid by KPMG for her services. Neither she nor KPMG disclosed this to SARS at the time when KPMG conducted its 'review' of events wherein which she was one of the dramatis personae.

It seems that an advocate of the Pretoria Bar Council became so concerned about these blurred lines back in 2008 that he wrote a 37-page opinion on the matter, and requested the Bar Council permission to report the matter to the NPA. The Bar Council, in its wisdom, sent a copy of the opinion to the woman, whose response was to launch an attack on the advocate, accusing him of, among other things, sexual harassment.

When the time came for her to testify at his disciplinary case, she declined to, on the grounds that 'too much time had passed'. But the man's career had by then been destroyed. And, needless to say, the complaint never reached the NPA.

Using much the same modus operandi, in 2013, she laid a 'complaint' on behalf of a 'client' against a very respectable SARS official who was ultimately found not guilty at a disciplinary trial. What SARS didn't know at the time, but what I can now prove, is that the 'client' who laid the 'complaint' was in fact never a client of hers, and that he was manipulated into laying the 'complaint' – he later confessed to me about this.

I have a list of people whose lives have been destroyed over the years in much the same manner.

What's more, KPMG was appointed auditor of British American Tobacco in 2015 – during the time that the auditing firm was busy with the SARS matter.

All this likely explains why nothing was mentioned by KPMG about the money-laundering, corruption and fraud that implicated the lawyer and British American Tobacco – and they had the gall to suggest that I was conflicted!

Thursday 25 August 2016

My time had finally come to face the CATS unit of the Hawks. My lawyers, Robert Levin and Bradley Thomas, were already in the office where the interview was to take place.

It had been more than a year and a half since I'd left SARS in as amicable circumstances as were possible at the time: in February 2015, SARS and I had basically agreed to part ways because I no longer fitted into the plans for the future of the organisation under Moyane.

Had I known how very unwanted I was when the new boss, Tom Moyane, had started there in October 2014, I would've just packed my bags and left. But that was not to be. Instead, I was relentlessly publicly humiliated, battered and bruised by one salacious and wild allegation after another. I was never given the opportunity to be heard or asked to respond to the allegations or allowed to defend myself publicly. Week after week, the *Sunday Times* carried sensational and untrue stories about me, usually accompanied by a picture of Ivan Pillay and me.

Now, finally, the Hawks had written to my lawyers, telling them that their investigation was complete, and saying that I had to provide them with a 'warning statement', which is usually the last step prior to submitting the evidence to the NPA for a decision whether to prosecute. In their letter, the Hawks accused me of having been corruptly involved in a fundraiser, and having contravened State intelligence legislation, specifically by managing the High-risk Investigations Unit, the so-called 'rogue unit', from 2010 onwards.

My attorneys and I agreed to hear out the Hawks and play by the rules. My view was that I was innocent and had nothing to fear.

I was also very keen to hear how we'd supposedly broken into homes, including Zuma's, and illegally intercepted taxpayers' communications; to find out where exactly the SARS brothel was located and who operated it; to learn more about the hundreds of millions in slush funds we'd supposedly spent on new homes and cars, and about the politicians we'd supposedly infiltrated and conducted lifestyle audits on – and about many of the other allegations that had by then been floating around.

The Hawks had only a few questions, most of which, curiously, required answers from me that they could very easily have obtained by simply examining public records, obtaining details from SARS or going onto the internet; very few of the questions concerned the 'rogue unit'. The thought crossed my mind that no prosecutor worth their salt could've seen and approved the questions; they would've just laughed them off.

I must say that I was dying to ask them whether they'd investigated those who were behind the smear campaign that had caused such harm to SARS, since those were real crimes against the State, but I bit my tongue and just listened. I realised fairly quickly that it must have dawned on the Hawks that all the stories were false.

Why they'd never thought it worth pursuing investigations into those who'd caused harm to SARS was no mystery to me, in any event. It was simple: they knew by then who the perpetrators were, and it was part of something more sinister unfolding; or they just didn't care.

The Hawks refused to give us a copy of the few questions they posed to me, and we were denied permission to record the meeting. My attorneys therefore carefully wrote down each question, and the conversations around them, and we asked for some time to consider the questions before we decided how best to complete the warning statement. I asked to be given until 15 September, to allow me some time to seek records from SARS, but they said no, that I had to get back to them by no later than 5 September because the case docket had to 'urgently' go to the NPA for a decision.

By agreement, at that meeting we completed only a portion of the warning-statement form in which my rights ('anything you say may be used against you …' etc.) were put to me and the specific allegations recorded, and I signed the incomplete document.

That very weekend, without waiting for my response, the NPA and the Hawks announced that the case docket had been handed to the prosecuting authority for consideration.

My lawyers immediately wrote to both the NPA and the Hawks, confirming the exact allegations against me and providing a list of the exculpatory evidence I would need to obtain from SARS in order to consider the questions I had yet to answer.

We never got a response.

Monday 10 July 2017

By early 2017, I was ready to go to court to expose the woman who was suing me, and everybody else behind the 'rogue unit' campaign. By then, a human-rights body had agreed to fund my case, provided that I didn't settle with the plaintiff. Their intentions were likely the same as mine: I wanted to air everything and anything relevant that I'd never been allowed to say publicly, or which I had said but which had just been swept under the carpet by the SARS 'panels' and the Hawks.

Then, in July 2017, SARS served me with a copy of an action it was bringing against the woman, to force her to proceed with the matter in court or argue against our respective objections. A telling extract in the SARS affidavit caught my eye. It quoted a letter from the plaintiff's lawyer admitting that she had no intention of pursuing the matter against SARS, and that the case was the only way of maintaining 'some sort of hold' over me, although precisely what 'hold' this was is anybody's guess. This was most certainly an absolute abuse of our courts although, to date, no action has been taken by the Law Society of South Africa or the Law Society of the Northern Provinces, which have oversight over her as a lawyer.

A few days later, a letter from her attorney arrived, acknowledging that the situation had placed both of us and our families in danger, and exposed us to criminals. It asked that I consider accepting her withdrawing the action, with all parties carrying their own costs. This time, it was I who didn't bother to reply; I decided to wait and see what would follow. I hoped that she would amend her claim so that I could file my plea and counter-suit against her.

On 10 July 2017, notice was served on my attorneys advising them that 'the plaintiff hereby withdraws the action instituted against the first [SARS] and second defendant [me] and tenders payment of their [SARS and my] costs to date hereof.'

I have since asked my attorneys to determine the costs I incurred in the process, which I'm allowed in law to claim back from her, and I presume SARS will have done the same for their costs incurred. Our difficulty in serving papers on her and collecting the costs is going to be compounded by the fact that she appears to no longer be registered as an attorney at the Law Society of the Northern Provinces, and I have no idea where in the world she is nowadays.

As for the Hawks and NPA looking at her and her cohorts' misdeeds, which include prima-facie evidence of improperly influencing SARS, the State Security Agency and the NPA, running interference in SARS investigations and profiting from this, racketeering, fraud, corruption and money-laundering, well, I suppose that they're not very interested in those matters either. What I do know, because I have evidence, is that she was (unlawfully) kept up to date with the investigation as it progressed by a specific Hawks official.

As an important aside, I've added up the direct losses to the taxpayer thanks to this woman and her compatriots over the years. Here's a quick breakdown of the ones for which I have incontestable evidence although there are, of course, more: there's a R50-million Lonrho-Rollex case that was manipulated and the money never recovered; another case cost the taxpayer over R25 million (not R20 million as SARS would claim) after she created a paper trail to deceive SARS; and yet another amounts to a staggering loss of over R600 million, where she also assisted a client to create offshore money-laundering mechanisms. The SARS official who was bribed is still at his post.

If SARS really wanted to make up for that under-recovery of R700 million in the 2017/18 fiscal year, they'd only have had to look to one person.[3]

Friday 9 March 2018

On the morning of 9 March 2018, after a year and a half of silence, I received a call from the Hawks. They were at my gate and wished to serve a summons on me.

The summons instructed me to appear before the Tshwane Regional Magistrate's Court on 9 April 2018, on charges of having 'agreed, approved or allowed, directly or indirectly' an amount of 'approximately R100 000' to a former member of the old Special Projects Unit, Helgaard Lombard, at an unspecified time and place, 'between August and September 2008'.

The summons named me as 'Accused Number 3'; my co-accused were Ivan Pillay and Andries Janse van Rensburg.

The summons itself was incredibly badly drafted: among other errors, it got my first and second names and surname wrong; my home address was wrong; and the annexures were misnumbered.

The allegations are utter nonsense, and that's all I'll say about them at this juncture.

On the very next Monday, 12 March 2018, my lawyers wrote to the NPA to raise the issue that the NPA had not sought nor considered my version or defence on the matter before deciding to prosecute me, as the Constitution and the NPA's own prosecution policy require, and to seek an explanation of the time lapse of over a year and a half since the investigation had been completed.

The NPA apparently responded, noting that they would allow me to make representations to them to reconsider their decision to prosecute me. Their reply letter was dated 14 March, signed by NPA special director Torie Pretorius on 17 March, and dispatched on 16 March; on top of this, the letter never arrived because it was sent to a nonexistent email address.

My lawyers sent another letter on 23 March, stating that if the NPA did not reply this time, I intended to approach the High Court urgently seeking to set aside their decision and delay the court summons.

We served urgent court papers on the NPA just before 16h00 on 28 March 2018.

Finally, the NPA replied to my lawyers' letters, on 28 March 2018 – but this time they sent their email not to the business email address clearly displayed on the correspondence, but to the email address of the law firm's marketing department, and only after my having served my urgent application on them, after business hours.

So it wasn't until the Sunday, 1 April, that we finally received the NPA's opposing papers to the urgent application, and only then did I finally read the two previous letters, which they'd attached as annexures.

Long story short, the NPA agreed to give us access to their complete case docket and allow us to make representations to them, which they would consider, and in return, we agreed to remove the urgent application from the court roll.

Monday 9 April 2018

I suffered in silence through the four 'panels' because I didn't want to cause any further harm to SARS and the Government than had already been caused by others. I stayed silent and swallowed everything thrown at me, through every smear campaign and article that ran in the media over the years, and through the Hawks investigations against me.

What I could publicly state, I did in the book *Rogue*, and through a few media releases and subsequent answers. But I was largely hamstrung in trying to defend myself because of taxpayer confidentiality and other similar laws. I just tried to get on with my life.

So I would've thought that having had my name splashed across television and media headlines as a 'rogue', been treated the way I had been by the 'panels', the 'day of the warning statements', and everything else that followed would've toughened me up for this day. It hadn't.

On Monday 9 April the humiliation continued as I took the stand next to my co-accused, Ivan Pillay and Andries Janse van Rensburg.

The magistrate's first question to NPA prosecutor Sello Maema was why the NPA was asking us to pay bail of R5 000 each when we'd complied with its summons to appear in court. Maema was unable to answer meaningfully.

The magistrate released us on warning and postponed the case to June, for the matter to be referred to the High Court, when we will appear again.

The financial burden and reputational harm caused by these events, and the psychological damage they caused me and my family, will never be remedied.

The future

I suspect there's still a long road ahead of us.

An obvious question is, if the Hawks and the NPA were so sure that I was guilty as charged, why did they not put questions to me regarding these allegations back in August 2016, when the Hawks first asked me to complete a warning statement – or, in fact, at any time over the next eighteen months? Why wait for more than a year and a half before deciding to prosecute me?

And why had they not bothered to first seek answers from me on the charges that they suddenly, a year and a half later, decided to prosecute me on? What if I had evidence that completely exonerated me?

And, finally, why did they choose to maintain, under oath, that they had, in fact, considered my version or defence on the new charges, when they'd done no such thing?

Make no mistake, if such a practice by our law-enforcement agencies is allowed uncontested, the South African public should be scared – very scared. It would mean that your worst enemy could lay a false complaint against you with the Hawks at any time; that the Hawks could pretend to seek to hear your version by asking you to complete a warning statement but then not wait for you to answer any questions, and ignore you when you ask them to hear you; they could then hand the case docket to the NPA, and years could go by before an NPA prosecutor could simply arbitrarily decide to prosecute you – on a totally different false allegation – while pretending that your version and defence have been considered, while also declining to hear you. In such circumstances, you would have no choice but to appear in court, incur costs and suffer humiliation.

It wasn't that long ago, before 1994, in the apartheid years, that supposedly eminent persons – officers of the courts, magistrates, medical doctors and experts, prosecutors and police officials – collaborated, with absolute impunity, to cover up the torture and murder of anti-apartheid activists in detention, in supposedly legally constituted inquests and court cases. Don't for a moment think that this can't happen again.

The Hawks and the NPA failed to deal with me fairly and procedurally. In particular, senior NPA advocates Torie Pretorius, Sibongile Mzinyathi and Sello Maema seemed uninterested in my version or defence of anything, least of all the allegations and charges on which they've decided to prosecute me. They've all gone under oath and stated that they have indeed considered my version and defence of the allegations and charges I face, and have also stated that the Hawks did indeed seek such of me prior to deciding to prosecute me.

I contest this in its totality. Neither the Hawks nor the NPA have ever given me the opportunity to answer any questions relating to the allegations and charges on which I'm now being prosecuted – and I can assure you that they will be unable to produce any evidence that they did so. I have no doubt that had they done so, they wouldn't have decided to charge me.

Now, finally, it seems, my time to challenge and expose matters openly in a truly independent public forum has arrived, and the public will come to know the whole truth.

I don't want to give away my case here, but I can tell you this much: I suspect that my list of witnesses is going to cause quite a stir, and I think that quite a few of them will by now know, or at least suspect, that I intend serving subpoenas on them. I am certain that, for some of them, life in the witness box is going to be a rather interesting experience.

I am innocent, and I will fight this case to the end.

Addendum 1

Extracts from Jacob Zuma's affidavit for review application submitted to Pietermaritzburg High Court on 23 June 2008

I now deal with the counts in the indictment relating to violations of the provisions of the Income Tax Act 58 of 1962 as amended.

These charges typify the improper convict Zuma at all costs 'leitmotif' which permeates the NPA's prosecution of myself. Should an application for a permanent stay become necessary this issue shall be vigorously pursued. In the application to set aside the search and seizure warrants I have already denounced the extension of the official investigation against me, allegedly on 8 August 2005 …

However, given the limited ambit of this application it is only necessary to refer to one aspect of the history and context of the alleged tax offences. The core of the averments regarding the so-called tax offences was summarised by Du Plooy, the NPA's deponent in its ex parte application for the search warrants as follows:

Addendum, Volume 8, p602, para 37.2 (d):

'The investigation regarding these offences was recently declared. The offences arise from the payments to or on behalf of Jacob Zuma by Schabir Shaik and/or the Nkobi group and/or Thomson/Thales. It is obvious from all the above that the payments were corrupt benefits bestowed upon Zuma in expectation of a quid pro quo. In this sense they were income earned by Zuma. There is a reasonable suspicion that they were not declared to the South African Revenue Service as required or to Parliament, particularly as it was Shaik's defence that his payments to Zuma were loans.'

In short, the contention was that Zuma should have declared the monies received from Shaik as a taxable benefit and probably did not do so. It is self-evident that these monies were not declared as income or a benefit by Zuma – in short he did not declare these as income and hence as bribes. Whether the income tax provisions were contravened or not, depended on whether the essential charge of corruption succeeded or not. If it did, it followed almost inevitably that the said provisions were contravened and vice versa.

With the greatest respect, this was an ancillary consequence of the corruption charges since 2001 when Zuma was first specifically intensively and officially investigated by the NPA.

The issue I wish to highlight is that in conjunction with the denouncement of the tax fraud investigation the following point was made by Zuma in the warrant application litigation after stating that he obviously had not declared the monies as income because the payments were not bribes: Zuma's founding affidavit: 'The allegations concerning fraud and contraventions of the Income Tax Act are apparently based on an allegation that I did not declare moneys allegedly received from Shaik or Shaik companies as income in the form of bribes to the SARS and Parliament. Analysis does not in any way ameliorate the patent absurdity of this approach.'

Para 58: 'SARS has the capacity to prosecute tax offenders and frequently does so. It has a battery of specific statutory provisions operating in its favour in this regard. I am advised and respectfully submit that it is, with respect, highly unusual for charges of misstating income to SARS to be prosecuted in the High Court by members of the first respondent's office. The accusation of a failure to declare the proceeds of robbery and theft could be levelled at just about everyone prosecuted in the High Court for theft or robbery during the past 20 years. I know of no such prosecution.'

Para 59: 'There is no allegation in Du Plooy's affidavit of any complaint by SARS in respect of the alleged fraud or contravention of the Income Tax Act. The respondents are challenged to produce such a complaint. A similar challenge is made in respect of the alleged declarations to Parliament.'

The NPA's answer was the following:

Para 36: '(a) A broad statement of the allegations concerning fraud and the contravention of the Income Tax Act is contained in paragraph 37.2 of du Plooy's affidavit in support of the warrants. Save as is consistent with that statement, paragraph 57 is denied.

(b) (i) The allegations made in the first three sentences of paragraph 58 are disputed. Tax offences are prosecuted by specialist prosecutors in the employ of the NPA. There are no statutory provisions affecting such prosecutions, but there are statutory provisions which operate in respect of tax investigations in favour of SARS.

(ii) The remaining allegations in paragraph 58 are not disputed. However, the first applicant himself points out that this is not an everyday case.

(c) The alleged contraventions of the Income Tax Act are integrally connected with the other charges being investigated, which fall outside the domain of a SARS investigation. In any event, the respondents remain obliged to investigate offences which fall within their mandate. In terms of Section 28(1)(c) of the Act, the Investigating Director may at any time during the conducting of an investigation, if he considers it desirable to do so in the interests of the administration of justice or in the public interest, extend the investigation so as to include any offence, whether or not it is a specified offence, which he or she suspects to be connected with the subject of the investigation.

(d) Whilst it is correct that no complaints have been received of the sort which the respondents are challenged to produce, the respondents remain obliged to prosecute crime where it comes to their attention. I accordingly respectfully submit that paragraph 59 is irrelevant.'

The NPA accepted herein that there was no complainant in respect of these charges. There is still no complaint from SARS in respect of these counts. The NPA is on an improper frolic of its own.

It is clear that the one entity which can readily determine in the event of a successful prosecution on the corruption charges or otherwise whether there was a contravention of the provisions of the Income Tax Act, would be SARS. They would have all the documentation and other evidence to establish what a tax payer declared or should have declared etc. unhampered by secrecy provisions of the Income Tax Act.

Clearly, SARS was not only the true complainant if there was to be a complainant, but on any basis it was a party with a very real and particular interest in any decision to prosecute or not to prosecute a person under the provisions of the Income Tax Act.

I have thus been advised that it is self-evident that SARS is the entity which is to determine whether a taxpayer is to be prosecuted and the extent to which the individual is to be prosecuted under the provisions of the Income Tax Act. The function of SARS to recover monies from tax-payers could otherwise be severely interfered with. It was wholly improper and unlawful of the NPA to institute such prosecutions under the Income Tax Act, without the necessary consultations and go ahead from SARS. Full legal argument will be advanced on this aspect.

It is contended that the NPA was very well aware of this. It was well aware of the fact that I had been in discussions with SARS in connection with my tax affairs. It was well aware that SARS would not have agreed to such prosecution and would indeed in all probability have been opposed to this. Its conduct in seeking a search and seizure warrant from Ngoepe JP of the TPD, in respect of SARS records demonstrates this. The NPA's conduct further blatantly ignored the Constitutional injunction in Section 41 of the Constitution, especially sub-sections (e), (f), (g) and (h).

The truth of the matter is that my legal representatives, and particularly my attorney, Mr Michael Hulley, have for some years now had discussions and negotiations to regularise my income tax affairs vis-à-vis SARS. I have been advised by my legal representatives to do so for it is the right thing to do for a person in my position and political role. I have been advised that even if I consider certain monies not to be income in my hands, to accept a globular assessment in this regard so as to ensure that my political enemies would not have any reason to make political capital out of my income tax affairs. I have accepted this advice. Needless to say, the Prosecution's case against me was a considerable complicating factor in the negotiations which followed.

In the end the dispute between myself and SARS was resolved with a large amount being paid to settle the amount of SARS's assessment. I can thus gratefully testify that the entire dispute between SARS and myself has been resolved, and SARS's claim has been settled in full. In this regard I point out that I had always, in the discussions with SARS, indicated my acceptance of any duly estimated amount of income tax. I point out that the amount assessed did not invoke any tax amnesty such as had been extended in the past to thousands of South Africans.

I have little doubt that the NPA has, throughout, been aware of the discussions between my representatives and the representatives of SARS. I refer to Section 73 of the Prevention of Organised Crime Act No 121 of 1998. The NPA has indeed been prying into my every financial affair for the past 7 years at least and indeed resorted to spying on me using intelligence gathering methods not authorised by any competent body. The absence of any consultation and the absence of seeking any representations from me (and my legal representatives) and SARS evident from the history of the litigation between myself and the NPA, come as no surprise.

The negotiations and settlement concluded between SARS and myself in terms of Section 88E of the Income Tax Act has been recorded in writing. The terms thereof are clearly confidential. I annex, however, a letter from Mr Hulley's office ('01') and the reply from SARS ('02') which confirms receipt of the payment of the amount assessed and the existence and basic outline of the agreement. The settlement was reached without any admission of criminal conduct on my part and on the basis that it disposes of and resolves all liability in respect of the said tax issues – both criminal and civil liability. There is with respect, no issue of criminal liability in this regard, left.

If the NDPP had at any time called for representations before the December 2007 decision, he would no doubt have been apprised both by myself and SARS that the negotiations had been ongoing for a number of years and that they were in an advanced state of reaching settlement. For reasons which I submit are obvious, the NPA simply deliberately refused to hear such representations.

Addendum 2

From: Gary Naidoo <gary@...co.za>
Date: 15 November 2013 at 17:35:29 SAST
To: Atul Gupta <atul@tnamedia.co.za>
Subject: Bloemfontein Sars

Hi Sir

I was given some info by my investigative contact that SARS was investigating the President.
While he was in the Free State this week he met someone from form SARS who mentioned that they are not investigating the President but rather people close to him. According to them is the following people:

1. Chief Douglas Zondo from Vryheid. He apparently had a contract to build part of Nkandla. His wife, daughter and son are also under investigation and they claim he owes SARS around R48m.
2. The Guptas
3. A Mr Parak from the Newcastle area
4. A Mr Mohamed from Durban or Pietermaritzburg who is apparently close to the KZN ANC structures and to the President.

The people mentioned below are part of the SARS investigation team who are based in Bloemfontein.

- Johann van Loggenberg
- [Names of other SARS officials redacted by author]

Regards

Gary Naidoo
Managing Editor, TNA Media (Pty) Ltd.

From: Atul Gupta <atul@...co.za>
Sent on: Friday, November 15, 2013 9:55:36 PM
To: Tony Gupta<tony@sahara.co.za>
Subject: Fwd: Bloemfontein Sars
FYI
Atul Gupta

Addendum 3

On 28 January 2016, someone sent an email anonymously to several media houses. A journalist gave me a copy because he wanted me to try and identify the author. I knew immediately who it was but declined to name the person out of concern for their safety. Because I couldn't verify the email or attribute it to a specific person, its contents were never made public.

Here, I publish this email publicly for the first time. I do so partly because of who it comes from and in honour of this person; and partly because, in a succinct way, it does sum up the climate at SARS over the years, and the unimpeachable character of Ivan Pillay in particular.

From: indefenceofsars <indefenceofsars@...com>
Date: 28 January 2016 at 7:38:07 PM GMT+1
Subject: In defence of Ivan and Johann

As a one-time colleague of both Ivan Pillay and Johann van Loggerenberg, I can no longer watch their reputations being tarnished and their lives ruined without at least contributing this cautionary tale.

They will both tell you they have feet of clay, and are open about their respective weaknesses (Ivan, perhaps for being a reluctant leader who prefers to work behind the scenes, and Johann, carrying the burden of a secretive past).

In their time at SARS they certainly made many enemies – many voices who would happily whisper rumours, and many voices who would be happy to see their fall from grace. No doubt they would have found their way to at least one of the various bodies that were tasked to investigate allegations of impropriety.

Indeed, many people in SARS had good reason to doubt, dislike and disapprove of them. They represented everything that criminal investigators hated. When they started at SARS, they were outsiders with no proven experience in formal criminal investigations, coming in to take over an empire of traditionally white male investigators who had gotten used a particular paradigm of operating. In this old-school paradigm, criminal investigators got to choose who to investigate, how often to investigate them and what for, using fluid processes, and not being held truly accountable for the outcomes. They represented an old-boys' club, and did not take kindly to the 'anti-establishment' duo that came to clean up. Because between them Johann and Ivan radically changed the way criminal investigations worked – over time, investigation cases were selected automatically, by an objective risk-profiling system, and randomly assigned to investigators, who were now required to use a structured investigations process, and who were being increasingly held accountable for the outcomes of cases.

Between them, Ivan and Johann not only changed the process of criminal investigations – they changed the entire philosophy behind how tax compliance risk should be managed, with what they called a 'comprehensive compliance approach'. Today, the approach they touted is widely accepted by modern tax administrations around the world: that taxpayer compliance is achieved through a balance of education, engagement, communication, service and enforcement – and that the threat of punitive action is not the only way of changing taxpayer behaviour. This was a radical departure for especially the criminal investigators and auditors at SARS, many of whom continue to believe in a command-and-control approach to securing compliance. The idea that simply engaging with taxpayers could change their attitudes and behaviours was anathema, and many viewed Ivan and Johann as heretics.

They also managed to alienate many of the lawyers at SARS. Lawyers in a bureaucracy by their very nature prefer stability and certainty. Many of them were equally cynical of the idea of engaging with taxpayers. Many of them were simply confounded by the idea that there could be a different way of applying or interpreting legislation. An example: income-tax legislation allows for making an 'estimated assessment'. It also allows for making an 'agreed assessment'. When Johann convinced drug dealers and gun smugglers to make payments against 'agreed estimated assessments', he was decried as unethical, for surely this construct had no basis in law. (If you have ever audited a drug dealer, you will know that they tend to not keep accurate records – certainly not to show a tax auditor. If you can think of a better way to assess the three million drug dealers you would like to tax, write a paper.)

It didn't help that they did not fit the profile of a typical criminal investigator. They are both profoundly deep thinkers, philosophers, humanitarians, with a real desire to leave the world a little better than they found it. This made them, in some ways, un-relatable. It does not, however, make them bad people.

Below the surface, of course, were the turf wars – if intelligence units in the police and the National Intelligence Agency were not cleaning up money laundering and other dirty dealings, SARS had the guts to fill the void. In the process they almost certainly stepped on some very big spy toes.

But more than this – they were brave in pursuing what they knew to be right. They wanted to change the paradigm – where you were never too big to be investigated; where you were never too connected to be called to answer. If the system didn't work, they would work to fix it. If the environment wasn't optimal, they would work to change it. It came at a big personal cost to them both. And in the process you can bet they made many powerful enemies.

Was there an intelligence unit at SARS? Of course there was – just like there is at any modern tax administration. Were they secretive about their projects? Of course they were – if you were investigating the triads and all-round bad guys, you would play your cards close to your chest too. Did they meet with taxpayers to discuss ongoing investigations? Of course they did – it is what a modern tax administration does. Was there what one would call a rogue spy unit? I am reasonably sure there was not.

Maybe we cannot blame Commissioner Moyane for taking a position on what could have been whispered to him by any one of the many enemies Ivan and Johann have made over the years. He is – arguably, possibly – as much of a pawn in this as many of us have been. Perhaps he does not know Ivan and Johann as men of honour – how would he? But men of honour they are.

By all means sully their reputations, for whatever hard evidence there may be of wrongdoing on their part. But let it not remain unsaid – they (and a few others like them) are the unsung heroes of the SARS we all became proud of. Instead of vilifying them, thank them for being brave enough to do what needed to be done.

Maybe this does nothing to change the course of public discourse. But just maybe, with some luck, it does.

Anonymous

Acknowledgements

I wish to acknowledge each and every SARS official I worked with throughout my years at SARS, especially those who collaborated on the cases that make up the stories in this book. I extend this acknowledgement to all the police officials, intelligence officers and external legal practitioners who worked closely with us, and all the prosecutors at the old NPA special tax units, who in a sense became part of the family. I hope this book is a fair testament to your efforts over the years.

I also want to thank the many social-rights activists I met following my departure from SARS, both those who're well known and those less so – the list is too long to name everyone here. You've inspired me and continue to do so. I have great respect for everything you've done for our country and its people. You're true heroes.

Thank you, too, to all the investigative journalists who make sure that the truth ultimately sees the light of day. You form part of the lifeblood of our young democracy and you have much more to do.

I thank Annie Olivier of Jonathan Ball Publisher for the opportunity to share these stories, for her unending support of the 'rogues', her advice and all her help in putting this book together. Thank you, too, to Tracey Hawthorne, my editor, for the guidance, editing and valuable assistance in putting the stories into a readable format.

Finally, I wish to acknowledge and thank Pravin Gordhan, Ivan Pillay, Shirish Soni, Adrian Lackay, Gene Ravele, Oupa Magashula, Goodnews Cadogan, Dan Mokgabudi and the late George Nkadimeng – mentors who in various ways over the years have provided the brightest light of purpose, inspiration and integrity that I could ever have hoped for. Thank you.

Endnotes

Foreword

1. Ivan Pillay is a former African National Congress (ANC) uMkhonto we Sizwe (MK) operative and member of the South African Communist Party (SACP). He lived in exile from the 1970s and returned to democratic South Africa after 1994 to take up a position in what was previously called the South African Secret Service. In 1999 he joined SARS as general manager: Special Investigations. He was appointed as one of four deputy SARS commissioners in 2009 and acted as SARS commissioner from 2013 to 2014. He resigned in 2015. He remains part of the ANC stalwarts and veterans grouping. He was charged by the NPA and Directorate for Priority Crime Investigation, together with the author and another, on 9 April 2018. At the time of writing, the criminal prosecution was continuing.

Chapter 2: Full circle

1. Cannabis from the Durban area, alleged to contain a higher concentration of the active component THC and therefore be more potent.
2. Mandrax (known as Quaaludes in North America) is a brand name for sleeping tablets (banned in South Africa since 1974) which, crushed into a fine powder and smoked with dagga, make what is known as a 'white pipe'.
3. By the time this criminal case came before court, in 1999, I'd moved on to other investigations and projects, and ultimately left the police.
4. *City Press* (2014) 'Sars man: the undercover cop who came in from the cold', 17 August. https://www.news24.com/Archives/City-Press/Sars-man-the-undercover-cop-who-came-in-from-the-cold-20150429 Accessed 12 April 2018.
5. Challenor, M (1999) 'Smith has 11 days to appeal asset swoop', IOL News South Africa, 18 October. https://www.iol.co.za/news/south-africa/smith-has-11-days-to-appeal-asset-swoop-16511 Accessed 26 August 2017.
6. Ibid
7. Delegations of prosecutorial powers were given to SARS prosecutors to prosecute in criminal courts by each regional prosecuting authority on a case-by-case basis. The court case that SARS relied on for the constitutionality of their criminal investigations was *S v Botha and Others*.
8. I came up with the idea, which I borrowed from the American model and a little from the police, to develop a very basic manual suspicious-activity report. These documents standardised the way in which people could report suspicious cases that they believed required auditing or investigation, and also standardised the way auditors and investigators could report feedback. The reports were completed by hand, then entered into an Excel spreadsheet database.
9. *S v Selebi* (25/09) [2010] ZAGPJHC 53 at para 46.2 http://www.saflii.org/za/cases/ZAGPJHC/2010/53.html Accessed 22 February 2018.

10. Sapa (2010) 'Motlanthe explains Sars lifestyle audits', IOL News South Africa, 11 March. https://www.iol.co.za/news/politics/motlanthe-explains-sars-lifestyle-audits-476059 Accessed on 2 September 2017.
11. I've stayed in contact with this man, and he's supported me, legally and otherwise, through some of my darkest days.
12. Singh, A (2003) 'The taxman pays a visit to Durban businessman', IOL News South Africa, 30 April. https://www.iol.co.za/news/south-africa/the-taxman-pays-a-visit-to-durban-businessman-105674 Accessed 26 August 2017.
13. Ibid
14. Ibid

Chapter 3: Dominoes

1. Gross Domestic Product (GDP) is the broadest quantitative measure of a nation's total economic activity, representing the monetary value of all goods and services produced within its borders over a specified period of time. (In this case, the percentage excluded software and services.)
2. The Directorate of Special Operations (DSO), popularly known as the Scorpions, was an FBI-style elite crime-fighting unit established by then President Thabo Mbeki in 1999 to fight high-profile crime and corruption cases. The unit was not part of the police but reported to the NPA. The Scorpions were disbanded by Government in 2008.
3. De Bruin, P (2001) 'Tax probe freeze in question', *Fin24*, 6 February. http://www.fin24.com/Economy/Tax-probe-freeze-in-question-20010206 Accessed 26 September 2017.
4. South African Revenue Service (2001). 'SARS v Tayob Family', Media Release Number 9 of 2001. https://www.ftomasek.com/archive/m080201a.html Accessed 23 March 2018.
5. Meintjies, M (2001) 'Tycoon must pay R15m of tax or do 16 years', IOL News South Africa, 24 May. https://www.iol.co.za/news/south-africa/tycoon-must-pay-r15m-of-tax-or-do-16-years-66971 Accessed 26 September 2017.
6. Ibid
7. Meintjies, M (2000) 'Don't grab our assets, says retail chain', IOL News South Africa, 1 December. https://www.iol.co.za/news/south-africa/dont-grab-our-assests-says-retail-chain-54564 Accessed 26 September 2017.
8. IOL (2001) 'Scorpions team up with SARS in fraud bust', News South Africa, 1 February. https://www.iol.co.za/news/south-africa/scorpions-team-up-with-sars-in-fraud-bust-60003 Accessed 26 September 2017.
9. Meintjies M and Sapa (2001) 'Ex-directors of Profurn flee SA tax scandal', IOL News, 8 February. https://www.iol.co.za/news/south-africa/ex-directors-of-profurn-flee-sa-tax-scandal-60563 Accessed 26 August 2017.
10. Mnyandu, E (2001) 'Hi Fi Corporation to pay R26m in tax dispute', IOL South Africa News, 19 January. https://www.iol.co.za/news/south-africa/hi-fi-corporation-to-pay-r26m-in-tax-dispute-55062 Accessed on 26 September 2017.
11. Hollowed-out bread loaves filled with vegetable or meat curry.
12. ITWeb (2000) 'Accord restates results after tax blow'. Financial, 31 October.

http://v2.itweb.co.za/index.php?option=com_content&view=article&id=100835 Accessed 26 September 2017.

13. Ibid

Chapter 4: Pay now, argue later

1. These powers of compulsion would later inform legislation in South Africa aimed at curbing organised crime and money-laundering.
2. In this 'pay now, argue later' scenario, if the SARS assessments were later found to be faulty, the taxpayer could claim back the amount paid, with interest.
3. *Metcash Trading Limited v Commissioner for the South African Revenue Service and Another* (CCT3/00) [2000] ZACC 21; 2001 (1) SA 1109 (CC); 2001 (1) BCLR 1 (CC) (24 November 2000)
4. Erasmus, D (2014) 'Taxpayers Rights When Audited By Tax Authorities In South Africa (Chapter 4 – 4.2.3)', *Tax Connections*, 17. https://www.taxconnections.com/taxblog/taxpayers-rights-when-audited-by-tax-authorities-in-south-africa-chapter-4-4-2-3/#.WdIP2_mCzIU Accessed 2 September 2017.
5. Ibid
6. Louw left SARS in early 2017.
7. *Metcash Trading Limited v Commissioner for the South African Revenue Service and Another* (CCT3/00) [2000] ZACC 21; 2001 (1) SA 1109 (CC); 2001 (1) BCLR 1 (CC) (24 November 2000)
8. South African Revenue Service (2000) 'Metcash Constitutional Court Judgment', Media Release Number 27 of 2000. https://www.ftomasek.com/archive/m241100a.html Accessed 26 September 2017.
9. Fin24 (2000) 'Metcash, SARS "defrauded"', 7 November. http://www.fin24.com/Economy/Metcash-SARS-defrauded-20001107 Accessed 26 September 2017.
10. Similar agreements existed between SARS and the Border Police, and SARS and different units in the prosecuting authority.
11. Ibid
12. Ibid
13. Ibid

Chapter 5: The Iron Duke

1. Seepe, J (2001) 'Pirates Boss's Dark Secrets', *News24*, 19 August. http://www.news24.com/SouthAfrica/Pirates-bosss-dark-secrets-20010819 Accessed 26 September 2017.
2. Sapa (2001) 'Sars has jumped the gun, says Khoza's lawyer', 26 August, IOL News South Africa. https://www.iol.co.za/news/south-africa/sars-has-jumped-the-gun-says-khozas-lawyer-73726 Accessed 2 September 2017.
3. The Frontline States were a loose coalition of African countries from the 1960s to the early 1990s committed to ending apartheid and white minority rule in South Africa and Rhodesia; they included Angola, Botswana, Mozambique, Tanzania, Zambia, and Zimbabwe.
4. Brümmer, S (2001) 'Ghosts Come Back to Haunt the "Iron Duke"', *Mail & Guardian*, 31 August. https://mg.co.za/article/2001-08-31-ghosts-come-back-to-haunt-the-iron-duke Accessed 26 September 2017.

5. Brümmer, S, Soggot, M and Deane N (2001) 'An Association with Apartheid Agent', *Mail & Guardian*, 31 August. http://allafrica.com/stories/200108300320.html Accessed 26 September 2017.
6. *The Irish Times* (2001) 'S Africa's soccer boss charged after raid', 18 August. https://www.irishtimes.com/news/s-africa-s-soccer-boss-charged-after-raid-1.393616 Accessed 26 September 2017.
7. Ibid
8. Ibid
9. Temkin, S (2001) 'Receiver Strikes a Deal With Iron Duke', *Business Day*, 21 August. http://allafrica.com/stories/200108210090.html Accessed 26 September 2017.
10. De Wet, H (2002) 'Khoza to hand R7,2m over to the taxman', IOL *Cape Argus* Sport, 2 August. https://www.iol.co.za/capeargus/sport/khoza-to-hand-r72m-over-to-the-taxman-90790 Accessed 26 September 2017.
11. Ibid

Chapter 6: Wheels of Africa

1. *Wheels of Africa*, Boley, J (2001) 'The Rise and Fall of Billy Rautenbach: How a South African entrepreneur challenged the establishment - and lost' Automotive News, 1 March. http://www.autonews.com/article/20000301/SUB/3010705/the-rise-and-fall-of-billy-rautenbach Accessed 13 February 2018.
2. The First Congo War (1996-7) was a foreign invasion of Zaire led by Rwanda that replaced President Mobutu Sésé Seko with rebel leader Laurent-Désiré Kabila, who renamed the country Democratic Republic of the Congo. Kabila then expelled all Rwandan and Ugandan forces, a major cause of the Second Congo War (1998-2003).
3. Ibid
4. *National Director of Public Prosecutions v Rautenbach and Another* (146/2003) [2004] ZASCA 102; [2005] 1 All SA 412 (SCA) (22 November 2004)
5. Ibid
6. Ibid
7. *Hyundai Motor Distributors (Pty) Ltd and Others v Smit NO and Others 2000 (2) SA 934 (T)* and *Investigating Directorate: Serious Economic Offences and Others v Hyundai Motor Distributors (Pty) Ltd and Others*, in re: *Hyundai Motor Distributors (Pty) Ltd and Others v Smit NO and Others* [2000] ZACC 12, 2000 (10) BCLR 1079 (CC), 2001 (1) SA 545 (CC)
8. *Business Report* (1999) 'Investigators raid Wheels of Africa offices', IOL Companies, 19 November. https://www.iol.co.za/business-report/companies/investigators-raid-wheels-of-africa-offices-790561 Accessed 2 September 2017.
9. Ibid
10. Ibid
11. Ibid
12. Sapa (2000) 'Constitutional Court upholds Rautenbach raid', IOL News South Africa, 25 August. https://www.iol.co.za/news/south-africa/constitutional-court-upholds-rautenbach-raid-48155 Accessed 2 September 2017.
13. Sapa (2000) 'Rautenbach's assets seized', *News24*, 19 September. http://www.

news24.com/xArchive/Archive/Rautenbachs-assets-seized-20000919 Accessed 2 September 2017.

14. See Sapa (2007) 'Rautenbach arrested in DRC', IOL News South Africa, 20 July. https://www.iol.co.za/news/south-africa/rautenbach-arrested-in-drc-362888 Accessed 2 September 2017

Part 2: The rise

1. IOL News South Africa (2007) 'Full text of Mbeki's State of Nation speech', Politics, 9 February. https://www.iol.co.za/news/politics/full-text-of-mbekis-state-of-nation-speech-314525 Accessed 13 December 2017.

Chapter 7: Many hands, light work

1. See, for example, Finance Standing Committee (2004), 'Budget Review 2004: briefing by Treasury and SARS; Budget hearing: Organised Labour and Tax Experts', Parliamentary Monitoring Group, 22 February https://pmg.org.za/committee-meeting/3474/ Accessed 12 April 2018.
2. Cadogan was years ahead of his time with the design of this model. In 2012 I attended a conference in Oslo, Norway, when the Organisation for Economic Cooperation and Development (an intergovernmental economic organisation with 35 member countries) introduced what it called 'the whole of government approach' to tackle organised and tax crimes in particular; I instantly recognised the model.

Chapter 8: Stashed cash

1. Maughan, K (2006) 'Crooks lose R1bn in property to State', IOL News South Africa, 21 November. https://www.iol.co.za/news/south-africa/crooks-lose-r1bn-in-property-to-state-304062 Accessed 14 April 2018.

Chapter 9: King

1. Chipps, R (2013). 'Chipps Jnr on his dad, the SARS investigator who nailed tax fugitive Dave King for R706m', *BizNews*, 9 September. http://www.biznews.com/thought-leaders/2013/09/09/chipps-jnr-on-his-dad-the-sars-investigator-who-nailed-tax-fugitive-dave-king-for-r706m/ Accessed 20 February 2017.
2. Heystek, M (2013) 'Dave King and I', *Moneyweb*, 4 November. https://www.moneyweb.co.za/archive/dave-king-and-i/ Accessed 2 September 2017.
3. This led to another criminal case (in which SARS had no involvement) and accusations that King had defrauded investors and lied to the Johannesburg Stock Exchange. The case died a relatively early death.
4. Dawes, N and Donnelly, L (2008) 'Dave King's Bermuda Triangle', *Mail & Guardian*, 30 May. https://mg.co.za/article/2008-05-30-dave-kings-bermuda-triangle Accessed 2 September 2017.
5. Ibid
6. *King v Commissioner for the South African Revenue Service* (08/38415) [2009] ZAGPJHC 1 (9 March 2009)

7. Ibid
8. A month later King brought an application before court to have his passport returned, in order to travel to Scotland to caddy for friend and business associate Gary Player and visit France's Bordeaux region to conclude 'some wine business' (see Whitfield, B (2002) 'Dave King's Passport Bid Fails', *Moneyweb*, 12 July. http://allafrica.com/stories/200207120598.html Accessed 12 April 2018). The application failed but soon enough, and without engagement with us at SARS, he did get his passport back from the NPA and was allowed to travel the world.
9. *News24* (2002) 'Tycoon arrested, gets R1m bail', 13 June. http://www.news24.com/xArchive/Archive/Tycoon-arrested-gets-R1m-bail-20020613 Accessed 2 September 2017.
10. *The Commissioner for the South African Revenue Service vs David Cunnigham King, Ben Nevis Holdings, Metlika Holdings and others* (Case number 4745/02) http://www.ftomasek.com/4745.pdf
11. Hawker Air Services was liquidated by SARS in 2006. Among the debt claims was a VAT-related claim of just over R73 million.
12. *Carmel Trading Company Ltd v Commissioner for the South African Revenue Services and Others* (447/07) [2007] ZASCA 160; [2007] SCA 160 (RSA); [2008] 2 All SA 125 (SCA); 2008 (2) SA 433 (SCA) (29 November 2007)
13. Ibid
14. Marais, J (2013) 'Why King agreed to R718m for a new start', *Sunday Times*, 1 September. https://www.timeslive.co.za/news/south-africa/2013-09-01-why-king-agreed-to-r718m-for-a-new-start/ Accessed 12 April 2018.
15. South African Revenue Service (2013) 'Joint media statement – settlement between the State and Mr DC King', 29 August. http://www.sars.gov.za/Media/MediaReleases/Pages/29-August-2013---Joint-Media-Statement-%E2%80%93-Settlement-between-the-State-and-Mr-DC-King.aspx Accessed 2 September 2017.
16. Ibid
17. Chipps, R (2013). 'Chipps Jnr on his dad, the SARS investigator who nailed tax fugitive Dave King for R706m' *BizNews*, 9 September. http://www.biznews.com/thought-leaders/2013/09/09/chipps-jnr-on-his-dad-the-sars-investigator-who-nailed-tax-fugitive-dave-king-for-r706m/ Accessed 20 February 2017.

Chapter 10: The scams

1. Lysergic acid diethylamide (LSD), also known as 'acid', is an illegal psychedelic drug used mainly recreationally. It's typically either swallowed or held under the tongue.
2. The VAT rate was 14% from 1994 to the beginning of 2018, but it was adjusted to 15% from 1 April 2018. Some basic items have always been excluded from the VAT regime.
3. If a business has a turnover of less than R1 million, registration for VAT is optional.
4. The world's oldest custom union, the Southern African Customs Union includes South Africa, Lesotho, Botswana, Swaziland and Namibia. The primary goal of this common customs area is to promote economic development through regional trade.

Part 3: Fissures

1. Serrao, A (2014) 'Sars target of tobacco industry backlash', IOL News South Africa, 31 July. https://www.iol.co.za/news/south-africa/gauteng/sars-target-of-tobacco-industry-backlash-1728457 Accessed 23 March 2018.

Chapter 11: Dirty tricks

1. One of the unit's last witnesses who provided an affidavit and was called on to testify in open court, related to a VAT fraud scheme in 2014. Two other witnesses were in the process of completing affidavits in early 2014, and one of them testified in a SARS-instituted liquidation inquiry in 2015. The latter two gave valuable evidence to us on the tobacco industry and would likely have become witnesses for the NPA had the unit not been closed down.
2. Kirk, P (2011) 'Murder of Customs official was a hit', *The Citizen*, 19 January https://www.security.co.za/news/17539 Accessed 29 April 2018
3. The NPA was approached to intervene and make a decision on these cases, and all were ultimately withdrawn.
4. The unit, which was established in March 2007, initially had no name since it was intended to go to the National Intelligence Agency. When this didn't happen, in July 2007 it was converted to a SARS unit, with a SARS mandate, and named the Special Projects Unit. I took it over in April 2008, and in May 2008 its name was changed to the National Research Group, with an even more refined SARS mandate. In March 2010, it was renamed the High-risk Investigations Unit. All its officials were formally employed by SARS.

Chapter 12: Death and taxes

1. Although typically attributed to American founding father Benjamin Franklin, it would appear that an even earlier version of this saying comes from Daniel Defoe's *The Political History of the Devil*: 'Things as certain as death and taxes, can be more firmly believ'd' (Defoe, D (1726) *The Political History of the Devil*. T Warner, London).
2. In October 2008, I would set out the events in an affidavit, supported by additional affidavits and evidence collected by then SARS anti-corruption head Clifford Collings, which were included in a criminal complaint registered with the police.
3. Dawes, N and Donnelly, L (2008) 'Can Dave King be linked to Agliotti?', *Mail & Guardian*, 9 November 2008 https://mg.co.za/article/2008-11-09-can-dave-king-be-linked-to-agliotti Accessed 13 April 2018.
4. Leonard Radebe was never a member of the SARS Board. He was a member of the SARS executive committee.
5. *Mail & Guardian* (2008) 'This might look a bit odd', 14 November. https://www.pressreader.com/south-africa/mail-guardian/20081114/281642481013819 Accessed 23 February 2018.
6. Sole, S (2011) 'Ex-con is Khulubuse's link to Chinese deals', *Mail & Guardian*, 7 January. https://mg.co.za/article/2011-01-07-excon-is-khulubuses-link-to-chinese-deals Accessed 13 April 2018.
7. E-brief News (nd) 'Dave King, SARS slug it out in high-stakes battle', http://

legalbrief.co.za/diary/legalbrief-forensic/story/dave-king-sars-slug-it-out-in-high-stakes-battle-2/pdf/

8. *Selebi v State* (240/2011) [2011] ZASCA 249 (2 December 2011)
9. Ibid
10. Davids, N (2014) 'Kebble killers haunted', *TimesLive*, 21 May. http://www.timeslive.co.za/thetimes/2014/05/21/Kebble-killers-haunted?PageSpeed=noscript Accessed 2 September 2017.
11. The Truth and Reconciliation Commission was a court-like body assembled in South Africa after the abolition of apartheid in 1994. Witnesses who were identified as victims of gross human-rights violations were invited to give statements about their experiences, while perpetrators of violence could also give testimony and request amnesty from prosecution.
12. Yutar, D (2000) 'Athlone bombing was God's will, says hitman', IOL News South Africa, 4 October. https://www.iol.co.za/news/south-africa/athlone-bombing-was-gods-will-says-hitman-49624 Accessed 23 February 2018.
13. *City Press* (2011) 'Apartheid hitman faces wrath of SARS', *News24*, 28 May. http://www.news24.com/Archives/City-Press/Apartheid-hitman-faces-wrath-of-SARS-20150430 Accessed 2 September 2017.
14. In those last few years at SARS, while the Central Projects Unit reported to me, I'd already begun the process of extending this capacity to other provinces. As I understand it, with the new 'operating model' at SARS that came about when Tom Moyane took over as commissioner, the unit was disbanded and many of its members left SARS. As for my Unfinished Business project – it remained just that: unfinished.
15. Ibid

CHAPTER 13 : 419S

1. The Gupta family migrated from the Indian state of Uttar Pradesh to South Africa in 1993. Based in Saxonwold, Johannesburg, and Dubai in the United Arab Emirates, they owned a business empire spanning computer equipment, media and mining. The family's strong ties to former South African President Jacob Zuma caused much political controversy and led to widespread claims of corruption, undue influence and 'state capture', a term referring to the Government acting for the Gupta family's benefit.
2. 'Radical economic transformation', a controversial topic in South Africa, means different things to different people. For some it refers to an overhaul of the economy, but for others, it's just a meaningless populist slogan.
3. A much-disputed term in South Africa, 'white monopoly capital' can mean everything from an oligopoly owned by a super-wealthy white elite that dominates large sectors of the economy, to business groups critical of corruption and alleged state capture within the administration of former South African President Jacob Zuma.
4. *The New Age Online* (2017) 'Hit list case is a scam, says magistrate as he grants bail', 8 May. http://www.thenewage.co.za/hit-list-case-is-a-scam-says-magistrate-as-he-grants-bail/ Accessed 13 April 2018.
5. Press Council (2013) 'Frans Richards vs City Press and Rapport', 19 November.

http://www.presscouncil.org.za/Ruling/View/frans-richards-vs-city-press-and-rapport-2542 Accessed 2 September 2017.

Chapter 14: Charlie and the rhinos

1. *News24* (2012) 'Hawks shoot dead Kruger poacher', 11 November. https://www.news24.com/SouthAfrica/News/Hawks-kill-Kruger-poacher-20121111?cpid=2 Accessed 23 February 2018.
2. CITES is an international agreement between governments that aims to ensure that international trade in wild animals and plants doesn't threaten their survival.
3. Later in 2013 Chumlong Lemtongthai appealed his sentence, which was reduced to an effective 30 years.
4. Parker, F (2012) 'Conviction deals blow to rhino horn syndicate', *Mail & Guardian*, 9 November. https://mg.co.za/article/2012-11-09-conviction-deals-blow-to-rhino-horn-syndicate Accessed 2 September 2017.
5. Crime Line is a private initiative, endorsed by the SAPS, that enables citizens to report crimes anonymously.
6. All Africa (2011) 'Joint Statement by the SARS and Crime Line - Another Blow for Rhino Syndicate', Government of South Africa (Pretoria), 4 November. http://allafrica.com/stories/201111080070.html Accessed 2 September 2017.
7. Rademeyer, J (2011) 'Hawks, Sars net trafficking "kingpin"', *News24*, 19 July. http://www.news24.com/SouthAfrica/News/Hawks-Sars-net-trafficking-kingpin-20110710 Accessed 13 April 2018.
8. Sapa and Parker, F (2012) 'Hawks nab alleged rhino poachers', *Mail & Guardian*, 11 November. https://mg.co.za/article/2012-11-11-hawks-nab-alleged-rhino-poachers Accessed 13 April 2018.
9. The successes of Charlie van Niekerk and his team were later recorded in the award-winning book by Julian Rademeyer, *Killing for Profit: Exposing the Illegal Rhino Horn Trade*, and in a BBC exposé on the subject.

Chapter 15 : How the 'rogues' helped to save the Springbok

1. Hasenfuss, M (2009) 'Brimstone to liquidate subsidiary', iFashion, *Fin24*, 27 January. http://www.ifashion.co.za/index.php?option=com_content&task=view&id=1541 Accessed 2 September 2017.
2. South African Revenue Service (2011) 'Introductory remarks to the Joint Portfolio Committees on borderline and border-post security on behalf of the various Government departments by commissioner of the South African Revenue Service, Mr Oupa Magashula', 8 November. http://pmg-assets.s3-website-eu-west-1.amazonaws.com/docs/111108iIntroductoryremarks.pdf Accessed 2 September 2017.
3. Masango, B (2008) 'Raid in Johannesburg nets counterfeit goods', iFashion, IOL, 18 November. http://www.ifashion.co.za/index.php?option=com_content&view=article&id=1225&catid=159 Accessed 2 September 2017.
4. Dolley, C (2008) 'China Town raid uncovers illegal garments', IOL News South Africa, 18 December. https://www.iol.co.za/news/south-africa/china-town-raid-uncovers-illegal-garments-429254 Accessed 2 September 2017.

5. Kriel, A (2009) 'SACTWU welcomes SARS raids', Congress of South African Trade Unions, 28 September. http://www.cosatu.org.za/show.php?ID=2442 Accessed 2 September 2017.
6. Ironically, among the documents contained in the criminal case lodged in May 2015 by SARS commissioner Tom Moyane against Ivan Pillay, Andries Janse van Rensburg and me ('Brooklyn CAS 427/5/2015'), which led to the aborted prosecution of then Finance Minister Pravin Gordhan, Pillay and former SARS commissioner Oupa Magashula during 2017, and the much later charges against us in 2018, is a copy of the actual affidavit obtained by the 'rogues'. Why it should be there is anybody's guess.
7. Thamm, M (2017) 'SARS unravels SA clothing industry: Tax leakages, job losses blamed on illegal imports', *Daily Maverick*, 9 March. https://www.dailymaverick.co.za/article/2017-03-09-sars-unravels-sa-clothing-industry-tax-leakages-job-losses-blamed-on-illegal-imports/#.WSQn52M6yP8 Accessed 2 September 2017.

Chapter 16 : Oh Tannenbaum, oh Tannenbaum

1. *Janse van Rensburg v Steyn* (66/10) [2011] ZASCA 71 (25 May 2011)
2. Rose, R (2013). *The Grand Scam: How Barry Tannenbaum Conned South Africa's Business Elite*. Zebra Press, Cape Town
3. Sapa (2009) 'Investors drawn into Ponzi scheme by greed', IOL News South Africa, 11 June. http://www.iol.co.za/news/south-africa/investors-drawn-into-ponzi-scheme-by-greed-446183 Accessed 28 April 2018.
4. Sapa (2009) 'SA rocked by R10bn Ponzi scheme', *Mail & Guardian*, 11 June. https://mg.co.za/article/2009-06-11-sa-rocked-by-r10billion-ponzi-scheme Accessed 28 April 2018.
5. Rob Rose received the prestigious Taco Kuiper journalism award for his coverage of the story throughout that year.
6. Brkic, B (2009) 'Barry Tannenbaum, from here to eternity', *Daily Maverick*, 28 October. https://www.dailymaverick.co.za/article/2009-10-28-From-here-to-ethernity#.WdJOP_mCzIU Accessed 2 September 2017.
7. Alcock, S (2009) 'Ponzi-scheme suspect Tannenbaum faces arrest', *Mail & Guardian*, 27 October. https://mg.co.za/article/2009-10-27-ponzischeme-suspect-tannenbaum-faces-arrest Accessed 2 September 2017.
8. FreshlyWorded (2013) 'What's happened to alleged Ponzi scheme mastermind and resident of Runaway Bay Barry Tannenbaum?' 24 June. https://freshlyworded.com/2013/06/24/whats-happened-to-alleged-ponzi-scheme-mastermind-and-resident-of-runaway-bay-barry-tannenbaum/ Accessed 2 September 2017.
9. Ibid
10. Dean Rees has apparently changed his name and now lives in the United Kingdom.
11. Venter, C (2013) '"I'll take an informed decision on Breytenbach"', *The Citizen*, 14 October. https://citizen.co.za/news/south-africa/68468/kgkgkg/ Accessed 15 March 2018.

Chapter 17 : The tax 'fixer' – Glenn Agliotti

1. Tromp, B (2011) '"Snitches, pimps, rats" off hook', *Pretoria News*, 6 April. https://

www.pressreader.com/south-africa/pretoria-news/20110406/281599532036875 Accessed 2 September 2017.

2. *Mail & Guardian* (2008) 'Agliotti and the fixers', 14 November. https://www.pressreader.com/south-africa/mail-guardian/20081114/281629596111931 Accessed 16 March 2018.
3. Ibid
4. Evidence of these scams, and of large sums of monies paid to Agliotti and others, is (strangely) included in the case docket 'Brooklyn CAS 427/5/2015' on which Ivan Pillay, Andries Janse van Rensburg and I were charged in March 2018.
5. *S v Shaik and Others* (CCT 86/06) [2007] ZACC 19; 2008 (2) SA 208 (CC); 2007 (12) BCLR 1360 (CC); 2008 (1) SACR 1 (CC) (2 October 2007)
6. Sapa (2004) 'Court mulls allowing Shaik returns', *Mail & Guardian*, 6 December. https://mg.co.za/article/2004-12-06-court-mulls-allowing-shaik-tax-returns Accessed 13 April 2018.
7. Sapa (2004) 'Sars won't testify in Shaik trial', *Mail & Guardian*, 7 December. https://mg.co.za/article/2004-12-07-sars-wont-testify-in-shaik-trial Accessed 2 September 2017.
8. Zuma, J (2008) 'Jacob Zuma's affidavit for review application', *PoliticsWeb*, 24 June. http://www.politicsweb.co.za/documents/jacob-zumas-affidavit-for-review-application Accessed 2 September 2017.
9. *City Press* (2013) 'Agliotti lifestyle audit reveals R78m tax bill', *News24*, 18 August. http://www.news24.com/Archives/City-Press/Agliotti-lifestyle-audit-reveals-R78m-tax-bill-20150429 Accessed 2 September 2017 Accessed 28 April 2018.
10. I retain possession of the recordings and have provided copies and transcripts of them to SARS, the Hawks, the State Security Agency, the Inspector General of Intelligence and SAPS between 2013 and 2016.
11. To date I have not been able to identify this person.
12. One other person was present at this meeting but he is irrelevant to this story.
13. I used the opportunity of this meeting to debrief those present on certain things concerning the 'rogue unit' allegations. I recorded it all. Perhaps one day I shall tell that story.

Chapter 18 : Document '02'

1. Basson, A (2008) 'The super JZ charge', *Mail & Guardian*, 4 January. https://www.pressreader.com/south-africa/mail-guardian/20080104/281552286530434 Accessed 2 September 2017.
2. Rampedi, P, Wa Afrika, M, Hofstatter, S and Rees, M (2014). 'SARS bugged Zuma', *Sunday Times*, 12 October. https://www.pressreader.com/south-africa/sunday-times/20141012/281479274659278 Accessed 23 February 2018.
3. Jacob Zuma's affidavit for review application submitted to Pietermaritzburg High Court, 23 June 2008 http://www.politicsweb.co.za/documents/jacob-zumas-affidavit-for-review-application
4. Broughton, T (2007) 'Zuma Pays R500 Admission of Guilt Fine Sars', *Cape Times*, 12 April. http://www.armsdeal-vpo.co.za/articles10/guilt_fine.html Accessed 26 April 2018.

5. All of these officials left in the wake of events at SARS in 2015. A detailed report that I had compiled on Zuma's non-compliance was (bizarrely) included in the docket 'Brooklyn CAS 427/5/2015' by the NPA, effectively placing it in the public domain.

Chapter 19 : The Young Man

1. Malema would go on to suggest that the 'dossier' emanated from within the State intelligence apparatus, but it did not.
2. Included in the attachments were the official mandates, structures and workflows of the Special Projects Unit and, later, the National Research Group, proving once again that the unit's existence had never been denied by SARS, as some would've had the public believe.
3. South African Revenue Service (2013) 'Responding to Mr JS Malema', Media Releases, 2 August. http://www.sars.gov.za/Media/MediaReleases/Pages/2-August-2013---SARS-Media-Release-%E2%80%93-Responding-to-Mr-JS-Malema.aspx Accessed 2 September 2017.
4. Attachment to *V Pillay v Commissioner for SARS*: Labour Court: December 2014
5. Seale, L (2013) 'Sars started Malema investigation in 2009', IOL News South Africa, 31 August. http://www.iol.co.za/news/crime-courts/sars-started-malema-investigation-in-2009-1561258 Accessed 2 September 2017.
6. Ibid
7. Public Protector (2012) *On the Point of Tenders*, http://www.pprotect.org/library/investigation_report/2012/Final%20Report%20Signed.pdf Accessed 28 April 2018.
8. Basson, A and Rampedi, P (2011) 'Malema's Secret Fund', *News24*, 24 July. http://www.news24.com/SouthAfrica/News/Malemas-secret-fund-20110724 Accessed 2 September 2017.
9. In August 2015 a criminal case against Julius Malema and Lesiba Gwangwa brought by the Hawks accusing them of fraud, money-laundering and racketeering – dating back to the initial charge in September 2012 allegedly involving a tender from the Department of Transport, Safety, Security and Liaison worth R52 million – was struck off the court roll (see Myburgh, RC (2015) 'Fraud case against Malema struck from roll', *Polokwane Observer*, 4 August. http://www.observer.co.za/fraud-case-against-malema-struck-from-roll/ Accessed 2 September 2017).
10. Letsoalo, M (2012) 'Malema's millions: Juju ally resists tax probe', *Mail & Guardian*, 18 May. https://mg.co.za/article/2012-05-18-malemas-millions-juju-ally-resists-tax-probe Accessed 2 September 2017.
11. Sapa (2012) 'Malema's business partner drops tax fights: report', *TimesLive*, 8 August. https://www.timeslive.co.za/politics/2012-08-08-malemas-business-partner-drops-tax-fights-report/ Accessed 2 September 2017.
12. South African Revenue Service (2013) 'Responding to Mr JS Malema', Media releases, 2 August. http://www.sars.gov.za/Media/MediaReleases/Pages/2-August-2013---SARS-Media-Release-%E2%80%93-Responding-to-Mr-JS-Malema.aspx Accessed 2 September 2017.
13. The Financial Investigations team was the forerunner of what would become

known as the Central Projects Unit. They focused on significant cases and matters that were likely to be considered controversial and of public interest. We needed to concentrate specific skills into a single unit to manage the complexities that came with this.

14. Ibid
15. Ibid
16. Rampedi, P and Motumi, M (2012) 'Broke Gwangwa gave Sars assets for unpaid taxes', IOL News *The Star*, 1 October. http://www.iol.co.za/the-star/broke-gwangwa-gave-sars-assets-for-unpaid-taxes-1392954 Accessed 2 September 2017.
17. SA History Online (2014) 'The 2014 national and provincial election results', 29 May. http://www.sahistory.org.za/article/2014-national-and-provincial-election-results Accessed 2 September 2017.
18. A consequence of the bizarre turnaround by SARS was that Malema decided to take the fight to SARS, asking the court to order that SARS honour the agreement. At the time of writing, the matter has yet to be completed in court.
19. Davis, R (2017) 'The Gathering: Maybe it's time for "crazy" ideas – Julius Malema', *Daily Maverick*, 24 November. https://www.dailymaverick.co.za/article/2017-11-24-the-gathering-maybe-its-time-for-crazy-ideas-julius-malema/#.Wl3kEvCWbIV Accessed 16 January 2018.
20. Evans, S (2014) 'Third time lucky: Malema strikes deal with SARS', *Mail & Guardian*, 26 May. https://mg.co.za/article/2014-05-26-malema-avoids-insolvency-ruling-with-sars-apology/ Accessed 18 April 2018.

Part 4: Rapid descent

1. Pillay, I (2016). 'The "rogue unit" narrative was a great disservice to public interest, and made up of lies and distortions', *Sunday Times*, 3 April. https://www.timeslive.co.za/sunday-times/opinion-and-analysis/2016-04-03-the-rogue-unit-narrative-was-a-great-disservice-to-public-interest-and-made-up-of-lies-and-distortions/ Accessed 20 April 2018.

Chapter 20: Walking quietly and carrying a big stick

1. amaBhungane (2015) 'Zuma's "deal" with Cape gang bosses', 19 November. http://amabhungane.co.za/article/2015-11-19-zuma-deal-with-cape-gang-bosses Accessed 19 March 2018.
2. The gold refinery was eventually liquidated.
3. A journalist sent me specific questions and quotes based on Meyer's allegations, which is how I came to learn of these stories.
4. *Sunday Times* (2017) 'Here they are: The emails that prove the Guptas run South Africa', 28 May. https://www.timeslive.co.za/sunday-times/news/2017-05-28-here-they-are-the-emails-that-prove-the-guptas-run-south-africa/ Accessed 19 March 2018.
5. Maughan, K (2017) 'Tom Moyane on why SARS currently not investigating evidence of corruption, money-laundering etc contained in #GuptaLeaks', Twitter, 3 July. https://twitter.com/karynmaughan/status/881804258194194436 Accessed 23 January 2018.

CHAPTER 21: TIGON

1. This affidavit forms part of the records of the corruption trial against former (late) national police commissioner and Interpol head Jackie Selebi.
2. Van Zilla, L (2003) 'Elaborate tax fraud dupes Sars "out of R3bn"', IOL News South Africa, 4 April. http://www.iol.co.za/news/south-africa/elaborate-tax-fraud-dupes-sars-out-of-r3bn-104059 Accessed 28 April 2018.
3. Slabbert, A (2017) 'The trial must go on – no time off for Tigon accused', *Moneyweb*, 3 August. https://www.moneyweb.co.za/news/south-africa/the-trial-must-go-on-no-time-off-for-tigon-accused/ Accessed 18 April 2018.
4. Copies of three versions of the KPMG report, dated April 2013, July 2015 and September 2015, are in my possession. The 3 September 2015 version is the 'final' version.
5. The case-management system that I introduced at the Special Compliance Unit had sequentially numbered projects; this particular project was the 32nd case undertaken by the unit.
6. *Mail & Guardian* (2007) 'Another rogue for Selebi's gallery', 1 June. https://mg.co.za/article/2007-06-01-another-rogue-for-selebis-gallery Accessed 13 April 2018.
7. See www.wachizungu.com
8. Department of International Relations and Cooperation (2013). 'The South African Embassy in Kazakhstan supports charity activities', 2013. http://www.dirco.gov.za/astana/events/south_african_embassy-charity.pdf Accessed 24 April 2018.
9. Soni's efforts in support of the fundraiser featured in a publication of the Department of International Relations and Cooperation which has been available on the internet since 2013. (See http://www.dirco.gov.za/astana/events/south_african_embassy-charity.pdf)
10. See www.wachizungu.com (Financial reports)
11. Letter in my possession.
12. Gavin Varejes confirmed to the media at the time that he was a complainant in Porritt's case, but declined to comment, probably because he may still have to testify against Porritt.
13. Faull, L (2016) 'Court rules Tigon duo must face charges', South African Institute of Tax Professionals, News & Press, 28 April. http://www.thesait.org.za/news/287016/Court-rules-Tigon-duo-must-face-charges-.htm Accessed 31 March 2018.
14. Ibid
15. Slabbert, A (2013) 'Porritt, Bennett and I committed deliberate fraud – Milne', *Moneyweb*, 13 September. https://www.moneyweb.co.za/news/south-africa/porritt-and-bennett-and-i-committed-deliberate-fraud-milne/ Accessed 16 April 2018.
16. Slabbert, A (2016) 'Who are Tigon's Porritt and Bennett: Indigent litigants or sophisticated scamsters?', *MoneyWeb*, 11 September. https://www.moneyweb.co.za/news/south-africa/who-are-tigons-porritt-and-bennett/
17. Slabbert, A (2018) 'Porritt averts contempt of court charge', *Moneyweb*, 13 February. https://www.moneyweb.co.za/news/south-africa/porritt-averts-contempt-of-court-charge/ Accessed 24 April 2018.
18. Slabbert, A (2018) 'Porritt acts just like Zuma, court finds', *Moneyweb*, 6 March.

https://www.moneyweb.co.za/news/south-africa/porritt-acts-just-like-zuma-court-finds/ Accessed 24 April 2018.

Chapter 22: It's a system, you see?

1. Ferreira, E (2017) 'Abrahams aims barb at Gordhan over Fica council', IOL News South Africa, 18 May. https://www.iol.co.za/news/politics/abrahams-aims-barb-at-gordhan-over-fica-council-9212300 Accessed 21 April 2018.
2. A 'politically exposed person' is someone who is or has in the past been entrusted with prominent public functions in a particular country, eg, a head of state, cabinet minister or senior judge.
3. It could be argued that some of our Chapter 9 institutions, like the Public Protector and Auditor General, also play a role, but it would be peripheral to their mandates.
4. 'Non-banking financial institutions' include insurance companies and pay agents.
5. Our financial-regulatory system does have some limited means to police culprits, such as suspending their licences or positions, and curtailing their financial activities – but these are narrow and none allows easy means to recoup lost outflows. Fines and administrative sanctions can be imposed, but individuals are hardly ever held to account by bodies within our financial-regulatory system.
6. In 2007 we conducted a very specific scientific process to determine the exact standard time for fraud investigations at SARS, which we then used to conduct our production planning and operate our case-management system.
7. The case against Delport formed part of SARS's investigations into the tobacco industry, and was one of the first of its scale.
8. Two of these are SARS's memberships of the World Customs Organisation and the African Tax Administration Forum.
9. The Presidency of the Republic of South Africa (2015) 'The Anti-corruption Task Team is fully operational', 27 January. http://www.thepresidency.gov.za/content/anti-corruption-task-team-fully-operational Accessed 16 April 2018.

Chapter 23: Fall from grace

1. At the time of writing, the matter remained unresolved and had yet to appear before a court. McKune, C and Sole, S (2016) 'Sars Wars: Influential "new guard" close to Tom Moyane's accused of power grab', *Mail & Guardian*, 19 February. https://mg.co.za/article/2016-02-19-sars-wars-moyanes-empire-strikes-back-1 Accessed 22 January 2018.
2. Pillay, I (2016) 'The "rogue unit" narrative was a great disservice to public interest, and made up of lies and distortions', *Sunday Times*, 3 April. https://www.timeslive.co.za/sunday-times/opinion-and-analysis/2016-04-03-the-rogue-unit-narrative-was-a-great-disservice-to-public-interest-and-made-up-of-lies-and-distortions/ Accessed 16 January 2018.
3. Du Toit, P (2017). 'Gordhan: There are some institutions that you just shouldn't mess with', *Huffington Post* South Africa, 22 February. http://www.huffingtonpost.co.za/2017/02/22/gordhan-there-are-some-institutions-that-you-just-shouldnt-mes_a_21719278/ Accessed 12 January 2018.
4. Vollgraaff, R and Vecchiatto, P (2017) 'Gordhan: SARS is a political project run by

people who can't manage tax system', *Fin24*, 18 September. https://www.fin24.com/Economy/gordhan-sars-is-a-political-project-run-by-people-who-cant-manage-tax-system-20170918 Accessed 16 January 2018.

5. Comrie, S (2016) 'Sars chief Tom Moyane's nephew linked to plum R220m tax debt collection contract', *Mail & Guardian*, 13 October. https://mg.co.za/article/2016-10-13-00-sars-chiefs-nephew-linked-to-plum-r220m-tax-debt-collection-contract Accessed 10 January 2018.
6. Bornman, J (2017) 'SARS lost 506 employees since start of year', *News24*, 6 December. https://www.news24.com/SouthAfrica/News/sars-lost-506-employees-since-start-of-year-20171206 Accessed 16 January 2018.
7. Paragraph 57 of the Sikhakhane panel report explicitly states that the panel was not convened to investigate allegations of a covert unit and that these allegations didn't form part of its terms of reference – but that it took it upon itself to include the allegations following media articles and after having interviewed me.
8. A SARS memorandum was leaked to the media, setting out how this unit sought to use undercover operations, a secret boardroom, safe houses and pool vehicles, and how they sought to hide their funding by setting off costs secretly against another cost centre.
9. Serrao, A and Basson, A (2016) 'New "rogue-type unit" operating at SARS, *News24*, 14 November. https://m.news24.com/SouthAfrica/News/new-rogue-type-unit-operating-at-sars-20161113 Accessed 28 April 2018.
10. Serrao, A (2016) 'Senior SARS employee involved with Zuma family-linked company', *News24*, 16 November. https://m.news24.com/SouthAfrica/News/senior-sars-employee-involved-with-zuma-family-linked-company-20161116 Accessed 28 April 2018.
11. Marrian, N and Ensor, L (2017) 'Tax office moves to discipline Jonas Makwakwa', *Business Day*, 23 February. https://www.businesslive.co.za/bd/national/2017-02-23-tax-office-moves-to-discipline-jonas-makwakwa/ Accessed 28 April 2018.
12. See https://www.facebook.com/TimesLIVE/posts/10154916249144617/
13. Cameron, J (2018) 'Feeling the heat: SARS Gupta man Tom Moyane shoots the messenger', *BizNews*, 19 March. https://www.biznews.com/good-hope-project/2018/03/19/sars-gupta-man-tom-moyane/ Accessed 22 April 2018.
14. Serrao, A (2017) 'SARS IT chief previously dismissed for misconduct', *News24*, 19 April. https://m.news24.com/SouthAfrica/News/sars-it-chief-previously-dismissed-for-misconduct-20170419 Accessed 28 April 2018.
15. Du Toit, P (2016) 'Exodus at Moyane's SARS continues', *Huffington Post*, 12 December. http://www.huffingtonpost.co.za/2016/12/12/exclusive-exodus-at-moyanes-sars-continues_a_21625971/ Accessed 28 April 2018.
16. Serrao, A (2017) 'Drama at SARS over R70m Gupta refund', *City Press/News24*, 4 June. https://www.news24.com/SouthAfrica/News/exclusive-moyane-okays-r70m-payment-to-guptas-20170604-2 Accessed 3 January 2018.
17. Lamprecht, I (2017) 'Sars unduly delays tax refunds in some cases, Ombud finds', *Moneyweb*, 5 September. https://www.moneyweb.co.za/mymoney/moneyweb-tax/sars-unduly-delays-tax-refunds-in-some-cases-ombud-finds/ Accessed 16 January 2018.

18. Le Cordeur, M (2017) 'Two more senior managers leave SARS, DA claims', *Fin24*, 17 April. https://m.fin24.com/Economy/two-more-senior-managers-leave-sars-da-claims-20170417 Accessed 28 April 2018.
19. This unit was apparently part of the new operating framework at SARS under Moyane.
20. Serrao, A (2017) 'Latest senior manager leaves SARS', *News24*, 1 March. https://m.news24.com/SouthAfrica/News/exclusive-latest-senior-manager-leaves-sars-20170301 Accessed 28 April 2018.
21. Serrao, A (2017) 'List of senior employees leaving SARS grows', *News24*, 23 November. https://www.news24.com/SouthAfrica/News/list-of-senior-employees-leaving-sars-grows-20171123 Accessed 28 April 2018.
22. African News Agency (2018) 'Sars welcomes tax administration inquiry', *The Citizen*, 19 February. https://citizen.co.za/business/1825851/sars-welcomes-tax-administration-inquiry/ Accessed 16 April 2018.
23. The National Payments Systems Act obliges pay agents to register with a central authority. In addition, the South African Reserve Bank issued two directives in terms of its legislation that governs pay agents. SARS should have, at the very least, conducted a basic diligence check to see if this company was registered as a pay agent.
24. Van Rensburg, D (2018) 'SARS accuses Guptas of lying', *Fin24*, 1 April. https://www.fin24.com/Economy/sars-accuses-guptas-of-lying-20180401 Accessed 24 April 2018.
25. Gouws, N, Skiti, S (2018), 'SARS boss Tom Moyane "told probe witness to feign illness", *Business Day,* 13 March. https://www.businesslive.co.za/bd/national/2018-03-13-sars-boss-tom-moyane-told-probe-witness-to-feign-illness/ Accessed 29 April 2018.
26. Cowan, K (2018), 'Revealed: Guptas claimed another R89-million in VAT', TimesLive, 25 April, https://www.timeslive.co.za/news/south-africa/2018-04-25-revealed-guptas-claimed-another-r89-million-in-vat/ Accessed 29 April 2018.
27. Versluis, J (2018), 'Guptas linked to R100m VAT scam', *City Press*, 29 April, https://www.news24.com/SouthAfrica/News/guptas-linked-to-r100m-vat-scam-20180428 Accessed 29 April 2018.
28. Cowan, K (2018), 'Lawyers snub SARS over bills', *Sunday Times*, 29 April 2018, https://www.pressreader.com/@Sangxa83775/csb_xAMBKhhnSkPlGkJ_Q2bDA1mWI84C6tPp3JuYEqs8fc8 Accessed 29 April 2018.

Chapter 24: Ivan's rugby ball

1. Merebank Justice Network Fundraising Committee (2016), 'Ivan Pillay – A son of the soil', *Chatsworth Rising Sun*, 27 October. http://risingsunchatsworth.co.za/74223/ivan-pillay-a-son-of-the-soil/ Accessed 2 September 2017.

Epilogue

1. *M Wingate-Pearse v Commissioner for SARS and Others* (2015) – this case, although filed before court and served on all parties, appears to have never been heard before the courts in 2015 or thereafter.

2. After Wingate-Pearse submitted tax returns for the years 1998 to 2005, in April 2006, SARS issued revised assessments for each of those years; with interest and penalties, these amounted cumulatively to some R41 million. Wingate-Pearse objected, and further revised assessments were issued, reducing his tax liability to slightly less than R23 million. Dissatisfied with these, he lodged an appeal with the tax court on 1 August 2007. Although this resulted in some downward adjustment, the accrual of interest substantially increased his overall liability. His appeal was heard by the tax court on 9 February 2015 and he lost.
3. In a bizarre manner, the 'Brooklyn CAS 427/5/2015' case docket has placed significant evidence of these matters in the public domain. It's astounding how neither SARS, the Hawks nor the NPA seem to have any desire whatsoever to recoup close to a billion rands in lost revenue to the taxpayer, and hold people accountable for this.

Index

D

E

U

V

W

X

Z

www.ingramcontent.com/pod-product-compliance
Ingram Content Group UK Ltd.
Pitfield, Milton Keynes, MK11 3LW, UK
UKHW020425250726
13967UKWH00007B/2822

9 781868 428090